Praise for *Partners in Passion*

"*Partners in Passion* is the perfect title because Mark and Patricia are just that—passionate about each other and passionate in their commitment to explore human sexuality together. They share how they have created and maintained a deepening erotic connection through their joint explorations of sexuality."

—Betty A. Dodson, artist, author, and PhD sexologist

"*Partners in Passion* is not only a sensible, compassionate, readable book; it is the best book I have ever read about the varieties of love and physical/emotional intimacy. The authors explain why basing marriage on the falling-in-love experience is a poor idea. They expose the common cultural myths that wreck so many contemporary relationships. They include sensible health advice minus the scare factor. They successfully synthesize Western and Far Eastern views about passion. This book is a must-read for all people, young and old, of whatever sexual persuasion and culture, who are on relationship adventures seeking fulfilling intimacy and passionate partnership. My clients will benefit hugely from reading it."

—Alice Kahn Ladas, EdD,
coauthor of *The G Spot: And Other Discoveries about Human Sexuality* and *Women and Bioenergetic Analysis*

"It's not every day that I learn something new about sex; the chapter on Tantra is among the best introductions to the topic I've ever come across."

—Ian Kerner, PhD,
New York Times bestselling author of *She Comes First*

"*Partners in Passion* is bursting with practical suggestions and sage guidance which will help couples become more sexually fulfilled, more intimate, and more fully human."

—Felice Newman,
author of *The Whole Lesbian Sex Book:
A Passionate Guide for All of Us*

"Creating an amazing sex life means more than learning some new tricks for pleasuring a partner. You also need to know how to have an amazing relationship—with yourself, with a partner, and with your sexuality. *Partners in Passion* is full of tools and ideas to make that happen, no matter what your relationship history or sexual preferences. Patricia Johnson and Mark A. Michaels have done a fantastic job of offering compassionate advice and clear steps to building the kind of relationship that can support and contain the sex life you deserve."

—Dr. Charlie Glickman,
coauthor of *The Ultimate Guide to Prostate Pleasure*

"Written with emphasis on the kindness, trust, and presence that are required in any healthy relationship, *Partners in Passion* illustrates delightful depths of insight, providing practical solutions to the very real issues that kill the passion and love in so many partnerships. Every couple needs to read this book!"

—Mikaya Heart,
author of *The Ultimate Guide to Orgasm for Women*

"*Partners in Passion* is the smartest and most comprehensive book on partner sex and erotic relationships available today. Brava, Mark and Patricia! I love this book."

—Barbara Carrellas,
author of *Urban Tantra: Sacred Sex for the Twenty-First Century*
and *Ecstasy Is Necessary*

"Patricia and Mark don't only write about being partners in passion; they are partners in passion. Drawing on their background in Tantra, their own long-term relationship, and the wisdom of other happy couples, Michaels and Johnson know just what it takes to keep things sparkling, sizzling, and sexy. Their book is an absolute must if you are in a relationship or hope to be."

—Jamye Waxman,
sex educator, coauthor of *Hot Sex: Over 200 Things You Can Try Tonight!*, and author of *Getting Off: A Woman's Guide to Masturbation*

"*Partners in Passion* is an outrageous, courageous, and much NEEDED endeavor. Michaels and Johnson distill the collective erotic wisdom of the ages, rewrite it with their own unique wit and generosity, and offer it back to us as a true gift! Their book raises the erotic consciousness and ushers in a new erotic paradigm for sexual relationships—such that all other erotic instructional manuals are merely supplemental. Read *Partners in Passion* first!"

—Jennifer Pritchett,
founder and owner of The Smitten Kitten

"*Partners in Passion* comes straight from the heart. Use this book as a gourmet guide to trust, touch, and ongoing adventures of discovery in the vast playing fields of loving relationship."

—Gina Ogden, PhD,
LMFT, and author of *Expanding the Practice of Sex Therapy* and
The Return of Desire

"These two passionate partners have done it again! *Partners in Passion: A Guide to Great Sex, Emotional Intimacy and Long-Term Love* ought to be the graduate's gift, the newlywed's gift, your lover's holiday surprise, and the birthday present for your best friend's 50th, too! Not only will you find intelligent, heartfelt information on many ideas and sexual concepts, your eyes will be opened to some of the myths that hold us back from fully finding pleasure and true intimacy. This is a grand blend of neuroscience, the most advanced thinking on relationship and sexuality education and practices—every lover's library needs one!"

—Suzie Heumann,
founder of Tantra.com

"Other than our need and desire to eat, sex is what we crave the most. It's what drives us. It needs to be fun and varied. Religion, politics, government intrusion, imposed morals, have all tried to suck the fun out of sex. *Partners in Passion* puts the fun back! It's a comprehensive and insightful guide for people who take their sex play seriously and are committed to leaving the bedroom with smiles on their faces. Even I can learn a few things from this fascinating book."

—Larry Flynt

"Speaking as both a certified sex therapist and a sex neuroscientist, I am awed by the magnificence of *Partners in Passion*, which is truly the most comprehensive, intelligent resource available to everyone interested in forging dynamic, joyful, and sustainable intimate partnerships. The authors thoroughly address the biological, psychological, and social aspects of relationship in a nonjudgmental, wise, and literate manner that instructs and inspires. Their rigor and scholarly attention to detail is impressive. Those seeking to create conscious, loving partnerships will find a compendium of concrete tools and resources in this important book. I will be encouraging clients, students, and colleagues to share this work. Bravo!"

—Nan Wise, PhD candidate
in congnitive neuroscience at Rutgers-Newark, and AASECT
certified sex therapist

"*Partners in Passion* by Michaels and Johnson is the most comprehensive compendium on sexuality to date. Erudite yet accessible, this book covers all the bases. Much more than just a guidebook to getting it on, *Partners in Passion* touches on many fields in sexology, including history, spirituality, anatomy and physiology, cultural constructions, gender differences, psychology, law, politics, art, and anthropology. An excellent book for college students who want a well-rounded text on sexuality, for partners engaging in the enhancement of their sexualities, or for those who are just curious about the messy complexities of human sexuality. This is a book for the whole family."

—Dr. Winston Wilde,
sexologist, sex therapist, marriage therapist, and author of
Legacies of Love

"Whatever your relationship might need for staying vibrant is here. A book that you and your partner will keep reading for decades."
—Joan Price, author of *Naked at Our Age*

"This book is an absolute must-read for everyone on this earth, as we are all sexual beings, many of us trying to navigate relationships which can be complicated and difficult. I love Patricia and Mark's gentle guidance on how to improve the communication in your relationship. The frank way they discuss taboo subjects is inspiring and informative. If you wonder where the spark went in your love life, pick up *Partners in Passion* to find your way back to a loving relationship with yourself and your partner."
—Jennifer Landa,
MD, OB/GYN, hormone specialist, and author of *The Sex Drive Solution for Women*

"Finally, a smart, sexy, and practical sex and relationship book! Mark and Patricia meld their knowledge of Tantra and alternative sexuality with accessible, practical techniques for building (or rebuilding) passion in long-term relationships. If you're a long-term monogamous couple looking to increase your connection or you're thinking about adding kink or openness to your relationship in a way that's healthy and caring, this book gives you the tools to build the relationship you crave."
—Jacq Jones,
sex educator and owner of Sugar the Shop

"Mark Michaels and Patricia Johnson are the authors of some of my favorite sexuality books, and in *Partners in Passion* they have taken their unique approach to intimacy to a whole new level. In this book, they offer a truly complete approach to sex, pleasure, emotional intimacy, and relationship building skills. Patricia and Mark have always made their readers feel welcome, safe, and appreciated. Their engaging and respectful style is evident in this book and is sure to help readers get the most from the valuable knowledge they provide in *Partners in Passion*. While many books give cheap ideas for short-term relationship improvement or a single creative night of sexy fun, *Partners in Passion* is dedicated to helping readers co-create lasting change in their love lives. From foundational information on anatomy and pleasure to confronting toxic relationship myths, every reader is sure to find important insights to use both right away and for years to come. *Partners in Passion* also includes several important chapters on advanced sexual practices, such as exploring kink, opening your relationship, and venturing into Tantra and Neo-Tantra. By combining foundational as well as higher level concepts, readers will be able to grow with this book and find content that is likely to meet their relationship right where it is. I look forward to recommending *Partners in Passion* to my clients!"

—Dr. Ruth Neustifter,
author of *The Nice Girl's Guide to Talking Dirty*

"At last! The new Holy Grail for how to sustain sexual fire and keep loving passion alive. The authors reveal the truths about ecstatic and joyful sexual expression, debunking common myths and providing understanding about sexual energy flow, while offering refreshing, sound, and sensitive guidance for couples seeking to thrive over time. I love this book."

—Dr. Patti Britton,
cofounder of SexCoachU.com, clinical sexologist, sex coach,
and author of *The Art of Sex Coaching*

"*Partners in Passion* is a contemporary sexuality book for both the novice and sexually experienced. The authors' practical and casual manner makes it easy to follow and appreciate the many topics ranging from sexual adventuring, safer sex, and designer relationships, to sexual communication, desire discrepancy, and aging. Reading it is like talking to a big brother or sister about all aspects of sexuality!"

—Sally Valentine,
PhD, FAACS, LCSW, AASECT certified supervisor
and sex therapist

Partners
in Passion

Partners in Passion:

A Guide to Great Sex,
Emotional Intimacy and Long-Term Love

**MARK A. MICHAELS
AND PATRICIA JOHNSON**

FOREWORD BY TAMMY NELSON, PhD

CLEiS
PRESS

Published in the United States by Cleis Press, Inc., 2246 Sixth St., Berkeley, California 94710.

Printed in the United States.
Cover design: Scott Idleman
Cover photograph: Moment/Getty Images
Text design: Frank Wiedemann
Illustrations: kd diamond
Internal Female Genitalia illustration © Tristan Taormino, used with permission.

First Edition.
10 9 8 7 6 5 4 3 2 1

Trade paper ISBN: 978-1-62778-028-5
E-book ISBN: 978-1-62778-045-2

Library of Congress Cataloging in Publication Data is available.

CONTENTS

LIST OF ILLUSTRATIONS

LIST OF TIPS AND TECHNIQUES

FOREWORD

TAMMY NELSON, PhD

I first met Mark Michaels and Patricia Johnson over a decade ago, when I took a private Tantra class with them. I was impressed by their knowledge and commitment to the process and to each other, well before their first book came out. In the intervening years, I have attended some of their public classes and have come to know them personally, and I've watched them grow both as teachers and as authors. I was delighted when they invited me to write the foreword to *Partners in Passion: A Guide to Great Sex, Emotional Intimacy and Long-Term Love.*

I was even more delighted after reading the manuscript. *Partners in Passion* is a wise, unique, and original book, informed by Michaels and Johnson's background in Tantra, as well as by their lived experience as married professionals and literary collaborators. It is peppered with useful tips and anecdotes, and with examples of long-term couples in satisfying relationships. Whether you are single and hoping to find a long-term partner, in a new relationship, hoping to make your committed relationship even happier, or seeking to renew your connection, *Partners in Passion* is essential reading.

As a relationship therapist, sex therapist, and board-certified sexologist, I have been working with couples and their sexual issues for many years. I have written books about sexual desire, about betrayal, and about passion. I have watched couples fall in and out of love and plunge back in for yet another try, braving the turbulent and sometimes dangerous waters of erotic monogamy. Being passionate partners with someone you love can be the hardest thing in life and also the most rewarding.

What makes it so hard? Almost every book, movie, and song we encounter is about love and passion. We all crave that sparkly, bubbling hot, inspired romance that makes our knees weak and never, ever leaves us bored or feeling tired of each other. But is that realistic? We all know that long-term relationships can create frustration, make us feel inadequate, and leave us craving something new or wondering why we can't trade this partner in for someone better.

Many people do just that. In fact, over half of us divorce, and many of those who stay together find some way to cheat on or betray the other at some point in their committed partnership. We need to change this. We need to find a way to make relationships work.

More couples than ever before are wondering if they can have a different type of relationship, a more intimate and connected partnership. They want more intense sex. They are also seeking a spiritual union that will lead to a more vibrant experience of love.

We have all heard that successful long-term relationships take work. What exactly is the "work" of a relationship? Some say it is communication. That's a great start, but communication is only the beginning of the hard work of getting through everyday life when both partners have jobs, are managing children and a home, and are trying to stay healthy. With all of these demands, how can anyone stay interested in what their partner says, make time for great sex, and still watch their favorite television shows together on a Sunday night?

Communication is not simply waiting patiently for the other person to stop talking so you can have a turn. It is also not merely verbalizing your own thoughts. Communication is a true form of connection, a deeper intimacy, a knowing, a listening, and a presence that most of us have never experienced. Many of us are so quick to assume we know what our partners are saying, before it is halfway out of their mouths, that we never hear them at all. Being heard and being seen for who we are is the deepest need we have as humans. Having partners who can truly hear us is an experience so profoundly healing that other problems in our lives simply slip away and become trivial in comparison. So what if your partner doesn't take out the garbage, if she or he is present, listening, and willing to try to understand your deepest desires and needs?

In *Partners in Passion*, Michaels and Johnson explore

this important key to healthy relating in great depth. They communicate to the reader what it means to really listen and be present, but in ways that may not be obvious. If you spend any time with them in person, you can see how connected and kind they are, how they empathize with each other, how their language of love is shared and validated. Writing just one book together is a Herculean task; the fact that they've written four is a testament to the depth of their connection. This book is not only about their lived experience as Tantra teachers; it offers a broader perspective on a new way of communicating and engaging. They are present for each other at these deeper levels, embodying a sensual and sexual connection that many couples strive for but have difficulty accomplishing. *Partners in Passion* will provide you with practical tools for creating a relationship that is rich, collaborative, and erotically engaged.

Therapists often look at sex from a clinical perspective. They are usually concerned with what isn't working, with sexual "pathology" or dysfunction. Clinicians usually try to determine what is broken and then work on how to fix it. Because they are teachers, Michaels and Johnson offer a different perspective: focusing on what works as the key to creating a more vibrant love life. They present sex in an open-minded, practical, and positive way. They strive to be inclusive of all orientations, identities, and relationship styles— traditional monogamy, polyamory, open partnerships, and even swinging. They present them all with empathy and sensitivity, without making us feel like we've missed the boat if we haven't had six sexual partners and an orgy in the past week. There is no judgment in this book, and it is just this absence of judgment that is crucial if relationships are to be collaborative and validating.

The authors' training and background bring a solid authenticity to their writing. They avoid stereotypes and clichés and endeavor to meet readers where they are, so people in more traditional relationships will not be left feeling "square" or alone. At the same time, those looking to expand their sexuality and explore the edges of their fantasy life together will find safe direction and a validating place to start.

The sexual focus here is on pleasure—how to give it and receive it—and how to have a satisfying relationship. The idea that sex should be a shared adventure, one in which each partner can remain open and curious to the other, adds lightness and a feeling of playfulness to the book. Where Tantric practices are included, they are purely experiential, practical, and undogmatic, with no demand to overthink the experience or strive to make something happen. In today's society, where hard work is revered, working hard at our relationships can seem overwhelming. And when things go awry, the feelings of failure can lead many into a spiral of shame and negative thoughts that create the opposite of what we really desire: lightness, joy, and mutual fulfillment.

Partners in Passion also has one of the most helpful and comprehensive resource guides of any book on relationships and sexuality available today. If you are curious about any number of sexual subjects, from online erotica to Tantric workshops to retreat centers to sexuality education, you can find it in this book. If you are thinking of opening your relationship and want to know how to go about it, or you want to know more about what the Tantric position Yab Yum entails, you will find it here.

This book is an ambitious project, and *Partners in Passion* delivers what it promises. One might expect such an encyclopedic volume to be superficial in its coverage, but this book is both deeply sensitive and filled with useful advice. In addition to providing a wealth of information, it gives couples an array of tools for deepening their connection. The focus of a relationship should be on what we may give to the other, what may bring the other pleasure, how we may deeply know the other, and what each may find erotic. These ideas are in direct opposition to the way most of us are conditioned to think about relationships. Conventional wisdom tells us to look at a romantic partner as someone who should meet our needs, give us what we want, and feed us, emotionally, sexually, and spiritually. This narcissistic view of relationships is doomed to fail, because no one can ever truly give us all that we desire, and any partner, no matter how perfect, will eventually disappoint us.

As Patricia and Mark put it: "Instead of striving to get one's needs met, mutually focusing on each other's fulfillment is the key to having better sex. Cultivating this attitude provides the basis for nurturing a long-term relationship that is fulfilling and enduringly erotic." This refreshing attitude is not only important for our personal relationships but perhaps for the world as a whole.

Michaels and Johnson write what they know because they are living what they write. I respect their love for each other and admire their vibrancy and determination to effect change in the world by creating happy, erotic, and committed long-term relationships. Great sex and a real, vibrant, and empathetic connection may just be the way to do that.

Tammy Nelson, PhD
Author of *Getting the Sex You Want* and *The New Monogamy*
www.drtammynelson.com

PREFACE

The tools it takes to have a vibrant, fulfilling, and expansive sex life are the same ones that can be used to create a satisfying long-term relationship. There are countless how-to sex manuals on the market. This is not one of those books. Merely finding the right moves or homing in on that perfect spot will not create a great sexual relationship. We seek to provide you with a foundation for an enduring and mutually satisfying erotic partnership. Our vision is holistic, and our intention is to give you the skills for creating a great sex life together, regardless of which tricks and techniques you care to use. Once you have refined these skills, we suspect those how-to books will prove to be a lot more useful.

This book is the upshot of an ongoing conversation that

began over fifteen years ago. We met in January 1999, when Patricia attended Mark's first public lecture on Tantra. Neither one of us was seeking or expecting to be in a long-term partnership, though there was a strong attraction from the start. We exchanged emails over the next couple of weeks and eventually met for lunch, at Patricia's invitation. During that first meeting, we decided to explore the sexual aspects of Tantra together, without having so much as held hands. By putting our interest in sex on the table from the start and being clear that it was very important to both of us, we bypassed a lot of the game playing and manipulation that is so common in the dating scene.

A few years into our relationship, we began writing a book on Tantra but abandoned the project, choosing to use the material for an online course instead. A year or two after this first try, we started working on a book based on a series of seminal lectures on Tantra that our teacher, Dr. Jonn Mumford, had given in the 1970s. We added some of our own research and ideas, and updated the content somewhat, so *The Essence of Tantric Sexuality* is in many respects a three-person collaboration. Our second and third books, *Tantra for Erotic Empowerment* (an expanded version of that online course) and *Great Sex Made Simple,* are more fully ours. This book both builds on and departs from our first three.

We were eager to write *Partners in Passion* because we want to reach people who wouldn't dream of buying a Tantra book. Our writing and thinking are informed by our background and training in the tradition. While we are convinced that thinking about relationships in a way that is informed by

Tantric principles can be valuable for any couple, this is only one stream among many that we've brought together here. This book sums up what we have lived, read, observed, and discussed over many years, and we hope our ideas will resonate with you.

Our collaborative process has evolved over the course of writing four books together, though the general contours have been consistent. We bring different personal histories, talents, and skill sets to our writing, so we thought it would be helpful to share a little on our backgrounds, how we work together, and our authorial voice.

Mark has written and translated plays (from French and Italian into English), has a law degree, and did graduate work in American Studies. In grad school, his coursework and research were focused on Native American Studies (which doesn't show up in this book), American popular culture, and human sexuality and reproduction (which do). He was strongly influenced by his exposure to feminist and queer theory. Patricia has approached our work from a more intuitive and less academic perspective, drawing on her career as a musician and performing artist.

This difference in background has also manifested itself in the division of labor. (This is a reflection not of gender but of our different talents and life experiences.) Patricia usually does a great deal of the preliminary work: transcribing our conversations about various subjects, outlining, and providing notes on the topics we want to address. Mark's background means he does the literary grunt work, writing the first draft based on the material we develop together and the initial notes

Patricia produces. After the first draft is completed, we seek outside input, do multiple readings of the manuscript both separately and aloud together, and propose and incorporate revisions when necessary.

Patricia sometimes says she sees herself as a muse, and she does play that role during the writing of the first draft. (In addition, she tolerates a lot of pacing and procrastination.) But muse is far too self-deprecating and is neither fair nor accurate. This book is an expression of who we are, individually and as a couple. Our authorial "we" may be a literary device, but it is also an honest expression of ourselves and how we create together.

The process of writing a book is intense, demanding, and emotionally charged; cowriting a book with your life partner, especially one about sex and relationships, is indescribably intimate. It requires fearlessness, flexibility, and a determination to keep the ego in check. We like to think of our life, our teaching, and our body of work in various media as testaments to the power of the collaborative relationship model we advocate. We hope this book will give you an embodied as well as an intellectual understanding of what is possible when you collaborate. We also hope it will inspire you to have productive and continuing conversations, just as we look forward to continuing the one we started more than fifteen years ago.

NEW RELATIONSHIP ENERGY

Do you remember how it felt when you were first falling in love? Or maybe you don't have to remember because you're lucky enough to be in that heightened state right now. Either way, the experience is intense, delicious, magical, something to be enjoyed to the fullest. All your physical and mental juices are flowing, and the experience is literally intoxicating. In new relationships sex tends to be exhilarating, and most new couples are eager to make love as often as possible. Nights may be long—with bouts of lovemaking interspersed with deep conversation and no concern about feeling sleep deprived. Those who are in this elevated and almost manic state are sometimes described as being in the throes of new relationship energy (NRE).

NRE can be a very heady and enjoyable state, and there's no reason to deny yourself the intensity and pleasure that accompanies it. As long as you remain mindful of the fact that it is temporary and something of an illusion, you'll be able to revel in it without being consumed by it. Similarly, remembering that the intensity will not last will make it much easier to transition from being in a new relationship to being in a longer-term one.

During this stage, the novelty of discovering a new partner, exploring and enjoying that partner's body, can create its own momentum. The same intensity is sometimes felt in casual sexual encounters. Novelty can be very alluring and can function as a powerful aphrodisiac.

NRE usually propels people for six months or so, but for some its effects can last as long as two years. As Helen Fisher has argued in *The Anatomy of Love,* NRE is (for the most part) a neurochemical phenomenon. It is very easy to make all kinds of promises and fantasize about having a life together when you are in this altered state of consciousness. Ironically, this is actually the worst time to decide whether this is the person you want to be with for the long term. Knowing that NRE is influencing (and possibly impairing) your judgment during this early stage can provide you some protection against being overwhelmed and making less than optimal decisions or promises that you'll end up regretting.

The emotions you feel during this period may seem like love, but they are probably better described as infatuation. Six months is not long enough to develop a real relationship and get to know another person. More often than not, your ideas about your beloved during this period are based on limited knowledge, projections, and fantasy. As infatuation fades and you start to gain a deeper knowledge of this other, you may realize that the person who captivated you is not the paragon of virtue that you imagined. It's easy to feel misled and deceived when this happens, but in most cases the deception is self-deception, and the disappointment is rooted in the other's inability to live up to your fantasy.

So love in the first six months is often frenzied, a kind of hallucination. Because everything is so heightened, it's a very exciting time, and it can be filled with drama, especially if you're afraid that the object of your affections and desire does not reciprocate. While this intense emotion may prove to be a foundation for a calmer, more balanced relationship over time, the drama that gets associated with new love, and especially with unrequited love, is not likely to be sustainable in a long-term partnership, even a passionate one, and we suspect that few people would want it to be.

NEW RELATIONSHIP
ENERGY FEELS LIKE...

Here are some descriptions of NRE from our friends on Facebook:

The exhilarating ambush of endorphins that results from a new emotional connection. Or just a new physical connection.

A rush up the spine for me and mine.

Let the self-revelation begin. Can't go anywhere REAL without it.

Like a kid in a candy store.

Maddening, delightful, dizzying, overwhelming. For me it's euphoria mingled with anxiousness before relaxing into contentment. And blushing. Lots of blushing.

It's like one of those puke rides at the Parish fair that leaves you feeling dizzy and a little queasy.

Modern popular culture, in the United States and in many other countries, conditions people to believe that new is better, that excitement, intensity, and fervor are equivalent to depth of feeling. In fact, intensity and depth are two radically different things. When you are in the throes of NRE, your feelings, though real, can't have the depth that they would have with someone you know well. There's a difference between falling in love and loving. You may be smitten by someone, or may have experienced "love at first sight." This isn't love; it's chemistry, though it's often the case that what triggers your response—whether it's vocal quality, a particular scent, a way of moving, hair, eye color, bone structure, or anything else—is deeply rooted in your biology and past attachments. This kind of deep sense of connection is important, but it is by no means a guarantee that you are truly well matched. The qualities that are revealed over time are the ones that are more significant in terms of long-term relationship satisfaction.

Some people feel disappointed or disillusioned as NRE starts to dissipate. This can lead to a breakup, especially among those who conflate love and infatuation or crave the intensity that NRE engenders. For others, the change is less dramatic, and the transition from infatuation or what psychologists call *limerence* to enduring love feels natural or even seamless. We will examine how this transition is frequently viewed as tragic in Chapter 12: Going the Distance, but for now, it's sufficient to note that the end of infatuation is the first major turning point in any partnership.

AFTER INFATUATION

Karen and Oliver have been together for just over four years, making them the shortest-term couple we'll be quoting. They are currently engaged, and Karen has a clear memory of making the transition from NRE to being in a partnered relationship. She has important things to say about the role of humor, the need to be flexible as one adapts, and the meaning of marriage.

After I moved to New York, our relationship began to develop into what it is today. Everything that attracted me to Oliver became everything that would frustrate, challenge, drive me crazy and, occasionally make me want to end the whole darn thing! So how did we go from initial infatuation with all those great qualities, to some utter frustration, to what is now appreciation, continued curiosity and love of all his wonderful qualities as well as all of his very human foibles?

One aspect that helped us grow was the sense of humor we both bring to the table. True, whenever I get really challenged, whether it's by his love of choice, his tendency to plan in his head rather than delegate, or the ways he's just like me (hey—only one of us can be lazy today, no fair!) my sense of humor might not be as readily available as his. Luckily, even through some of the really tough spots that first year or two, we both always seemed to come back, ready to forgive and forget and even laugh about the "fight" we had just had. I'm not perfect, I absolutely hold on to gripes or annoyances longer than I "should." And I fess up and can't help but laugh at my own foibles, as well as his.

I really love and appreciate Oliver for: his honesty about who he is in the moment, his willingness to accept his own and my changes, his desire to keep learning and exploring the world, his dedication to the people in his life, the way he has responsibly dealt with loss, his never-give-up attitude, and his remarkable openness and acceptance of all people.

After four years together, we have decided to get married. In truth, we very nearly already are. And we possibly could continue to grow and move forward on our own without marriage. Oliver and I have chosen to be each other's family. Without marriage, that remains our own, personal choice, beautiful, but kept tight within a bubble of our own small world. While I have had many "chosen" family members in my life—family friends whose importance grew beyond the simple title of friend—I feel that this marriage means that we have not only "chosen" each other but that we are on a road to create something new and potentially even larger. By joining ourselves in union, we also succeed in linking our families—my parents and his daughter, my cousins and his, even his ex-wife—who somehow become joined in a greater web, a bigger circle of people and influences, and with that comes greater potential, greater power to offer good in the world.

While the energy of our relationship may no longer be so-called new relationship energy, I feel that there will always be the new energy of each experience, and part of the joy in that is experiencing the journey we go on together.

Oliver was in an open relationship, with a live-in partner and other lovers, both male and female, when he met Karen at a party. He describes that first meeting as electrifying, with a strong attraction when their eyes first met; however, she was not interested in open relationships, and lived in San Francisco, while he lived in New York. Despite these hurdles, he pursued her and invited her to dinner on his next trip to the Bay Area.

On my trip back a month later I hadn't heard from her. Asking around through friends from the party, I got her info and sent her an invite for that dinner date I had wanted. She answered, but the easy flow and intensity had been replaced with guarded apprehension.

When we finally met up a couple days later, as soon as Karen opened the door to greet me, I could read on her face what the obstacle was. She was sure I was just a player looking to hook up. I saw myself through her eyes and realized, yeah, I'm a stranger, and she has no reason to think my motives for wanting to meet again are anything other than self-serving.

We went to dinner and as the hours passed we talked. I learned of her family, her thoughts, and what she wanted to explore next in life. The heat and intensity of our first meeting wasn't there, but a warm and sharing person of a different nature was. That was the start of a pattern that would become the bedrock of our relating.

It's four plus years later now. In that time members of my romantic circle ebbed and flowed. Many, including my original partner, moved on organically into friendships. Karen joined and found her own place both within the circle and in New York, growing our relationship into what we have currently created.

As things stand now it is us, and no others, as lovers. We are in many ways in a much more conventional and traditional place as primarily monogamous, living together, and recently engaged. We carry the knowledge of shifting relationships, personality dynamics, and openness to explore within us and throughout our relationship. Many of our friends turn to us for advice and guidance knowing that we have not only built an enviable coupling but have firsthand experience on the changing nature of caring for people while discovering ourselves.

The next turning point in many relationships takes place when people move in together or get married. This sometimes occurs more or less simultaneously with the transition from infatuation to enduring love, but the issues and challenges this change presents are somewhat different. That said, these challenges do relate to the shift that takes place when people stop dating each other, having separate lives, and getting together when it's mutually desirable and convenient to do so. As Esther Perel observed in *Mating in Captivity,* there is a tension between the domestic and the erotic. It would be foolhardy to pretend that this tension is not real. The person you are dating is a lot more mysterious than the person with whom you wake up every morning, whose odors, illnesses, and changes in mood become a part of your everyday existence.

Some may think this is a pessimistic view of love and long-term relationships, but we prefer to see it as a realistic and empowering one. Recognizing these biological facts makes it possible to act in ways that will strengthen your bond and keep your erotic connection vibrant as you transition from infatuated to enduring love or from dating each other to being a couple. Even if you're a long-term couple, we encourage you to keep on dating each other.

Whether you are brand-new lovers or you have been together for years, it's crucial to become skilled at relating both in and out of bed. As time goes on, you may have to become more active in choosing to remain sexually engaged. While this may take effort at times, your knowledge of each other, your shared base of experience, and the goodwill you've built by repeatedly demonstrating your dedication to having a great erotic life are likely to enrich both your relationship and your lovemaking. If you're in a new relationship, this book should help you manage the transitions gracefully, and if you've been together for a while, you should discover ways to reconnect and rekindle your passion for each other.

GOOD RELATIONSHIPS: THE TEN BIG MYTHS

New relationships can be intense and all-consuming and may often include the desire for a kind of total merger with one's beloved. By contrast, long-term relationships require people to maintain intimacy as well as separateness, comfort as well as passion. These aspects of a partnership can often feel like antitheses. The key to having a vibrant relationship lies in finding a balance and embracing all aspects of these apparent polarities. This is particularly true in the realm of sex, and in the coming chapters we'll share an array of tools for doing just that.

Good sex is closely tied to the general health of a long-term relationship. Misguided beliefs about the nature of sex, love, and what it takes to have an enduring relationship are deeply embedded in Western culture. These cultural myths affect us, whether we believe in them or not, because they are so persistent and pervasive. They frequently send us mixed messages, create unrealistic expectations, and lead us to reduce living human beings to stereotypes.

For this reason, it is valuable to examine some of these myths and the burden they place on all of us when we're interacting with real people. By recognizing the way these myths affect us, both consciously and unconsciously, we can reframe them, discard them, or at the very least minimize their power over us.

This is the first step toward making relationships richer, more rewarding, and more genuine. It will help keep sex fresh and ensure that it stays pleasurable for as long as you are together.

MYTH #1: YOU NEED TO FIND A SOUL MATE

In contemporary society, there is a very common superstition that finding one's soul mate (sometimes called a "twin flame") is the key to having a true pair-bond, and that in the absence of this "other half," no intimate relationship will be fully satisfying. Two very damaging concepts are implicit in this belief: first, that there is a single, ideal partner out there in the world for every individual, and second, that people are incomplete until they find their "other half."

This belief in the soul mate is so pervasive that there are hundreds of books on the market with "soul mate" in the title. The notion was perhaps most succinctly expressed in

THE MYTH OF
THE MISSING OTHER HALF

The origins of this myth are very old, dating back at least to ancient Greece. In *The Symposium,* Plato has Aristophanes tell a story in which humans originally had four arms and legs and two faces until Zeus severed them, thus forcing people to spend their lives looking for their missing other half. This vision of human incompleteness gained even greater currency in the twentieth century, as the idea that romantic love should be the foundation of enduring relationships became the cultural standard.

the emotional tagline from the 1996 film *Jerry Maguire,* "You complete me," which was also the title of a hit song by Keyshia Cole in 2008. This is clearly a concept with enduring popular appeal.

Some matches are indeed better than others. People who are not well matched on multiple levels are not likely to have satisfying relationships. Despite the fact that Internet dating services often promote their ability to help subscribers find their soul mates, the real secret behind Internet dating is the use of algorithms to identify compatible qualities more accurately, weeding out the poor matches.

The pursuit of a perfect or ideal mate is misguided. The idea that a twin flame exists somewhere may have a certain allure, but it is a prescription for relationship dissatisfaction, because it is based on a fantasy. In reality, there are multitudes of potentially good partners out there, for anyone. You need to have enough in common—values, interests, sexuality—for a relationship to have potential, but there will inevitably be differences. It is important to bear this in mind for the long term, no matter how well matched you may be. The idea that you have to be in total harmony all the time is just as toxic as the idea that you need to find a perfect match.

Since you're reading this book, you may already have found a partner who is a good match for you, or perhaps you are in a new relationship and want to develop the skills for having a more fulfilling long-term partnership. To ensure that things continue to function smoothly in the long run and to keep your sex life vibrant, focus on the areas where you fit together well and develop the flexibility to accept and perhaps even appreciate those areas where you differ. This applies both in and out of the bedroom.

TIP: Explore Your Commonalities and Differences

Make two lists: one of qualities and tastes that you share, and another of ways in which you differ. Try to be as specific as possible in identifying how the similarities and differences enrich your relationship and sex life. To provide a concrete example from our own lives: we bring a number of different strengths to our writing. For one, Patricia's background as an opera singer has given her the ability to be very disciplined and consistent in work habits. Mark is more prone to procrastinating, waiting until inspiration strikes, and working extremely hard as deadlines loom. Over the years, we have found that these very different approaches to working have been an asset. We have influenced each other, but we both retain the same general makeup. The combination of these two qualities has had a synergistic effect, enabling us to write four books together.

MYTH #2: THEY LIVED HAPPILY EVER AFTER

This myth (and it really does have mythic origins) is very closely related to the concept of the soul mate. Both predate the belief that romantic love is the foundation on which long-term relationships should be built. Both are archetypes that exist in similar forms in many different cultures and that appeal to deep-seated human yearnings. And both have increased their grip on the contemporary psyche, in part because they have been amplified and modified in popular culture.

As you are most likely aware, the expression "and they lived happily ever after" originated in fairy tales. Contemporary Americans are most familiar with the Disney versions of the tales, which gloss over many of the darker, more violent aspects of these stories to make them palatable for mass consumption. Similarly, the modern, Disneyfied renditions tend to create the impression that happily ever after refers to romantic love. In reality, these tales followed two primary formulas. One involves restoration. *Sleeping Beauty* is perhaps the best-known example; *The Ramayana* is another, more ancient version from a different culture. In this form of tale, a person of noble background is brought low, forced to suffer, and is then restored to his or her proper station. The other form of tale involves the rise of someone from poverty to wealth, often through marriage to a noble. *Cinderella* is a prime example, though in many of the earliest "rise tales" the hero is male.[1]

---

1   Ruth B. Bottigheimer, "Fairy-Tale Origins, Fairy-Tale Dissemination, and Folk Narrative Theory," *Fabula* 47, no. 3–4 (September 2006), 211–221, abstract online at http://www.degruyter.com/view/j/fabl.2006.47.issue-3-4/fabl.2006.023/fabl.2006.023.xml.

Thus, in its original form, happily ever after seems to have little to do with love or emotional connection between the hero and heroine. Instead, these are stories about wealth and class, about suffering and reward, or in the case of *The Ramayana*, about purity and doing one's duty (and Sita and Rama don't exactly live happily ever after).[2] Modern adaptations of these tales—the film *Pretty Woman,* for example— often rely on the "rise" formula and celebrate the change in station, but they differ from the originals by emphasizing the personal qualities and lovable traits of the prince. There was a prince but no Prince Charming in the original fairy tales; the appellation is a nineteenth-century invention.[3] Similarly, in all likelihood, we twenty-first-century Americans understand happily ever after in a way that differs vastly from

---

2   *The Ramayana* is an Indian epic with deeply symbolic and esoteric meanings. Despite its origins in a culture quite different from our own, it is a kind of double restoration tale, albeit a more ambiguous one, with a more complicated ending in some versions. To make a very long story (or group of stories) short, the couple in *The Ramayana*, Sita and Rama, are both noble, and Rama is the heir to a kingdom. After they marry, Rama's stepmother prevails on his father to pass the throne to a younger sibling and banish the couple. Sita, Rama, and their entourage are contented in their exile, until a demonic figure named Ravana kidnaps Sita. Rama raises an army, and with the help of the monkey god Hanuman, defeats Ravana and his minions and rescues Sita. After the rescue, he accuses her of having been unfaithful. Sita insists that her love has never wavered. The story varies, but Sita either throws herself on a funeral pyre or is subjected to a trial by fire, which she survives thanks to divine intervention. Rama is then restored to the throne. In some versions of the tale, rumors of Sita's infidelity persist, and Rama banishes her. In these versions, she bears him two sons while in exile, and when she next encounters him, she asks the Earth, her mother, to swallow her. For a good, brief discussion of the complexities of reading *The Ramayana*, see USC Professor Vinay Lal's site, Manas, http://www.sscnet.ucla.edu/southasia/Religions/texts/Ramaya.html.

3   The Merriam-Webster Online Dictionary, http://www.merriam-webster.com/dictionary/prince%20charming, states that it first appeared in 1856.

what our ancestors understood a couple of centuries ago.

The old understanding was not relationship-based; it was about one's station, and "they lived happily ever after" was a formulaic recitation that was followed by "The End." In contemporary culture, the meaning of the phrase has morphed and has taken on an altogether different air of finality. Because we value romantic love in a way that our ancestors did not, we are likely to think of it as the source of happiness. This is a kind of subtle entrainment that can impair our ability to realize that relationships are dynamic and subject to change. The idea, as so crudely yet memorably dramatized in *Pretty Woman,* is that once you meet your Prince Charming, everything will work out wonderfully, even if there are a couple of initial bumps in the road.

Although it is modern, this mythology is so deeply ingrained in our culture that, like Christianity, it influences virtually everyone, no matter how sophisticated you are and how much you've struggled to free yourself from limiting ideas. It is likely that a great deal of relationship disappointment has its roots in "happily ever after." It can lead to unrealistic expectations, an unending quest for the perfect partner, and the mistaken belief that a mere rough patch is a catastrophe. The truth is that even the happiest and most harmonious partnerships can sometimes be difficult.

Relationships change and evolve, and that is something to celebrate. When it comes to Prince or Princess Charming, forget about the quest. Find aspects of that ideal, mythical being in your current partner, and focus on them. Don't compare yourselves or your relationship to other people, especially to characters that never existed.

MYTH #3: YOU SHOULD WORK ON YOUR RELATIONSHIP

America was founded in large part on Puritan values, and the "Puritan work ethic" is often seen as a cornerstone of our society. While there is certainly nothing wrong with hard work, the tendency to overvalue it can lead to a grim and joyless worldview that treats playfulness as childish frivolity. Maintaining a playful attitude is one of the keys to having great sex and an effective way to keep your relationship happy and well balanced.

This emphasis on the need for work directly conflicts with the happily ever after mythology we just discussed. Many people seem to believe in both ideas, despite the contradictions. Love is effortless, and involves prancing off, hand in hand, through a field of flowers, forever and ever. At the same time, you must buckle down and make it work. Neither of these beliefs is particularly healthy, and entertaining both of them at once can only lead to unhappiness.

Too often, the idea of work enters people's minds at a time when the relationship is already in trouble. People say things like, "We need to take some time to work on our relationship." Sitting back and waiting until things are bad, and then deciding to go to work, is not a very effective way to get through difficult times. It is better to nurture your connection on a daily basis. If you can do this, you are far less likely to be overwhelmed during rough patches.

Sustained effort and attentiveness to your partner are important if a relationship is to thrive, but effort and work are not synonymous. Relationships are not jobs and should not be drudgery, so we encourage people to change their language. One way of reframing the idea of work is to think about your relationship in the language of business or art. If you apply the term *joint venture* (or even better, *joint adventure*) to your partnership, you are likely to get a good return on your investment.

We also like the term collaboration, though it has its roots in "labor," which is synonymous with work. Despite this etymology, collaboration is usually used in the context of creative and artistic undertakings. Approaching your life and your love as a creative process will help you discover more joy and pleasure in all of your interactions.

Both of these linguistic modifications have the added benefit of implying mutuality and sharing. Changing terms may seem like a small thing, but words matter. In fact, they matter a lot.

Changing terms changes the way you think, and changing the way you think can enhance your erotic life together. The more playful you can be about your sex life, the more happiness and enjoyment you will find. If you can reimagine your relationship as a joint adventure, try imagining your sexual encounters (and adventures) as opportunities to play together. This will help you avoid one of the pitfalls that couples commonly face: difficulty talking about sex. People often think that addressing their sex lives requires a big conversation. It's far better to talk about sex a lot, and in as light-hearted a way as possible. Sex can be quite silly, after all, so make talking about it a priority, and retain a sense of humor. This is not to say there will never be times when you have to be more serious. Every light and humorous sexual conversation you have is a way of creating goodwill, of investing in each other, and if you make that investment, the more difficult conversations won't drain your resources.

TIP: Talk about Sex

Include the subject of sex in three or more conversations a week. Keep it light and general at first. If talking about sex is new to you, you can make the conversation playful and less personal by repeating slang and clinical words for sexual body parts and activities. Take turns saying each word at least four times. Try to top each other with ridiculous sexual terminology. Pussy, pussy, pussy, pussy! Schlong, schlong, schlong, schlong! Wank, wank, wank, wank! You're likely to be laughing before long. This can lay the groundwork for talking about sex in general terms: "I've heard that some apes resolve conflict by having sex. Can you imagine what life would be like if that were how humans acted?" As you get more comfortable, you can move into talking about what you enjoy about sex: "I never feel as relaxed as I do after an orgasm," or "When you take me into your mouth, I feel like my entire body is enveloped. It's wonderful."

MYTH #4: MEN ARE FROM MARS; WOMEN ARE FROM VENUS

This phrase is no doubt familiar to most. It is the title of a perennial best seller by John Gray that was first published in 1993 and remains popular over twenty years later. Gray's thesis was undoubtedly influenced by "different voice feminism," especially the work of psychologist Carol Gilligan and linguist Deborah Tannen. Gray's book was a phenomenon; it made Gray a sought-after speaker and generated numerous sequels and spin-off products.

Gray took the scholarly research, which itself errs on the side of gender essentialism, to an extreme and thereby reinvented it as stereotype. We're not the first to observe that people of all genders are from Earth. Beyond that, men and women have more in common with each other than with any other creature on the planet. To make blanket generalizations is not helpful except on the most superficial level. Gray's model builds on older myths—the concepts of "opposite sexes" and "the battle of the sexes"—and reconfigures them in therapeutic terms. Despite this reframing, the model is still an adversarial one, and adversarial models are not optimal for nurturing harmonious relationships or fueling sexual passion (except in very small doses). Having the sense that you're on opposing teams will only foster conflict.

The myth that men are from Mars and women are from Venus emphasizes what makes us different instead of what we have in common and also neglects the many individual variations that exist among human beings—how we are shaped by culture, class, ethnicity, and family background, to name a few. It is far more valuable to develop an intimate understanding of your partner's style—in all forms of communication, whether verbal or nonverbal.

There is a common belief that men want sex and women want love, but sometimes men need to feel heard emotionally before they can be sexual. Similarly, certain men may value cuddling and other forms of physical intimacy more than they value sex. We think it is essential to point out that this stereotype is a modern invention. In the pre-Modern period, men were believed to be naturally chaste but subject to seduction by wanton, lust-driven women, an equally stereotypical belief that persists mostly below the conscious level in contemporary Western culture. The best approach is to understand your own ways of being, your own styles of communicating, and your own sexualities, as individuals and as a couple.

Some of these may fit the stereotypes, and others almost certainly will not. Remember that none of these things are static. Although we all may have certain patterns that remain with us for most of our lifetimes, we also change, grow, and respond differently depending on a multitude of factors. If you're stuck in the belief that men want to fuck and women want to cuddle, or that men want to dominate and women want to communicate, you're not treating your partner as a living human being. The more carefully you can tune in and recognize when your partner wants to cuddle and then fuck, fuck and then cuddle, or fuck, get dressed, and go out, the more fun you both will have. This is true even if your partner needs to talk and doesn't want to fuck at all. So forget the other planets; just pay attention to what's happening here on Earth.

MYTH #5: RELATIONSHIPS AND SEX ARE ABOUT GETTING YOUR NEEDS MET

There's a popular belief that getting your needs met is the key to relationship satisfaction. All people have needs, and it's human nature to try to ensure that these needs are met. Nevertheless, we believe that focusing too intently on your own needs while buying into the myth that your partner is obligated to fulfill them imposes an impossible burden on a relationship.

This focus on "needs" is common to the point of being pervasive in our society. Many approaches to improving relationships treat getting your needs met as paramount, frequently without exploring what the phrase really means. This has been a subject of debate among psychologists for decades, and there are a number of different ways of defining and categorizing human needs.

The best known of these is Abraham Maslow's model, which he called the "hierarchy of needs." It is pyramidal in structure. Maslow posited that our most basic needs are physiological. The next level up in the hierarchy is safety, followed by love and belonging (including sex), then esteem, and self-actualization.[4] Maslow's theory has been both expanded upon and criticized, but it remains very useful for thinking about life and how to find fulfillment and meaning in a modern, individualistic society.

At the same time, it seems to us that Maslow's model conflates actual needs with wants and desires. Everyone needs food, shelter, air, and both physical and emotional interaction with others. (Physical contact is crucial for infants, and complete isolation generally leads to mental illness in adults.) However, beyond these biologically determined requirements, things are considerably more complicated, and the influence

---

4   A. H. Maslow, "A Theory of Human Motivation," *Psychological Review* 50, no. 4 (1943), 370-96, full text available at http://psychclassics.yorku.ca/Maslow/motivation.htm.

of culture and other factors is far stronger. For example, most people also feel a desire to have sex (which can feel subjectively like a need), though this varies a great deal from person to person and from time to time. We both love sex; having it is very important to us; but it's also true that we could live without it if we had to.

As we see it, what people usually mean when they say they aren't getting their needs met is actually that they aren't getting what they want or desire. In the realm of sex, distinguishing between needs and wants can be crucial, especially if your libidos are not well matched. If you think you have a need, and your partner isn't fulfilling it, you're stuck, since the language implies that something essential, perhaps for your very survival, is lacking. Conversely, if you say that you want something but aren't getting it, you have more options. You can negotiate; you can adjust internally; or you can choose ways to get what you want that aren't driven by the feeling of desperation that needing something and not getting it are sure to inspire. Framing something as a want rather than a need also makes it much easier to avoid blaming your partner for failing you when you aren't getting it.

In addition to distinguishing between needs and wants or desires, we suggest that shifting the focus from the self to the *other* is the most effective way to get what you want in your relationship, perhaps most dramatically in the context of sex. It's a bit of a cliché to say that what we get tends to be commensurate with what we give, but this has been our experience. We'll discuss Tantra and Neo-Tantra in more detail in Chapter 7. For now, we'd like to point to one important element from the classical Tantric tradition that provides a useful model for how to approach both sex and relationships in general. In Tantric sexual ritual, the practitioners have very specific roles to play—each is there to help the other reach a state of extended, mystical ecstasy that can be attained in prolonged lovemaking. Thus, the attitude of both partners in the Tantric ritual is one of service. The focus is on the other, not on the self. This focus on the other is crucial.

It is true that, on a certain level, relationships have a transactional dimension. It is also true that we all feel needy sometimes. Even without the cultural messages we've internalized, most of us will feel disappointed in our partners for not living up to our hopes and expectations, at least from time to time. But if you can develop this attitude of service and bring it into your life, recognizing that your purpose both in and out of bed is to take your partner higher, the higher you are likely to be taken in return. This will only work if the two of you can agree upon it together and apply it. This way of thinking can be a challenge. It requires a conscious effort to overcome deeply held cultural beliefs, but it has been at the core of our relationship for well over a decade. We can say very confidently that it works.

MYTH #6: DESIRING SOMEONE ELSE IS A FORM OF INFIDELITY

This myth is closely related to the belief that monogamy is both natural and optimal (see Myth #7). It also relates back to the myths about soul mates and living happily ever after. Implicit in this idea are the beliefs that if you truly love someone, that person should be everything to you and that feeling attracted to others is both morally wrong and a sign of serious problems in your relationship.

This belief frequently extends into the realm of sexual fantasy. For some, fantasizing about anyone outside the primary relationship is virtually the same as cheating, and much of the moral outrage about pornography is based on a form of this myth. According to self-help superstar Dr. Phil McGraw, "Watching Internet pornography or engaging in cybersex is a short step to cheating." McGraw goes on to urge his readers to tell their partners to "choose between the pornography or the relationship."[5] While the Internet may encourage certain compulsive behaviors, McGraw's premise seems to be that directing any sexual energy or desire outside the primary relationship is the first step on a slippery slope.

It's somewhat paradoxical that many people (including some who would be extremely jealous if their partners so much as looked at another person) contend that anything short of genital intercourse is not sex. This is another example of the mixed, confused, and confusing beliefs about sex and relationships that pervade American culture. The way out of this jumble is to examine the messages you've been receiving and to experiment, explore, and discover what's true for you, with the awareness that circumstances may change. For example, you may enjoy viewing Internet porn or have a casual flirta-

---

5   Dr. Phil McGraw, "Is Internet Pornography Cheating?" http://www.drphil. com/articles/article/54.

tion with someone at work. These things may be perfectly OK with your partner at one time but not another. The disloyalty is not in the behavior or any specific actions; it has far more to do with your attitude and your agreements.

To frame this more positively: allowing yourself to feel and openly acknowledge desire for another can actually nourish your bond. If you like watching porn, masturbating to it, and can tell your partner about your activities, you can get turned on and then bring that energy into your relationship. This is true even if you are a man who is masturbating to orgasm, though not to the exclusion of having sex with your partner. It's often the case that denying and suppressing desire leads to a more generalized lack of interest in sex, especially if what you're denying is a core part of who you are sexually. If you can embrace your sexuality, including desires that may not be socially acceptable, and bring that passion into your relationship, your shared sex life is likely to be a lot more fulfilling.

It's not uncommon for people who are having affairs to feel renewed attraction to their long-term partners. It can be valuable to bear this in mind when you're thinking about mere attractions or fantasies involving other people and activities that may not be part of your shared sexual life. You can use these attractions and fantasies as aphrodisiacs. If you're walking down the street with your partner and someone catches your eye, talk about it. You may discover that open discussion of your erotic impulses and your turn-ons fuels your desire for each other. If you can alter your thinking just a little and be honest, you'll realize that desire is limitless. Viewed from this perspective, outside attractions (whether or not you act on them) have the potential to inspire new and exciting conversations about your sex life and deepen your emotional connection.

MYTH #7: MONOGAMY IS NATURAL AND OPTIMAL

The myth that monogamy is natural and optimal undergirds the belief that desire for another is tantamount to cheating. The origins of these beliefs are ancient in Western culture. By no means were all the marriages in the Bible monogamous (Jacob had twelve wives), and the nature of marriage was quite different before the modern era. Nevertheless, both the Old and New Testaments (especially the New Testament) tend to emphasize some form of monogamous union and to treat it as the preferred form of relationship.

In more recent decades, evolutionary psychology (and especially the popularized version thereof) has been enlisted to justify the kind of monogamy practiced in modern America as being evolutionarily determined. According to the crudest form of this narrative, contemporary relationship structures are rooted in the behavior and biology of our Pleistocene ancestors. It holds that men by nature want to spread their seed and have sex with as many women as possible, and women are looking for a provider, using their sex appeal to ensnare an alpha male. When a child is produced, the bond with the child tames the man, keeps his urges in check, and ties him down to a life of supporting his mate and their children, unless and until his old instincts are triggered, usually by some younger, more alluring woman.[6] We've come a long way since Shakespeare's era, when female nature needed to be "tamed."

In their brilliant and important best seller, *Sex at Dawn: How We Mate, Why We Stray, and What It Means for Modern Relationships*, Christopher Ryan and Cacilda Jethá do an effective job of demolishing this stereotype. They make a very strong case, based on ethnography, data about other primates, anatomy, and the human sexual response cycle, that our Pleistocene ancestors lived in small bands and engaged in sex in a more open, egalitarian way. Ryan and Jethá argue that preagricultural human sexual behavior more closely resembled that of bonobos (our closest primate relatives, known for their robust sexuality) than the norms that prevail in modern society. Although these arguments and the supporting data are compelling, there is also a good deal of evidence—based on ethnography and on studies of the brain and hormonal influences on sex and parenting—to suggest there is some truth to the evolutionary psychologists' argument that we are wired for pair-bonding.[7]

If human biology inspires us both to form intimate pair-bonds and to seek contacts outside of those bonds, then what makes for a healthy relationship is considerably more complex than dogmatic advocates of monogamy (or nonmonogamy

---

6   David Brooks and Gail Collins, "Why Househusbands Are the Future," http://opinionator.blogs.nytimes.com/2010/02/17/why-househusbands-are-the-future/. Brooks has been one of the leading popularizers of this simplistic gloss on evolutionary psychology.

7   Patrick Clarkin, "Humans are (Blank-) ogamous," http://kevishere.word-press.com/2011/07/05/part-1-humans-are-blank-ogamous/. Dr. Clarkin's multipart discussion of *Sex at Dawn* and biological anthropology is thorough, balanced, and well worth reading.

for that matter) would have us believe. At the same time, the impulse to bond deeply with another is not something that should be dismissed lightly. Our species varies a great deal, and it's as much of a mistake to think about absolutes when it comes to monogamy and nonmonogamy as it is to state flatly that men are from Mars, and women are from Venus. Since this is a book for couples, we will assume that the overwhelming majority of our readers are already in a pair-bonded relationship. How you choose to deal with the other side of the equation—that desire for outside sexual contact—is entirely up to you. The important thing is to define your terms, be clear and honest with each other, and recognize that things can change.

The biggest problem with monogamy as currently practiced is that it is a default mode—a relationship style that is taken as a given, as morally right, as the only healthy option, as a way of being that cannot be examined, let alone questioned. When monogamy is advocated in this unconscious manner, it's very difficult even to define it. We think this reflexive monogamy is the source of much heartache, and it is one of the primary reasons why various forms of cheating are so prevalent. For many, compulsory monogamy is an impossible standard to live by, so they cheat, even though they simultaneously believe that cheating is the worst possible thing they can do. This is a uniquely modern and largely American attitude. While adultery is considered to be a sin and has been treated as a crime throughout the Western world, it has also been expected and generally tolerated in European cultures, when engaged in discretely.

If you can move away from thinking of monogamy as the ideal and recognize it as just one form of human behavior, something that you can choose, you can arrive at a more specific, genuine, and personal understanding of what choices are right for you. Begin by asking yourself what really matters to you right now and what being monogamous means to you. You may feel that monogamy is primarily emotional—some people are untroubled by sexual infidelities but are pained by the thought of a partner's emotional intimacy with another. You may think it's all about the sex—some find the thought of a partner making love to another to be unsettling or worse but are untroubled by deep friendships. You may not be comfortable with either one of these models, or your feelings may depend on the circumstances.

Developing this more nuanced and fluid understanding of relationships will help you recognize that monogamy is not monolithic; it may work for some but not for others, or it may be appropriate at some times and not at others. Once you know this, you can begin a dialogue about what you want and what you think would be best for both of you. Then, if you choose to be monogamous, you'll be doing so consciously and will be far less likely to experience it as a kind of prison. Similarly, if you choose to explore opening your relationship, you can do so in a way that is honest and mutual and thus avoid the pain that cheating and deception so often inflict.

TIP: Define Monogamy for Yourselves

Discuss what monogamy, infidelity, and cheating mean to you. Each of these may include both sexual and nonsexual components. This is just an intellectual exercise. Treat it as an opportunity to think about these subjects in a more methodical way, not as a conversation about what you might do in the future. These terms are not easy to define, and you may need to have more than one conversation to arrive at your own understandings. Engaging in a dialogue about monogamy and what it means to you will help you think about sex and relating in a more conscious and intentional way. This is likely to give you a deeper understanding of your own relationship dynamics and your underlying and often unspoken assumptions. Bringing awareness to these aspects of a relationship is a great way to build intimacy.

MYTH #8: SEX SHOULD BE SPONTANEOUS

Now that we've examined some of the biggest myths about relationships, it's time to take a look at some misconceptions about sex. It would probably be possible to write several volumes on this subject, but in our experience, the myth that sex should be spontaneous is very common and very damaging. We have been surprised at the resistance we've faced when we point out that this belief can be a source of problems, even as we acknowledge that spontaneous sex can be delightful.

The insistence on spontaneity seems to be tied to some of our cultural ideas about relationships, the belief in soul mates and happily ever after in particular. If relationships should be "natural" and effortless, it stands to reason that sex should be too—that you should come home from work, fall into each other's arms, tear each other's clothes off, and make mad, passionate love on the kitchen table. Of course, when this happens, it's great, but we suspect that it's rare for most long-term couples (and even many short-term ones).

The ideal of spontaneous sex is not rooted in reality. People lead busy lives, and most have to plan their days and evenings. They come home from work tired and distracted, and if children or aging parents are in the picture, there are additional demands to be met. It's hard to feel like jumping each other's bones when there are so many obstacles in the way. This may sound like a fairly grim picture of modern life, but we think it's a generally accurate one.

For most couples, dating is effectively a form of engaging in scheduled sex. When people don't live together, they plan their meetings, prepare for their dates, and get together at an appointed place and time, perhaps for dinner and maybe a movie. All of this is frequently just a buildup to the main purpose, a sexual encounter, and the buildup enhances the entire experience. Even if sex in this context feels spontaneous, it has actually been planned, and in a way that is as structured as many a well-crafted short story or play. Thus, scheduling sex is OK for most people, in certain contexts and provided they don't openly acknowledge the scheduling.

We live together and work together, mostly at home. We have no children, and in theory, we could have sex whenever we want. In this respect, we're more fortunate than people who have to commute, navigate parental responsibilities, or both. Nevertheless, we've found that if we don't put sex on the schedule, we're far less likely to have it. We are confident that the same is true for the vast majority of couples who are less fortunate than we are. We've found that scheduling sex not only ensures that it will happen, it keeps desire alive between us and increases the odds that we will have spontaneous sex on those days when we haven't put it on our to-do list.

There's another reason why scheduling sex is a valuable and effective way to keep your partnership vibrant and erotically charged. By making the time for encounters to happen, you are treating your lovemaking as something important and worthy of your attention. This is a way to treat your relationship as a living organism that calls for your mutual nurturing. Far from being unromantic, having unspontaneous sex is actually a way of maintaining and deepening intimacy, of showing, in perhaps the clearest possible way, how much you care for each other and how much you value your connection.

TIP: Make Time for It

Schedule at least two erotic encounters a week for the next month. It's up to you whether these encounters include orgasms for one or both of you. Take note of how this affects your general level of desire. Our friends Pierre and Stacy take extra-long lunch breaks every Thursday so they can meet at home for an early afternoon tryst. They delight in anticipating this weekly ritual and tell us that it keeps them feeling hot for each other.

MYTH #9: THE SEX IN MOVIES, ON TV, AND IN PORN IS GOOD

Of all the myths we've discussed, this one is perhaps the most widely repudiated and, at the same time, the most subtly pervasive. Virtually no one dares suggest that sex as it's depicted in the mass media is realistic or is a model that anyone should emulate. Nevertheless, media images influence and can even shape us, whether we recognize it or not.

Before the invention of the motion picture, people got their ideas about how to have sex from still images, the written word, and (in more instances than many of us who grew up with closed doors can probably imagine) from direct observation of people in the act. While Freud thought that a child's witnessing "the primal scene" was an intrinsically traumatic incident, it was, in all likelihood, a commonplace for most of human history. No doubt, children in the small bands of hunter-gatherers, so effectively evoked in *Sex at Dawn*, would have seen adult sexual activity on numerous occasions.

Things changed dramatically with modernity and the introduction of the moving image. We suspect that the overwhelming majority of American adults have never watched other people having sex, but most have probably seen at least some pornography, and virtually all have seen Hollywood depictions in the movies and on television. Filmed sex, whether actual or simulated, is not reality. Instead, it is informed by many of the myths we've already discussed. This unrealistic aspect is exacerbated by the demands of the medium itself.

Many mainstream movie depictions of sex emphasize the spontaneous, romantic ideal. Foreplay is seldom shown. (This is also true in pornography.) People frequently just seem to go at it, and it is usually over very quickly. Older, overweight, or less than beautiful people are often ridiculed for having sex, and sex in general is often mocked.

Sex can certainly be funny and even ludicrous, and most if not all cultures have some form of off-color humor, but in many Hollywood sex comedies—think the long-running *American Pie* series or *The Hangover* franchise—sexual humor degenerates into sexual disgust. Another common cinematic approach is to treat the sex as secondary to the romance and the buildup. After the participants finally tumble into bed where everything happens between the sheets, they manage to awaken with perfect hair and makeup. All of that said,

GOOD SEX ON-SCREEN

Tell Me You Love Me received critical acclaim for its frank portrayal of sex in relationships. The series is even more explicit than the recent and also excellent film about a sex surrogate, *The Sessions*, with Helen Hunt. In both cases, the sexual content is central, in terms of both character development and plot. *Tell Me You Love Me* suggests that sex can improve as people age. The most satisfying (and in our opinion) erotic encounters are between the therapist (Jane Alexander) and her husband (David Selby). At the time of writing, *Tell Me You Love Me* was available on DVD through Netflix, and *The Sessions*, an Academy Award nominee, was still in theatrical release.

in recent years there have been some admirable attempts to depict sex in more honest and realistic ways, notably the HBO series *Tell Me You Love Me* (which lasted only one season), but efforts such as these remain the exception.

In the early days of the Internet, many people started posting homemade pornography online. During that period, it was easy to watch people having very realistic sex, though back then the quantity was nowhere near what it is today and download speeds made viewing difficult and time-consuming. In recent years, pornography that is more commercial has become the rule on the Internet. While we enjoy watching pornography from time to time, most of it provides a terrible model that, unfortunately, some people seem to confuse with reality. In commercial porn, the positions depicted are intended for the camera. The performers are like athletes; many of them spend hours training their bodies and minds for the performance. And despite their skills, the sex often looks contorted, and in many of the scenes, it is questionable whether there is real pleasure involved.

Pornographic films seldom show the application of lube (except for saliva, which works but is hardly the only or optimal lubricant). In many cases, acts that have significant health risks—such as vaginal penetration following anal intercourse with no washing in between—are commonplace. In addition, notwithstanding the emergence of a talented group of feminist pornographers, most pornography is made by men, for men. This is true even though, anecdotally, it seems that the number of younger women who watch Internet porn is growing, so most depictions of female sexuality are based on and designed to appeal to least-common-denominator male fantasies.

Just as we enjoy some pornography, we like a good film or television series and can get caught up in a romantic story as easily as anyone. At the same time, the misleading messages that mass media depictions of sex send to the audience are troubling. There is no way to escape these media depictions, but when you encounter them, remind yourself, *This is only a movie,* and always strive to discover your own authentic form of sexual expression. Ultimately, this will be more satisfying than anything you've ever seen on screen.

MYTH #10: THERE IS A RIGHT WAY TO BE SEXUAL

This myth has much in common and is entwined with the idea that sex should be spontaneous. It also relates to the influence that motion pictures have on people's erotic lives. Our background is in Tantra, and we've encountered some in our field who have very strong beliefs about right and wrong ways to interact; some groups that have been influenced by the Tantric approach even insist that certain types of clitoral stimulation are superior. Others suggest that female ejaculatory orgasms are the ultimate sexual experience and that nonejaculatory orgasms are the male ideal. Similarly, the emphasis on simultaneous orgasm that remains a mainstay of beliefs about heterosexual intercourse is nothing if not a dogma about the right way to have sex.

There are many other beliefs about right and wrong ways to

have sex. Some people still think of oral and anal intercourse as unnatural or degrading. We were surprised to discover that there have been discussions on several blogs among women who feel varying degrees of discomfort about receiving cunnilingus, especially since the common stereotype is that a significant number of men are reluctant to perform it.[8] There are many—some influenced by Freud, others by religion, and still others whose ideas were shaped by more generalized cultural factors—who continue to view masturbation as either entirely unacceptable or as a poor substitute for intercourse, an activity that is wrong for people in relationships. We've heard claims that vibrators are "addictive" and therefore shouldn't be used. The list of misguided beliefs could go on and on. The wrong way to have sex is when it involves an abuse of power, inflicts harm on others, or is nonconsensual. Beyond that, if your lovemaking leaves you unsatisfied or unhappy with yourself, you may be trying to conform to some set of idealized beliefs about what is good sex rather than focusing on what is right for you.

This belief that there's a right way to be sexual can cause a lot of misery. To give one concrete example, as sex-advice columnists on the website dick-n-jane.com, we received a question from Steven, who was distraught because his girlfriend came very rapidly, while he required more time. This sexual response pattern is not typical. Indeed, it is the opposite of what is commonly deemed to be normal. Generally

8   Jamye Waxman, "Women Really Do Have a Fear of Oral Sex," http://thestir. cafemom.com/love_sex/125780/women_really_do_have_a.

speaking, men do come more rapidly than women, but this is by no means always true, and the questioner was clearly very troubled by this perceived abnormality.

He also indicated that he was uncomfortable talking with his partner about the situation. We did our best to encourage communication and suggested that if she was finished with intercourse well before he came and was merely tolerating it, they should work around this difference. Oral sex, manual stimulation, and self-pleasuring are just as valid as genital intercourse and were quite likely a better way for this particular couple to conclude their lovemaking.[9]

The emphasis on genital intercourse as an ideal is perhaps the most dramatic form of the myth, and it is still prevalent. This emphasis by its nature treats same-sex relationships as inferior to heterosexual ones. In reality, as Lou Reed wrote more than four decades ago, "And no kinds of love are better than others."[10] If we can free ourselves from the many myths we unconsciously accept, the possibilities are limitless.

---

9   "She Orgasms Too Quickly," http://dick-n-jane.com/2011/08/she-orgasms-too-quickly.html.

10 Lou Reed, "Some Kinda Love," *The Velvet Underground*, MGM Records, 1968.

3

A NEW PARADIGM: KEYS TO CREATING AN ENDURING AND EROTIC RELATIONSHIP

It's easy to be critical of social norms, especially when discussing relationships and sexuality. Misguided and damaging myths are abundant when it comes to these subjects, and the myths we addressed in the preceding chapter are by no means the only ones that prevail in our culture. Now that we've offered a critique, and some implicit alternatives to the conventional model, we will start exploring a radically different approach to love and sex.

In this approach, self-awareness, especially sexual self-awareness, treating relationships and lovemaking as collaborative activities, and cultivating an adventurous, exploratory attitude are central to having a satisfying sex life. As you may have surmised from the previous chapter, this model involves framing sex and partnership in terms that differ quite dramatically from beliefs that are current both in popular culture and in much of the therapeutic community.

Great sex and lasting relationships are mutual undertakings that are nurtured by selflessness, the deliberate cultivation of what we call *profound interest* in one's partner, a determination to be as kind as possible, even during difficult times, and a recognition that, while openness and honesty are important, discernment about when and how to be open and honest is equally important. Verbal communication plays a major role in developing the capacity to relate in this way; however, nonverbal skills are frequently of more consequence. Connecting nonverbally and becoming skilled at recognizing nonverbal cues are central to building vibrant sexual and interpersonal relationships. In terms of sex, it's essential to be able to talk about it, but too much talk at the wrong time can be an antiaphrodisiac.

Whether you're communicating verbally or not, developing the ability to be empathic and flexible is central to the process. This too involves moving beyond the emphasis on getting one's needs met and fantasies about an idealized partner. It means recognizing that this other with whom you're interacting will forever be somewhat mysterious, even as you attempt to know that person as deeply as is possible. It also means recognizing that change is the only constant in life. Certain themes may recur in our lives; for many of us, the basic template of our sexual tastes is established fairly early, but there is always the potential that new interests and desires will emerge.

From the perspective of performance and desire, most men

hit their peak in their teens or twenties. For most women, this peak comes much later in life. On the surface, this may seem to be a cruel irony, but there is more to sex than performance, and quantity is not the same as quality. Performance and desire are only the most dramatic areas in which changes in sexuality may express themselves over a lifetime. There are many other more subtle and nuanced shifts that take place. Thus, in addition to the qualities we've mentioned above, maintaining a high degree of flexibility—in terms of how you approach lovemaking, how you think about sex, and how you define your relationship—is crucial. There is no one-size-fits-all approach to any of this; if you can stay open and flexible, you will be far better equipped for the long term, and if you develop certain skills, you should be able to keep things hot for many years to come.

KNOW YOURSELF SEXUALLY

Since time immemorial, in cultures around the world, self-knowledge has been seen as a very important, if not the paramount, value in human life. This was true even in cultures that differed immensely from our own and in which individualism, as we know it, would have been a thoroughly alien concept. In the Taoist tradition, for example, it is said, "He who knows others is wise. He who knows himself is enlightened."[11] A similar belief was inscribed on the Oracle at Delphi and expressed by many Greek philosophers, and

11 Lionel Giles, trans., *The Sayings of Lao-Tzu* (London: Orient Press, 1904), 44.

variants on the saying "Unless you know yourself, you cannot know God" have been current in various branches of Judaism, Christianity, and Islam for many centuries. Our training in traditional Tantra included a very strong emphasis on cultivating the ability to observe ourselves and examine not only our mental processes but also our bodies and how we experience them.

Given this history and the transcultural recognition that self-knowledge is central to living a meaningful life, it is somewhat ironic that contemporary Western culture, for all its emphasis on individualism and personal fulfillment, often treats self-knowledge and meaningful self-exploration as mere self-indulgence.[12]

Of course, in all likelihood, most of the ancient sages (except perhaps the Tantric and Taoist sages) were not thinking about sex when they emphasized self-knowledge. In the Western world, the value of sexual self-knowledge seems to have gone mostly unrecognized until the modern era and specifically the age of psychoanalysis. Freud and Wilhelm Reich, whatever their personal and theoretical flaws, deserve great credit for recognizing that sexual self-knowledge is central to living life fully and that the process of getting to know yourself sexually is a crucial step toward liberating yourself.

Freud and Reich's psychoanalytic approaches have fallen out of favor today, and their ideas about sexuality—especially

---

12 While it is beyond the scope of this book to examine the reasons for this apparent paradox, we feel it is important to note that a self-aware person is not likely to be a very compliant consumer.

Reich's—were never fully embraced by mainstream American society, notwithstanding their influence in some circles. If self-knowledge is no longer seen as an admirable goal, sexual self-knowledge remains even more deeply buried, except within the growing community of sex-positive people. Many of us still carry a legacy of sex-negativity that is deeply embedded in American society.

SEX-POSITIVITY AND SEX-NEGATIVITY

Sex-negativity is the belief that some or all human sexual activity is intrinsically harmful, immoral, or distasteful or that sexual activity is only appropriate in the context of marriage or for the purpose of procreation. Sex-negative attitudes are often, but by no means always, rooted in religion. Sex-positivity is the celebration and embrace of consensual human sexual expression.

In a lecture on her book *Satisfaction: Women, Sex, and the Quest for Intimacy,* psychiatry professor Anita Clayton described her clinical experience treating preorgasmic women and revealed that many of her patients, when asked if they ever masturbated, said no, sometimes replying, "Of course not. I'm married." This is but one example of how sexual self-knowledge remains a taboo.

Knowing yourself sexually is really a process. This is true not only because we change and grow, and what is intensely plea-surable and exciting at twenty may not have the same appeal at forty, but also because even the most self-aware person can never attain complete self-knowledge. While you may know that something specific turns you on and may be able to articulate some of the reasons for that response, there will always be a certain element of mystery in the realm of sexuality. Thus, this search for sexual self-knowledge may seem quixotic, and perhaps it is, but the quest is what matters most.

In the context of a long-term partnership, the same principles apply. If you can't ever know yourself fully, knowing another is even more elusive. Being a couple entails bringing together two individual sexualities and thereby creating a third, shared sexuality, a realm in which you both overlap but are not fully congruent. Anyone who pays attention can discover certain things that are sure to please a partner. Nevertheless, there will be aspects of your beloved that are beyond reach and that will remain forever mysterious. Even within the areas where you overlap, there's still the potential to be surprised.

We have already intimated that knowing yourself sexually begins with self-pleasuring. This is not an idea that Freud (who considered masturbation to be immature and a poor substitute for partnered sex) or Reich (who had only a somewhat more tolerant perspective) would have embraced. There has been considerable progress since the early to mid-twentieth century. This is due in large part to Betty Dodson and others of her generation who taught women to become familiar with their genitalia and use vibrators as a tool for becoming orgasmic. Despite the progress that has been made since the 1960s and '70s, there is still a long way to go. Our society has yet to produce a male answer to Betty Dodson, perhaps because the underlying assumption is that men know instinctively how to pleasure themselves. While this may be true on the crudest level, to date there has been little recognition that many men would benefit from exploring self-pleasuring in a more conscious way. Joseph Kramer's work is an important exception, but unfortunately, his influence on the heterosexual male community has been limited, whereas Dodson has been able to reach women of all orientations and has almost singlehandedly inspired a revolution in thinking about female sexuality.

Thus, masturbating, while paying close attention to what kinds of stimulation and what parts of the body give you the most pleasure, is the first step in developing sexual self-knowledge. But it is only the first step. As an aside, masturbation can also be very useful for becoming more flexible sexually. In this context, you can explore different positions, different kinds of stimulation, and different fantasies, without having to worry about performance or your partner's reaction. While we always encourage couples to cultivate an open, exploratory attitude toward their sexual lives together, treating some of your self-pleasuring sessions as solo laboratory experiments can be a great way to discover new things about yourself. You can then share these discoveries with your partner if you choose.

TIP: Masturbate to Learn about Yourself

Pleasure yourself for the purpose of learning more about your personal way of responding. Make this a regular ritual. It is easy to fall into the pattern of masturbating in habitual and limited ways that guarantee a quick orgasm. If you seek new information about yourself during each session, you are likely to find new sensations and orgasmic responses. Do this by touching other parts of your body, not just your genitals, while you are aroused. Experiment with different sex toys, different positions, and times of day, or while watching yourself in a mirror. In addition to gaining greater insight into your inner sexual landscape, you will also reap the many health and emotional benefits of the hormonal rush that accompanies an orgasm. While partnered interactions are pleasurable and can lead to new discoveries, this process can be random. Knowing your own body and being able to describe in detail what you have learned about yourself through sexual self-exploration tends to be a better recipe for making partnered encounters more pleasurable. If you understand what works for you and how you respond, your partner won't have to resort to guessing.

Similarly, masturbating in front of your partner can help you develop self-knowledge as a couple. It can be very intimate—a form of sexual show-and-tell—especially if you can talk about what's happening for you and whatever fantasies you may be using to turn yourself on. This can be a great form of foreplay; it can be done simultaneously, or you can turn it into an erotic display for your partner's voyeuristic enjoyment. And keeping in mind the fact that you're seeking to develop knowledge of each other can serve to deepen your emotional bond as well.

It's not uncommon for people to feel some measure of shame about their masturbation and about their fantasy lives. This feeling of shame, and the accompanying need to hide, often seems to fuel compulsive and unhealthy behaviors. By bringing both masturbation and fantasy into the light, you may find that you feel much better about yourself sexually.

Separateness and some measure of privacy are important in any relationship, but hiding and shame are not the same as having a healthy sense of personal space. If you can be open with your partner about your masturbation and your fantasies, at least some of the time, the shame and intense need to hide certain aspects of yourself are likely to dissipate. Beyond that, your shared sexual knowledge is likely to make your erotic life as a couple far richer.

In addition to the things that turn you on, there are a multitude of other factors to consider when exploring your sexuality together. The more freely, comfortably, and openly you can talk, the more opportunities you'll have to develop a fuller and more varied sexual life. In this context, it's extremely important for the listener to be respectful and kind. Avoid making shaming or judgmental statements about your partner's interests. If you are engaging in this kind of exploration, it's equally important to make sure you don't treat the expression of an interest or a desire as a demand for an activity or as a criticism. By agreeing to make a consistent effort to communicate about your sexuality in a way that is mutually supportive, you will create an environment in which these discussions can be a turn-on.

Some people find it difficult to think about their partners' sexual histories, but this can be a very rich area that presents many opportunities to learn from each other. If you can talk about past lovers, past experiences, what worked well for you and what didn't, you can give each other valuable pointers about what your turn-ons are, just as long as you refrain from making hurtful comparisons. Similarly, if you can talk about your formative experiences, from childhood to first date to what it was like to lose your virginity—creating your own erotic autobiographies—you can learn much about the landscape of your present erotic life.

Watching erotic movies—both mainstream and explicit—can also fuel the conversation. *Secretary, Bandits, Last Tango in Paris,* and *9½ Weeks* are some classic films that deal with sexuality in unconventional ways. Vintage pornography of any kind and instructional explicit films can provoke interesting discussions. You can also buy books about various sexual practices and thumb through them together. This can fuel discussions about how some of the things you haven't tried might affect you.

As you become more practiced, you will be able to start going deeper, and begin examining and understanding your individual and shared sexualities in a more nuanced way. For some, this can serve as a precursor to sexual adventuring, which we will discuss in depth in later chapters. At this stage, just paying attention and bringing sexuality into a realm of conscious awareness and conversation can be liberating.

In our many years of teaching Tantra, some of our student couples have made it clear that they don't talk about sex except during their sessions with us. While we are delighted to provide a safe environment for doing so, we find it unfortunate that they need it. While communicating openly about sex may be a challenge, having the courage to do so will enable you to grow and explore together.

LOVE IS PROFOUND INTEREST

Do you remember how you behaved when you were first falling in love? In all likelihood, you listened intently to what your partner had to say, found something magical in the most mundane biographical details, missed each other, and were eager to be together whenever you were apart. You probably went out of your way not only to listen to this new person in your life but also to do things to make that person happy— anything from very grand, romantic gestures to small acts of consideration, and you in turn received similar gestures with gratitude. If you're like most people, and you've been together for a while, chances are your way of interacting has changed considerably, and you're less thoughtful, less focused on your beloved, and less appreciative. You have the power to change this and recreate some of what it was like during the early stages of the relationship. And in reality, it doesn't take an enormous effort to do so.

People generally think of love and hate as polar opposites, and this is reasonable; intuitively, the feelings seem antithetical, but in some respects they are more similar than they are different. They are both intense. They both demand substantial emotional and mental energy. Most people devote more attention to those they love and those they despise than to those about whom they feel neutral. Thus, in a very significant way, it is more accurate to say that indifference, not hate (or fear), is the opposite of love.

The inspiration for this understanding comes from our

Tantra teacher's teacher, Swami Gitananda Giri.[13] He defined love as "profound interest." This observation not only illustrates our perspective on love and indifference; it also points to a practical method for keeping love and passion alive. All you have to do is actively maintain an interest in your partner.

How do you begin? The first step is to cultivate the ability to pay attention. As any experienced meditator knows, the capacity for sustained attention will fluctuate; similarly, your capacity to be profoundly interested in your partner will vary from time to time and situation to situation. It would be impossible, and undesirable, to be profoundly interested in your partner all the time and during every interaction. As with meditation, the fluctuations are to be expected; the value lies in making the effort and communicating your interest as best you can.

To frame this concept in somewhat more conventional—and clinical—terms, the couples therapist John Gottman uses the phrase "turning toward." According to Gottman, you should, "be aware of bids for connection and turn toward them. The small moments of everyday life are the building blocks of relationship."[14] Every effort to display profound interest in your partner is at once a bid for connection and an act of

---

13 Swami Gitananda was of Indian-Scottish ancestry and was born and raised in India, where he studied with some of the most accomplished and renowned yogis of the early twentieth century. (One of his teachers, Swami Kanakananda, "The Sleepless Saint," is mentioned in *Autobiography of a Yogi*.) He was also an MD, and he spent much of his adult life practicing medicine in Canada before returning to India to establish an ashram. He was thus a person who was able to live in at least two worlds.

14 John Gottman, "The Gottman Theory for Making Relationships Work," http://www.gottman.com/54756/About-Gottman-Method-Couples-Therapy. html. Gottman discusses the concept of "turning toward" in considerably more depth in his books.

turning toward. This can be as simple as taking a few minutes to listen to something your beloved is saying, even if you'd rather be doing something else. Consistently turning toward each other, and receiving and acknowledging the bids for connection whenever possible, will create a positive feedback loop that reinforces the mutuality of your profound interest. When it comes to lovemaking, keeping profound interest in

PROFOUND INTEREST IN PRACTICE

Francesca and Caroline have been together for 14 years and have been married for 12, half of that time legally, in their home state. Francesca is a writer, business owner, and sexuality educator; Caroline is a dancer and somatics teacher in a college-level acting program. Leading a conscious and intentional sexual life together has been central to their relationship from the start. They sometimes function as mentors and role models to friends and acquaintances in their community. We asked them how they display profound interest in each other sexually.

We bring intention to our sexual life together in how we set up time for sex. We make sure we have a date night every week, which we intend as a time of sexual connection. We also attend events, like BDSM workshops and conferences, where sexuality is the focus of a weekend. We get a big dose of external stimulation, which reenergizes us. Our work lives are cyclical—one of us is an academic with summers off, the other's work can be very demanding for weeks at a time and then ease up. When we notice we are not as connected as we'd like, we plan for a "thirty in thirty"—a month in which we have sex every day. After four weeks of daily sex we find we are in the bubble, aligned in the most delicious way. We both believe that it's essential for each of us to have down time, time that is for personal growth and reflection. It's much easier to be available to each other at a profound level when one is available to one's self.

We intentionally keep our erotic lives lively—and in the forefront of our life together. We flirt, strip, sashay, entice each other in the kitchen as much as in the bedroom. We appreciate each other's sexiness. And neither of us tamps down her appreciation of other people's sexiness. It's fun to watch each other's momentary attractions and we even encourage it. The more each of us experiences sexual heat, the hotter we are together.

We love the different moods and levels of intensity of our sexual life together. We think "married" sex is good sex. In fact, sometimes when we think we are about to have ordinary middle-of-the-week sex, suddenly something shifts, and we find ourselves in a state of charged fucking that feels new and uncharted. It's the ongoing practice of intimacy—like weekly date night sex—that allows the unexpected to occur.

We are more likely to ask each other questions and have in-depth discussions when we are planning a BDSM scene or an encounter with another person. We are profoundly engaged with each other, and profoundly curious, but it doesn't really come out through asking each other questions. Our engagement with each other is cultivated through the practices we spoke of above—being intentional with time, liveliness, appreciation, etc.

We do tell each other about our fantasies and explore them together, either through storytelling or role play. It's not the most important part of our sexuality at this point in our life.

When we met, we had really clear D/S roles that are still part of our sexual lives together. We've explored other roles occasionally and have plans to continue that exploration. Mostly we find married sex to be so hot that we engage less in specific role-playing and scenes than we used to.

We find that when we are each individually engaged in her sexual fantasies, interests, etc., our shared sex life benefits. This might mean having a good chat with a friend about sex, or editing sex writing, or giving advice to friends, or hanging out in the sex-positive community where sex is always valued as a topic of conversation. Many people we know don't really talk about sex very much and we think that contributes to the flattening of their sexual interest.

mind can be crucial. It is an important component in the process of developing sexual self-knowledge as a couple. If you aren't deeply interested in your partner's sexuality, you won't be able to gain much insight into your sexual life together, even if you know yourself and your body. If this is true in the broad sense of developing knowledge of your sexual life together, it is perhaps even more important in the context of any given sexual encounter. Good lovers need to cultivate the ability to tune in and notice what's happening internally, while simultaneously observing the way a partner is responding. Being able to focus intently on your beloved's state (without losing track of your own) is the key to giving pleasure. While many people think that love means your partner will anticipate your every need, this ability is really the product of repeated checking in—both verbally and nonverbally—of building a body of

WHAT SUBTLE CHANGES CAN TELL YOU

While everyone is an individual, and we recognize that gender is a continuum, there are some general observations to make about men and women. Sexual arousal in men is usually fairly apparent and visible; the signs tend to be less obvious in women, so it is important to monitor changes in skin tone, body movements, and breathing patterns. This is also true if your partner is a man; you need to know how to back off, to be aware if he is about to come, and to determine whether he's ready to move in the direction of ejaculation or would like to delay it. This can be even more difficult during genital intercourse. If you allow your arousal or your orgasm to overwhelm you, you can leave your partner behind or pull him over the edge before he's ready.

knowledge that's based on profound interest.

To refine this ability to tune in, you have to be able to talk about sex, specifically, and in explicit terms. It can be very useful to discuss an encounter that was less than fully satisfactory, provided you do it long after the event and take care to avoid saying anything critical about your partner. This will not be an abstract conversation about what turns you on or what works for you. It requires talking about your encounter and describing the stimulation you received and the sensations you felt in as much detail as possible. For example, if you were out of sync, and one of you came before you wanted to, it can be incredibly valuable to describe what the orgasm felt like and what triggered you to go over the edge. It's important to reduce the emotional charge around an experience that didn't work out so well and to treat it as a learning opportunity.

This approach to post-sex debriefing also entails, as a first step, talking about what works when things go well. We recommend saying a minimum of three positive things before saying anything vaguely negative or critical. For instance, you can begin with something like this: "You know I always feel happier after sex with you. It is such a turn-on that you're so enthusiastic. I love the way your eyes light up as you kiss your way down my abdomen when you're about to give me head, and when you use your lips and tongue. Sometimes, the feeling of your teeth can be a little too much for me. If you can be gentler and use more lips and tongue, it will be easier to relax and fly higher with you."

This is investing in your relationship and building goodwill. It will create the trust and support that can transform the less enjoyable experiences into learning tools and make those conversations much easier. Making a conscious decision to talk about your encounters in this way will encourage you to stay more aware during sex. When something feels really good, make a mental note of it, so you can describe it clearly to your lover. Being specific will encourage a repeat performance.

TIP: Twenty Things That Make You Happy

List ten things that make your partner happy, and list ten things that your partner does that make you happy. This can be in any realm, sexual or otherwise. Compare lists. Periodically expand on these lists, and make plans to do at least one item a week.

VIEW YOUR SEXUAL LIFE TOGETHER AS A CO-CREATION

As we have already indicated in our discussion of sexual self-knowledge, people bring their individual sexualities into each of their relationships. Thus, the shared sexuality that you have as a couple is created and shaped by your individual sexualities and prior experiences. While these factors will influence your relationship, they need not control or determine it.

By their nature, relationships are co-creations, and it is always helpful to bear this in mind, in good times and in more difficult ones. When things are going well, this awareness will serve to nurture your connection. If you can remember that you are not operating in isolation when you encounter difficulties, you may be able to look at your partner and whatever you are facing in more compassionate and less blaming

THE ART OF RELATIONSHIP

Armand and Isadora are passionate about their art and their relationship. We asked them to comment on how they bring the interrelationship between their creativity and their love for each other.

Armand replied:

Although my experience of our relationship is organic and our collaboration came to life without much planning or thought, I feel that our relationship is a reflection of our creative lives and that each aspect mirrors and enriches the other. We spend pretty much all our time together, and our daily lives are devoted to our creative processes, whether we're working separately or together. Our sex life is creative and fulfilling, and it influences and is influenced by our creative work—Isadora's burlesque performances and my photography, which is often quite sexual. The erotic aspect of our creative work also keeps us focused on our sexuality and requires us to remain in sync.

According to Isadora:

Before I met Armand, I had never worked with a lover on anything. I find that working with him enables me to love him even more. When things don't go as planned, we are able to help each other manage whatever has come up and often to avoid what would otherwise be very stressful. In my own creative work, I trust him and take his advice about any technical or creative challenges I'm facing. Being with him has helped me grow into being a better person and a better artist, and that feeds back into our life together. Our loving partnership is very special. It's a living, loving work of art.

terms. Thinking this way is likely to make it easier to navigate the challenges and generally lead to a happier and more balanced way of being together. When it comes to sex, every encounter with another person is a co-creation. From this perspective, you can view your relationship as a third entity and a third sexuality that is created by your coming together.

This concept of co-creation can be a very valuable one. If you are jointly creating this third entity, this relationship, then it is something that you can nurture and build together, something that will thrive based on the quality of your attention. Another way to think of this is to view your relationship as a process, a collaboration, a work of art.

If you can bring this artistic sensibility to your relationship and recognize that sex is, among many other things, a form of expression—an expression of how you are together, your feelings for each other, the way you think about the world, and how you inhabit your bodies—you will discover another way of approaching and becoming absorbed by the transcendent potential in sex.

There are several ways to clarify this at least superficially abstract idea that you should treat your lovemaking as a form of artistic expression. In the simplest terms, as Mikhail Baryshnikov is purported to have said: "The essence of art is to have pleasure in giving pleasure."[15] While Baryshnikov's

---

15 Mikhail Baryshnikov quoted, http://thinkexist.com/quotation/the-essence-of-all-art-is-to-have-pleasure-in/535149.html. We have not been able to identify the original source of this oft-cited statement, which is sometimes rendered as "The essence of all art..." The aphorism has also been attributed to Dale Carnegie, but the source of that attribution is a 2007 book with no accompanying footnote, http://en.wikiquote.org/wiki/Dale_Carnegie.

observation pertains to art, the same can be said about the essence of great relationships and great sex.

The words of Albert Einstein are perhaps even more apt: "The most beautiful thing we can experience is the mysterious. It is the source of all true art and all science. He to whom this emotion is a stranger, who can no longer pause to wonder and stand rapt in awe, is as good as dead: his eyes are closed."[16] If we can maintain just a little awe and wonder at the mysterious power of sex (even as we gain intellectual knowledge of the subject), there will always be the potential for delight and appreciation in our lovemaking. In addition to being forms of expression, both art and sex can open us up to the mysterious and possibly even the mystical. By remembering that your sexuality is a form of expression, you can begin to think about what you are expressing. Consider how every gesture, every touch, every sound, every movement conveys something to your partner. With this awareness, you can direct your expression in ways that are interesting and potentially profound.

If you cultivate this attitude of openness, curiosity, and creativity, you are likely to discover new ways of being sexual together that will bring greater variety and more pleasure into your encounters. Thinking about sex as a form of artistic expression can make it easier to begin the process of exploration. People who dedicate their lives to exploring the mystery of sex, and do so in a conscious way, generally bring enormous creativity to the process, and you can too.

---

16 Albert Einstein, "Mein Weltbild" (The World as I See It), translation online at the American Institute of Physics website, http://www.aip.org/history/einstein/essay.htm.

TAKE PLEASURE IN SERVING EACH OTHER

We've already alluded to the value of developing an attitude of service in the context of critiquing the notion that relationships are all about getting your needs met. We have also explained that this attitude is an important component of the Tantric approach, and that this is something we strive to incorporate into all aspects of our relationship. We'd like to examine this concept in more depth, as it runs so strongly contrary to many commonly accepted social norms.

The origins of this emphasis on getting needs met in a relationship are more deeply embedded in Western, and especially American, culture, with its tradition of individualism and the very common belief that the purpose of life is self-fulfillment. At its worst, this kind of individualism treats life as a zero-sum game in which there are winners and losers. Even in its milder forms, this emphasis on the individual tends to encourage us to forget that human beings are social animals, and that the individual can only flourish in a context of relatedness and interdependence. We deceive ourselves about our need for others at our peril.

This suggestion may seem radical, but the best way to find fulfillment is to focus more on others than on the self. We've experienced this many times in the context of teaching. We may feel tired or stressed from traveling; we may have had an argument, be in a low mood, or feel otherwise completely uninspired. When one or both of us is in any of these states, the thought of getting up in front of an audience and being charming and informative can seem daunting. Despite all of this, once the class begins, our attention invariably shifts away from whatever may be troubling us, and we focus on our purpose—sharing our knowledge with people who are there to learn.

In these situations, we are literally forced to forget ourselves. This is a little more difficult when the need to focus on the other is strictly interpersonal instead of something that's compelled by external circumstances. Nevertheless, the same principle applies. If you can turn your attention away from your needs or wants, your partner's failure to meet them (or your hope that they will be met), and your emotional state, and instead focus on another person, you are likely to be taken outside of yourself. You will soon lose track of whatever troubling thoughts you might be having.

This point applies to all aspects of a relationship, and as with so many other principles that we think are important, it is not something that you can or should expect to be able to achieve at all times. There has to be room for a meltdown or two, and it is important to express your desires. If you're feeling deprived or neglected, it's generally a good idea to find a way for your feelings to be acknowledged and addressed. What we're advocating is really a change in emphasis that involves both the recognition of your interconnectedness and a conscious choice to focus on the other rather than on the self.

Having said all of this, there is a place for selfishness. Many people feel deeply disempowered, believe that they have spent their entire lives in service of others, and take the view that they have never gotten their needs met. This feeling can be very intense, and it frequently manifests itself in those who have devoted themselves to child rearing. As we've already implied, we sometimes feel it too, since so much of our lives involves service, whether as teachers or in the environmental work we do. Even in these situations, however, we get significant rewards from the others we are serving. In the context of a partnership, the idea is that if you are prepared to serve and give to your beloved, you will receive even more in return. This is true both in terms of the relationship in general and in terms of sex. If anything, the potential for getting back more than you give is greatest in the sexual realm.

It may seem paradoxical to emphasize focusing on the other rather than the self as a way to find more satisfaction. You may be wondering how this can possibly work when you're making love, or you may be thinking that we're talking about a kind of economy, an exchange, in which the focus is on the quid pro quo.

There is frequently an economy in sex (including sex in long-term relationships), and for some there can be an explicit quid pro quo. This is sometimes the source of rather tasteless (and sexist) jokes about the exchange of jewelry for sexual favors, but the more typical pattern is considerably more subtle, unconscious, and unarticulated. It plays out in many everyday encounters. In this form of exchange, the partners go through a series of sexual maneuvers, each doing something to please the other with the hope (or even the expectation) of getting pleasured in return. This can work well up to a point, and you may not want to reject it entirely. Nevertheless, we'd like to propose a more radical and more potentially rewarding scenario.

Instead of focusing on pleasing your partner for the sake of the reward you may receive, try focusing on drawing pleasure from the pleasure you are giving. The fact is that virtually everybody does this during sex; it's just not always a conscious process. Each partner's arousal increases the other's, so we're suggesting that you become aware of something that's going on in the background anyway. Again, this is a subtle shift, one that doesn't require you to make major changes.

If you can recognize and embrace your partner's being turned on as a source of excitement, you'll end up not only giving your partner more pleasure but also getting more pleasure yourself. The real secret of great lovers is in their ability to get pleasure from giving pleasure. While we'll be discussing empathy in more depth, what's at work in this context is related. You are identifying with and taking pleasure in what the other person is experiencing, thereby stepping into that person's skin, just a little.

It's OK to allow for ego gratification in this context as well. You can take pride in your skills as a lover. The first step is to remember a specific instance when you really pleased a partner and focus on how that experience made you feel. The second step is to nurture those feelings, and apply the confidence they inspire while you are making love. Think about that feeling of mastery and start to apply it, and you will be well on your way to experiencing the joy that can be found in serving your beloved.

CULTIVATING CONFIDENCE

Jed says that one of the ways he became a confident lover was to replay sexual encounters in which he felt masterful during masturbation sessions. His insight is an important one. His approach was effectively implanting this sense of mastery into his unconscious. It is a form of what some would call sex magic. You don't have to believe in magic to recognize that focusing on those moments when you feel skillful builds confidence, and confidence is crucial.

It is important for you both to approach sex with this attitude. This is about a mutually rewarding give-and-give (not give-and-take). If one person is doing all the giving, and the other is doing all the taking, things will probably go awry very quickly, but if you can both decide to take pleasure in giving, the effect is likely to be synergistic.

MAINTAIN A SENSE OF MYSTERY

We've heard it said that intimacy means "into-me-see." This wordplay is not particularly clever, and the model for relating that's implied is both overly intrusive and somewhat superficial. The definition is partially redeemed by the fact that it does not stress verbal communication, which many modern relationship experts have conflated with intimacy. True intimacy is often, and perhaps most often, something that exists outside the realm of verbal expression.

There is both less and more to being intimate than seeing into someone. For starters, there is no way you can truly see into another. Your view will inevitably be incomplete and shaded by your own perceptions and prejudices. Attempting to see and understand your partner's inner world is valid and has its place (just as communicating verbally has its place), but the effort is better understood as an imaginative act. Trying to see into someone is a step toward building empathy, but it is not the only factor, or even the primary factor, when it comes to creating intimacy. It's more productive to think about intimacy in a relationship as a process that involves some very careful balancing, something that evolves with time and cannot be forced. True intimacy is about having the skill to be at once separate and connected and being able to tolerate the sometimes paradoxical demands of striking this balance.

As Esther Perel observed in *Mating In Captivity:*

> When the impulse to share becomes obligatory, when personal boundaries are no longer respected, when only the shared space of togetherness is acknowledged, and private space is denied, fusion replaces intimacy and possession co-opts love. It also becomes the kiss of death for sex. Deprived of enigma, intimacy becomes cruel when it excludes any possibility of discovery. When there is nothing left to hide, there is nothing left to seek.[17]

Thus, some forms of intimacy can be stifling. Perel also wisely explains that notions of intimacy used to be founded

---

17   Esther Perel, *Mating in Captivity: Reconciling the Erotic and the Domestic* (New York: HarperCollins, 2006), 46.

on respect, and relationship success was understood as being contingent on a shared sense of purpose and project. She makes a strong case that the exalting of intimacy is a new development in human society, emerging in conjunction with the modern idea that romantic love should be the basis for marriage or any long-term relationship. But Perel's most important point is that this modern form of intimacy, with its focus on verbal expression and its tendency to be intrusive, is likely to suck the erotic energy out of a relationship.

The truth is that most people find sexual encounters with new partners to be particularly exciting, though not always as gratifying as being with someone familiar. Either way, there's a huge difference between having sex with someone you barely know and having sex with a partner you've been with for a decade. If they're honest, most people will acknowledge some measure of craving novelty; part of novelty's allure has to do with the mysterious nature of the new partner and the excitement associated with exploring that person's unfamiliar physical and mental territory. Seduction involves both mystery and the promise of at least partial disclosure. Although every "other"—even someone with whom you've spent many years—remains fundamentally opaque and mysterious, it's easy to forget this when you know a great deal about another person and have spent a lot of time together.

And in the realm of sex, if you have easy access, there's usually no need to put a lot of effort into seduction. While it is said that familiarity breeds contempt, and that's true in some instances, we suspect that it more frequently breeds boredom and lack of interest, which are the real antitheses of love. Bear in mind that your partner will always remain a mystery, at least in some ways. This mysterious element is often negated by the intrusive demands of "into-me-see." Instead of denying the mystery, we suggest that you celebrate it.

A first step in this process is recognizing that you don't have to share everything with your partner and that retaining some measure of personal privacy, both physical and mental, is not wrong, is not a rejection, is not a refusal to connect. We all need our solitude and our private realms, even though we live in a society that demands ever-increasing self-disclosure, and in which privacy seems like a very quaint notion. In many societies that are less materially well off, there is little personal privacy, and as Perel observes, people in these societies often have no wish for more intimacy. In the pre-Internet era, individual privacy became very important in the Western world, but today many forms of privacy are mere memories. We are thus advocating a way of being that goes against much of the thrust of contemporary culture, but maintaining a realm of personal inner space is important for anyone who wants to lead a balanced life.

We like to distinguish between what's private and what's secret. Some measure of privacy is important no matter how intimate you are. Defining that realm of privacy is highly individual. There's no formula for it, and it will undoubtedly change over time in any relationship. The distinction between privacy and secrecy (or the corrosive form of secrecy we're describing) is not always obvious. Recognizing it, and being honest with yourself about which is which requires a high degree of self-awareness and some vigilance. When behaviors start to feel compulsive or you repeatedly find yourself quitting your web browser hurriedly when your partner enters the room, you're probably no longer just keeping something private.

It may seem self-contradictory in the extreme for us to define love as profound interest, suggest that a collaborative attitude is a key to having a fulfilling relationship, advocate open and frank discussion of sex and fantasies, and at the same time suggest that there's a need for a private realm and that too much intimacy can be stifling. The apparent conflict is a consequence of the way people have been trained to think, not of what we're advocating. The essential point is that there's a need to balance these aspects of a relationship for things to work well. It's crucial to maintain a mutually respectful attitude, to develop a shared sense of adventure and exploration, to take pleasure in giving pleasure, and to find ways to connect, while being comfortable with the reality that we all need to turn inward at times. Indeed, we have to wonder whether some of the behavior that gets labeled sex or pornography addiction (and the secrecy that so often accompanies these activities) represents a rather desperate and counterproductive response to the excessive demands for intimacy and connection that our culture imposes on relationships.

Thus, one aspect of maintaining a sense of mystery involves recognizing and allowing for separateness, even in the closest of relationships. It's up to you both to define what kind of separateness is optimal for each of you. It may involve keeping certain fantasies private, accepting that a partner can masturbate without telling you about it, or watching porn alone. For some, it can mean opening the relationship. We don't have any moral judgments about this, and it is up to you to arrive at a mutual understanding.

The demand for total disclosure is the source of a great deal of unnecessary suffering. If it is not OK to have fantasies and desires other than ones that involve your long-term mate, yet you experience those fantasies and desires, the only option is to stifle your urges and your sexuality. This will affect your relationship. Allowing these feelings and, indeed, acknowledging the reality that it is at least theoretically possible to act on them can keep things vital. Perel calls this "the shadow of the third" and suggests that in a healthy relationship, it must be acknowledged, at a minimum.[18]

Beyond acknowledging (or welcoming) the shadow of the third into your bedroom, there are practical ways to keep the sense of mystery alive in your relationship. You can begin by looking for the unexpected and allowing yourself to be surprised by your partner. Sex may seem routine, but that's an intellectual judgment.

The reality is that even if you have been with the same person thousands of times, you never know exactly what is going to happen, and there's always the option of trying something different: having sex in another room, in a new position, or at a different time of day. You may even discover that your partner enjoys something you never dreamed she would.

Whatever the variation, the important thing is to refrain from having a goal other than observing. Avoid becoming attached to a specific outcome. In this context, we're suggesting that the

---

18   Ibid., 188–198.

experiment involve something that's reasonably close to things you've already done together; this isn't about exploring deeply held fantasies or pushing boundaries. Instead, this is an opportunity to notice new things in the context of a slight departure from the routine and especially to be surprised by something in your partner's response. It can be very small and subtle, but the point is to recognize and celebrate it, so that you will remember that your partner is and always will be at least somewhat mysterious. And even if you don't observe anything new, if each of you can create the mere expectation that surprises are possible, you may start to see each other somewhat differently.

TIP: Small Adjustments Can Change Your Experience

It is often harder to change your routine than it is to recognize that you have one. Here are some suggestions that should get you started.

Candlelight—there's nothing like a warm glow to help you see your lover differently.

Change of clothing—this doesn't have to be expensive lingerie and can be something as simple as a silk shirt.

Play music—you can have fun with this by trying anything from Barry White to "Ride of the Valkyries."

Change your position—there's no need for acrobatics; this can involve minor adjustments from changing the angle of your hips, to standing, or challenging yourselves with the ancient college rule that "one foot must remain on the floor."

Try a different lube—this can be subtle, but you'll discover that using different types of lube produces different sensations. Avoid brands that claim to be warming; they can irritate the skin.

Change your location—even if you need to remain in your

bedroom, you can still create small changes in your environment. Bring in a bench, massage table, or footstool.

Once you start playing around with these small changes, you may realize that there's no need to make love the same way twice.

———————————————————————⬤———————————————————————

BEYOND THE KEYS:
HOW TO LIVE
THE NEW PARADIGM

Now that we've introduced you to some fundamental principles and techniques for keeping long-term relationships vibrant
and sexually rewarding, we'd like to provide you with some
additional tools for inventing or reinventing your life together.
Some of the techniques, attitudes, and language will likely be
familiar but possibly not in this particular context, and some
may be new to you. We emphasize certain words and mental
attitudes in this chapter with the intention of suggesting
different ways of thinking. People underestimate the importance of language at their peril, and there's a growing body
of research that indicates that "our emotional state is largely

determined by what we attend to."[19] While there are limits on the human capacity to control what we attend to both in life and in a partnership, employing some of these techniques and maintaining the right attitude should help you avoid falling into the old paradigm of getting your needs met, thinking about *quid pro quos,* or focusing on what's wrong with your relationship or sex life instead of what's right.

CONNECT FIRST—TALK LATER

By now, you know we think that much of the contemporary emphasis on verbal communication skills is misguided. It's useful to know your own mind and sexuality, and it is good to be able to express your desires in a kind and supportive way that encourages your partner to do whatever is possible to meet them. Becoming skilled at nonverbal communication, using nonverbal tools to nurture your connection, is even more important. This is true both in sex and in life generally. Many people become somewhat nonverbal when making love, and there's a large body of research that shows we respond to an array of nonverbal cues at a level below conscious awareness; for example, recognizing an angry facial expression without even realizing it.[20]

Multiple senses are involved in reading nonverbal cues. We often consciously or semiconsciously take note of tone of voice, body language, facial expressions, breathing patterns, skin

---

19 Daniel Kahneman, *Thinking, Fast and Slow* (New York: Farrar, Straus, and Giroux, 2011), 394.
20 Ibid., 1.

tone, and gestures. Although they involve the voice, laughing and crying are nonverbal expressions of emotion. These are only a few of the most obvious forms of nonverbal communication. We can convey emotion through touch as well, and there are even more subtle cues that are communicated at a level that is entirely unconscious. It is well known that smell is important to sexual attraction, and human pheromones have been studied since the 1960s. Subtle changes in scent can be indicators of changes in emotional states. Thus, nonverbal cues affect us on multiple levels. By contrast, most verbal expressions (except spontaneous eruptions in immediate response to an intense stimulus) are mediated by our intellect.

There is nothing wrong with the intellect, and many great relationships involve great conversation. There is much that can only be conveyed verbally. People, and especially lovers, have to use words to communicate, but words are only part of it. Because verbalizing—including writing and speaking in sign language—involves rational thought, it can frequently create distance. In the context of disagreements, this rational component of speaking is likely to be a polarizing factor that puts each partner in a frame of mind in which being "right" is more important than being connected.

Although falling in love is a process that operates on multiple levels, we'd suggest that verbalizing is less important than some other elements. In the early stages of a relationship, you probably spent a good deal of time in silence, simply gazing into each other's eyes. Yes, you got to know each other by talking, but consider the possibility that instead of gazing at each other because you were falling in love, you were actually falling in love because you were gazing at each other. Even if this is an overstatement, the fact remains that gazing into each other's eyes was a key component in the process of falling in love. You can make the conscious choice to keep this element in your relationship (or to reintroduce it) no matter how long you have been together. By doing so, you will be repeatedly reevoking the intensity of the connection you had in the early stages of your relationship and reminding yourselves of the emotional and erotic charge you felt at the time.

TIP: Eye-Gazing

Stand facing each other about two feet apart.

Maintain eye contact. In order to avoid the urge to shift your gaze, we suggest that you focus on your partner's left eye with your right eye.

Allow the muscles around your eyes to relax, and blink gently when you need to.

Focus on the act of gazing; this will eventually silence any mental chatter.

Do this practice daily for 3–5 minutes as a way to establish a nonverbal sense of connection.

Once you've made this a habit, you can use it as a tool for defusing conflict.

This simple and profound technique can bring you into harmony both physiologically and emotionally. If you are experiencing some disruption in your bond or are feeling an argument brewing, you can take a "time-out" and gaze into each other's eyes. This will help you feel less polarized and bring you into balance. Eye-gazing is effective for a number of reasons, not least because it's a way of deliberately and repeatedly recreating the circumstances that enabled you to fall in love.

There is more to say about nonverbal communication, and becoming a skilled lover certainly involves learning to read nonverbal cues. At the risk of overgeneralizing about gender, we find that this tends to be more challenging for men than it is for women. This is probably due to both cultural and biological factors. Sex is often treated as a commodity: women are generally conditioned to withhold it, guard it, or parcel it out, and men (beginning in adolescence) tend to think that they have to get it while they can. Thus there can be a tendency to go straight for the genitals, ignore foreplay, or rush through intercourse, perhaps because as a teenager it seemed as if you had to get it over with quickly in case she changed her mind, or (all kidding aside) you feared being discovered. Similarly, women may not always be sensitive to male sexual response, which is frequently more urgent, genitally focused, and fragile due to anxieties about erection and the associated assumptions about sexual performance and masculinity.

These are broad, general statements about gender and sexual response, which vary a great deal from person to person, irrespective of anatomy. Couples who are naturally well matched are fortunate. For those who are less in balance, the value of becoming skilled at reading nonverbal cues is even greater. It will enhance your ability to meet in the middle and be more effective at pleasing each other. Some of this is simple—pausing to notice your partner's breathing, the hardness of his erection, her lubrication, the way she is moving, whether his face is starting to flush. It is a good idea to become skilled at slowing down, shifting your focus away from what you are doing or how you are feeling sexually, and pausing to observe what is happening with your partner. As you become more adept at reading them, these nonverbal cues can become extremely erotic in and of themselves. It is a turn-on to know that you are turning your lover on.

TIP: Focusing on Nonverbal Cues

Here's a simple exercise that should hone your ability to focus on nonverbal cues. It only takes a few minutes.

Agree on a body part, other than the genitals, that you would like to have caressed.

One person is the giver, and the other receives.

Gaze into each other's eyes as you do this exercise.

Experiment with different kinds of caresses—light strokes, kneading, rubbing, tapping, scratching gently, or any form of sensual and slightly erotic touch that appeals to you.

Remain silent. The receiver should communicate any response through the eyes alone.

Reverse roles after 3–5 minutes.

Treat this as an experiment, an exploration. There is no success or failure. Keep it light and playful, and in time, you are sure to become more sensitive and attuned to your partner's nonverbal cues.

You can also try a form of this exercise in a more full-on sexual encounter. Try making love wordlessly yet also as observantly as you can. Communicate your responses to each other without speaking. It's not difficult to develop this skill set, which is one of the keys to becoming a great lover; all it takes is a little practice.

BUILD TRUST AND CREATE GOODWILL

Trust and goodwill are very closely related conceptually, so much so that we think of them as nearly synonymous; both are crucial in maintaining a strong relationship. There are some distinctions. Goodwill pertains more to emotion, to feelings about your partner that are built up over time, but without deep and abiding trust, there can be no goodwill. This is why affairs can be so devastating for some relationships; the breach of trust can cancel even many years of accumulated goodwill.

The concept of trust is very complex. In many cases, we have an intuition about whether a person can be trusted or not. This is an operation of what Daniel Kahneman calls "System 1," a loose and unscientific term for that component of consciousness that makes snap judgments. According to Kahneman:

> We are endowed with an ability to evaluate, in a single glance at a stranger's face, two potentially crucial facts about that person: how dominant (and therefore potentially threatening) he is, and how trustworthy he is, whether his intentions are more likely to be friendly or hostile.[21]

Kahneman goes on to explain that we make these instant assessments of dominance based on facial structure, and our gut instincts about trustworthiness are determined largely by the expression of the person we're encountering—smiles suggesting

---

21 Ibid., 90.

safety and trustworthiness, and frowns suggesting danger.

These initial impressions may have evolutionary value as a survival mechanism; however, they can be entirely unreliable if the person is deliberately being deceptive or ingratiating, or due to any number of other factors that can cloud our judgment. Kahneman makes it clear that System 1 is essential for day-to-day functioning but that excessive reliance on intuition can lead to all kinds of trouble. Thus, an initial feeling that someone is trustworthy differs a great deal from the kind of trust that is developed and nurtured in the context of a long-term relationship.

This initial feeling that someone is trustworthy undoubtedly plays a role in attraction and in the selection of casual partners, but most of us have trusted the wrong person—in dating, friendship, or business—at least once and probably many times. Poor choices aside, when the intuitive sense that a person is trustworthy starts to be borne out in a series of interactions, the conditions for a deeper, more enduring relationship are established. This is the beginning of true trust building, and while intuition may continue to be a factor, this more enduring form of trust is not a product of Kahneman's System 1. Instead, this deeper trust is instilled by experience and multiple interactions. For some, this can begin to build fairly rapidly, and if so, it's probably best to be cautious. For others, especially those who have experienced deep betrayal, it can be a very slow process. If you've ever cared for an animal that has been mistreated, you know how much time and effort it takes to create a sense of safety in your pet. The same is true for most human beings.

Unfortunately, many of our cultural constructs around dating and sexuality do very little to encourage trust building. This is especially true when it comes to heterosexual courtship. Popular books aimed at both men and women, *The Rules, Secrets of the A Game,* and *The Game* among many others, profit from treating courtship, dating, and seduction as a game. They play on stereotypes: women should want to attract a man who's a keeper and need to manipulate him into nesting; men just want sex and should use guile to lure women into bed—it's only fair, after all, because women want to trick men into settling down. While some of the stratagems described in these books may be effective in some cases, their emphasis on gaining an advantage over a mysterious adversary who belongs to an "opposite" sex creates an obstacle to building trust from the very outset. More generally, this way of thinking about sexual relationships denies women the fullness of their sexuality and desire. It reinforces the idea, fairly common among men, that they have to beg, borrow, or steal in order to get laid. Such stereotypes are deeply embedded in modern culture, and books such as the ones named above both partake of and reinforce these stereotypes.

If it were up to us, we'd propose an entirely different approach to courtship, one in which people were upfront about their sexual tastes and interests, didn't play games with each other, and were generally forthright. The game playing and manipulation may be accepted (but should not be acceptable) in high school, when people are struggling to find appropriate ways to relate to the objects of their attraction, but many adults continue to engage in this kind of behavior. It shouldn't be surprising that so many people are left wondering what has gone wrong in their relationships when they have done so little to build trust and persist in thinking of their partners as crude stereotypes or, worse still, as enemies who must be defeated.

Building trust is not really all that complicated, leaving aside situations of past betrayal or where personal history has created obstacles. All it takes is honesty—not radical honesty, just a basic determination to be truthful and forthright—tempered with kindness. It also involves being reliable—calling when you say you're going to call, showing up on time, taking responsibility if you make a mistake. There may be a little bit of self-sacrifice involved, especially if you are chronically late, for example, but taking these steps will demonstrate that you are "radically taking the other person into account."[22]

Having frank conversations about your sexual interests, your sexual tastes, and your sexual history—including any history of sexually transmitted infections—is also crucial for building trust. As we've noted, some people find it difficult to talk about past lovers. It's worth moving beyond limitations like these, which are based on very old-fashioned ways of thinking about sex—that it's proprietary, only for marriage, and only to be shared with one person in your entire life. Of course, it's never a good idea to be excessively effusive or wistful when describing past lovers. But talking openly about sex, sharing your interests (even if your partner's interests are

---

22   Mira Kirshenbaum, *I Love You But I Don't Trust You: The Complete Guide to Restoring Trust in Your Relationship* (New York: Berkeley Publishing Group, 2012), 20.

different) and your sexual histories in ways that are mutually supportive, will not only make it possible to get more pleasure out of your lovemaking, since you will know each other more fully—it will also build trust and intimacy. Where there is trust, there can be no "battle of the sexes."

BE BRAVE: HAVING THE COURAGE TO BE OPEN ABOUT SEX BUILDS INTIMACY

Building and maintaining a meaningful and enduring connection takes courage, and so does making the choice to keep your relationship vital both emotionally and sexually. It is hard enough to be sexually free and open as an individual. The challenges can be even greater in the context of a partnership, but so can the rewards. Sex is a loaded subject for everyone, regardless of how liberated we may think we are. We all have entrenched beliefs about ourselves, and it can be very unsettling to recognize, let alone embrace, the fact that our sexual proclivities don't always match our self-images or what we would like our partners to believe about us.

We can say confidently that if you're not doing harm to others, behaving compulsively, or engaging in overly risky behavior (endangering health and safety or doing something that's likely to get you arrested), the benefits of both exploring and embracing your authentic sexual nature far outweigh the challenges of adjusting your self-image to accommodate new insights and behaviors. Denying your sexuality because of beliefs about propriety or judgments about what is "normal" is more likely to be damaging than is acting in accordance with your true nature. The same goes for withholding or concealing your desires and interests from your partner.

Making the decision to live differently always takes courage. Being sexually free in a society that remains at once extremely sex-negative and overly obsessed with sexuality takes courage. To choose to be sexual when things aren't "perfect" is to be truly vulnerable. Even talking honestly about sex with your partner, or anyone else, requires a break with convention.

In our experience, people who are not part of the community of sexual explorers often get very uncomfortable when we talk about our work, our writing, and our lives. Simply choosing to know yourself sexually, simply wanting to grow, and simply not being silent about sex are often less than acceptable socially. Making others uncomfortable isn't easy, nor is experiencing their disapproval. Nevertheless, the rewards for being courageous usually outweigh these costs, and in the context of a partnership, being open and honest about your desires can be a powerful way to create solidarity and deepen your emotional bond.

KEEP KINDNESS AS YOUR TOUCHSTONE

Striving to be kind, especially when things are not going well, is essential for maintaining an atmosphere of love and caring for each other. Bearing in mind the importance of kindness, even when you are feeling angry or upset, can serve as a check on any impulse to be brutally honest. (More on honesty in the next section.) If you keep kindness as your touchstone, it is far more likely that your partner will be able to receive your words, even if what you are expressing is difficult and perhaps not entirely welcome. Doing so will also enable you to be discerning, and with practice, you're likely to become adept at knowing intuitively when and how to express yourself in a way that is well received.

Negative comments and rhetorical questions about a partner that are categorical, whether general or sexual— "You're such a slob, why do you always leave the house in such a mess?" or "You always come too quickly and leave mc unsatisfied. Why don't you ever think of my pleasure?" for example—may be truthful expressions of emotion and the reality of the person who is making the statement. Because these comments are absolute and unkind in the way they are stated, the person on the receiving end is likely to feel both harshly judged and utterly disempowered. If she's a hopelessly messy person or if he is unable to satisfy her, there's no room for discussion, let alone any potential for change. In addition, if you give feedback framed in a way that suggests you anticipate failure—a communication style that seems to be very common in couples, especially unhappy ones—you will get that result. Instead, try to express yourself in a manner that conveys confidence in your partner's ability to do what you ask. If you can do this, you are much more likely to get the desired response than if all you do is criticize and point out inadequacies.

Similarly, being kind involves developing discretion and discernment about when to speak. Never say anything even vaguely critical during or immediately after lovemaking. Most people are in a highly vulnerable state when they're turned on and after a sexual encounter. Of course, if something is not working for you in the moment, and certainly if an activity is causing you any discomfort, it is good to speak out, but again, it is best to do so in a way that is not colored by blame or judgment. Thus, it's much better to say something along the lines of "I'm not sure I love that. Could you try this instead?" This is likely to be much more effective than saying, "Why are you doing that? It feels awful." If something happens during sex, and you feel the need to discuss it, kindness (not to mention enlightened self-interest) often dictates that you should save the conversation for later.

"Don't go to bed angry" is a somewhat controversial bit of conventional wisdom, though some recent research tends to support the idea.[23] While it may not be humanly possible to avoid ever going to bed angry, doing your best to minimize conflict in advance of sleep is kindness in action. Have those difficult conversations in a way, at times, and in places that will minimize their potential for disrupting your connection. Thus, you should also avoid arguing in bed.

---

23 A. M. Hicks and L. M. Diamond, "Don't Go to Bed Angry: Attachment, Conflict, and Affective and Physiological Reactivity," *Personal Relationships* 18 (2011), 266–284, abstract online at http://onlinelibrary.wiley.com/doi/10.1111/j.1475-6811.2011.01355.x/abstract.

TIP: Put Disagreements in Their Place

Dedicate a space for your disagreements. If you're getting ready for bed and are having an argument or feel one brewing, choose to take the discussion into that dedicated space and wait until things have cooled down before calling it a night.

Most couples have most of their sex in bed, and it's difficult enough to eroticize your shared sleeping space. Thus, it's a good idea to refrain from creating an association between your bed and conflict. Being kind is not an abstraction; it's all about making choices that demonstrate your esteem for your partner and send the message that, even if you're furious about something, your anger in no way diminishes your regard.

It's also important not to assume that just because your intentions are kind, your words and actions are being received that way. Pay attention to the way your partner responds. If the conversation stops, slows down, or body language and facial expression are indicative of distress, you may have misspoken and expressed your feelings in an injurious way. The mere belief that you did not intend to hurt does not absolve you of responsibility if your words caused pain, so it is important to distinguish between your intention and the actual impact of what you say. When in doubt, check in and ask.

Similarly, it's easy to take expressions of strong emotions like anger as if they were personal attacks or signs of serious problems. If you are prone to reacting this way, you may need to remind yourself that it's just an emotion, and it will pass. It's also helpful to have a conversation about how these incidents make you feel, though not in the midst of an argument. This can help the more volatile partner be more mindful and also serve as an opportunity for you to reassure each other and rededicate yourselves to being as kind as you can. It's inevitable that you will have arguments, and some of them may be heated. In these situations, kindness means taking care that you are expressing anger or frustration as specifically as is possible and not engaging in personal attacks.

BE HONEST IN MODERATION

The idea that it's important to be honest with your partner may seem simple. In fact, the subject of honesty is more complicated than it appears. Chronic dishonesty is almost always a sign of serious problems in a relationship, but honesty takes many forms, and it is not always healthy or helpful.

It *is* very important to be honest with your partner, but the way you go about it is crucial. We have encountered quite a few couples for whom the statement "I'm just being honest" is really a justification for emotional battery. In intimate relationships, total honesty is not always the best policy, since total honesty is often brutal. Being forthright in a way that is helpful requires some skill.

"*Radical honesty,*" an approach developed by psychologist Brad Blanton and detailed in his book by the same name, has gained a sizable following, especially among segments of the alternative sexuality and polyamorous communities. (*Polyamorous* means "loving many"—see Chapter 9: Advanced Sexual Adventuring.) Practicing radical honesty requires you to "speak everything regardless of how the person you're speaking to may react."[24] We do not feel that this is helpful. It often encourages a nonrelational way of communicating that can be totally self-involved. We've seen people use it as a club for beating up their partners. They're often oblivious to how their message is being received and have no willingness to take responsibility for the damage they've done because being "honest" gives them an excuse.

Honesty tempered by prudence is a much healthier approach. We are not suggesting that you suppress or deny all of your feelings; nor do we want you to think that if something important to you or the relationship comes up, you should squelch it. But being promiscuous with your honesty, having no discernment about how hurtful words can be, is not productive or sexy. For this reason, when you want to express something, it is wise to take stock of your motives before speaking.

---

24 Tristan Taormino, *Opening Up: A Guide to Creating and Sustaining Open Relationships* (San Francisco: Cleis Press, 2008), 44.

TIP: Is Honesty Appropriate?

Some of the following questions have been attributed to the Buddha or to Vac, the goddess of speech in Hinduism. They actually reflect beliefs about when and how to speak that exist in many spiritual traditions, both Eastern and Western. Before you decide whether it's appropriate to "speak your truth," ask yourself:

Is it true?

Is this an appropriate time?

Is it necessary?

Is it kind?

Is it helpful?

Does it improve upon the silence?

Note that we are advocating discretion and self-awareness, not dishonesty. Actively deceiving a partner—unless you're planning a surprise party or something of that nature—is not going to be good for your relationship and will almost certainly damage trust. Worse still, an ongoing pattern of active deception, of any kind, can be thoroughly corrosive.

There is a widespread tendency to associate honesty with negative statements. The expression "to tell you the truth" often seems to be employed in the context of confessing to something, saying words someone may not want to hear, or giving criticism. Remember that being honest also includes the positive. There's no need to be parsimonious with praise.

TIP: Over-the-Top Honesty

List five things you admire or appreciate about each other and describe them in the most hyperbolic terms possible. Be sure to include at least two sexual appreciations. You're likely to discover that praise feels good, even when it's delivered with a hefty dose of humor. See if you can praise each other into embarrassment.

Finally, it's perhaps most important to be honest with yourself; this is not easy and indeed may be impossible. Having a sense of self is a survival mechanism, and it is very easy to engage in protective self-deception when some behavior or trait does not align with this sense. It is worth resisting this tendency to self-deceive to the extent possible. Doing so will make it easier to exercise discretion in your honesty with others.

ENGAGE EMPATHICALLY

We've already mentioned John Gottman's concept of turning toward. (See Chapter 3: A New Paradigm.) One way to think about empathy is to understand it as a radical form of turning toward. People tend to define empathy as a capacity that is related to negative emotional states—being able to put yourself in the place of or feel the emotions of a person who is in pain. In reality, empathy has a much broader meaning, encompassing the full spectrum of human emotion and experience. For this reason, developing your ability to be empathic has significant implications in the realm of sex, both in terms of becoming a more skillful lover and in terms of getting turned on by your partner's arousal.

Developing and displaying your capacity for empathy is one of the keys to true intimacy. It can also be profoundly healing, both in very broad terms and in terms of dealing with the inevitable conflicts that will emerge in any long-term relationship. Although the word *healing* has been so overused that it can border on being meaningless, especially in the realm of sexuality, bringing a healthy dose of empathy into your relationship can be very helpful in repairing past hurts and preventing future ones. Some psychoanalysts have rejected the Freudian model in which the analyst remains neutral and detached, suggesting instead that the key to successful therapy lies in maintaining a stance of "sustained empathic inquiry—an attitude ... that consistently seeks to comprehend the meaning of the patient's expressions from a perspective within rather than outside the patient's frame of reference."[25] Bringing a similar attitude to engaging with your partner can be beneficial (although you should never think of yourself as your partner's therapist) and is one way of expressing profound interest.

Although we're talking about sex and love, not psychoanalysis, the point is particularly significant as it pertains to certain popular communication techniques, including active listening, which involves the neutral mirroring back of a partner's words. "If I hear you correctly, you're saying 'I sometimes feel pressured to have sex.'" We have always found these

---

25 Robert D. Stolorow, Bernard Brandchaft, and George Atwood, *Psychoanalytic Treatment: An Intersubjective Approach* (Hillsdale, NJ: Analytic Press, 1987), 10.

techniques to be risky, because they can easily be experienced as distancing and may even seem patronizing. If empathy is effective in a therapeutic context, then the same is likely true in the context of relating to your partner. Our personal experience suggests that engaging empathically when emotions are intense and communication is difficult can be the best way to deal with whatever issue has arisen.

To say that empathy is very important is not to imply that you should abandon your emotional boundaries or that you should always seek to feel what your partner is feeling. When people talk about picking up on someone else's energy, they are often describing the experience of feeling flooded due to the intensity of the emotion involved. It's one thing to do your best to see and feel things from another person's perspective; allowing yourself to be swept away by another's emotions is something else. There may be times when you have to protect yourself, but that does not negate the value of cultivating your capacity to be empathic.

It is perhaps not surprising that empathy gets a very bad name in certain circles. President Barack Obama was attacked (and continues to be criticized) by some on the right for suggesting that empathy is a good quality for a Supreme Court justice to possess, as if empathy were something soft, weak, contrary to the ideal of equal justice, and somehow "un-American."[26] In reality, empathy is anything but that.

---

26 James Christophersen, "Obama's Empathy Rule: Alive and Well in the Second Term," *National Review,* April 9, 2013, http://www.nationalreview.com/bench-memos/345108/obamas-empathy-rule-alive-and-well-second-term-james-christophersen.

It takes courage to be empathic, especially when you're in a situation that involves conflict, but that's exactly the time to empathize. Developing the capacity for empathy means developing the ability to crawl into your partner's skin, to understand intellectually, emotionally, and even physically what your beloved is experiencing. This requires both imagination and the ability to put aside your own feelings and self-interest, at least temporarily.

There is a significant difference between empathy and *compassion*—a word that is widely used and perhaps more comfortable for many people. Compassion is more akin to sympathy. Where compassion implies a certain standing apart, to a degree that can sometimes seem patronizing, empathy is more engaged and egalitarian, since it entails an effort not just to feel sorry for the other person but also to experience (or imagine) what the other person is going through. In addition, unlike empathy, compassion is linked to suffering as opposed to the full spectrum of emotion.

COMPERSION: TAKE PLEASURE IN YOUR LOVER'S PLEASURE

Compersion is a term that has become popular in some polyamorous circles. Poly people often use the term to refer to experiencing pleasure when a partner is being sexual with someone else. It can also be employed in reference to more generalized circumstances in which jealousy would be the expected response. As you will see, our definition is somewhat more expansive and is not limited to sexual situations or those that would inspire jealousy. In any case, people who have refined their compersion skills can perform a kind of alchemy, transforming what might otherwise be a negative response into a celebratory one.[27]

Empathy and compersion are closely related, and compersion can be considered a specific form of empathy. Compersion involves taking pleasure in your partner's pleasure, whatever the source. This can include a new interest or activity in which you have no desire to participate. It can also involve getting turned on by the fact that your partner is turned on. There is ample research showing that people respond with similar emotions when they observe emotional reactions in others. Some claim that the source of this ability is hardwired, produced by what are known as mirror neurons, but this is still the subject of scientific debate.[28] Whatever the nature of the biological mechanisms, it seems likely that we all have some innate capacity to experience compersion. This is a capacity that can be refined and developed.

To give you a more concrete understanding of this emotion, you can think of it as being the satisfaction that some people take in cooking for others, even if they don't eat the food themselves. For some, this is a profound pleasure. We also

27 See Eric Francis, "A Crazy Little Thing Called...," http://planetwaves.net/compersion.html. Francis has been thinking and writing about compersion for many years and has played a leading role in advocating for its value. He introduced us to the concept over a decade ago at a polyamory conference.

28 For a skeptical view of mirror neuron theory, see Ruth Lays, "'Both of Us Disgusted in *My* Insula': Mirror Neuron Theory and Emotional Empathy," *Nonsite*, no. 5, March 12, 2012, http://nonsite.org/article/%E2%80%9Cboth-of-us-disgusted-in-my-insula%E2%80%9D-mirror-neuron-theory-and-emotional-empathy.

appreciate Open Love NY board member Murray Schechter's metaphor. He told us that compersion is the feeling you have when you're driving around looking for a parking space, and you turn onto a street and see someone else backing into a spot, and you feel happy for her. Schechter's metaphor is one to ponder; the cooking example is probably a more familiar emotion, one that may make it easier to recognize compersion as you start to feel it.

TREAT YOUR RELATIONSHIP AS AN ONGOING EXPLORATION

We often describe the Tantric practitioner as experimenter, experiment, and laboratory. The experiment is the activity; the laboratory is the body; and the experimenter is the part of you that observes what's happening without judging, collecting data as a scientist would. Whether or not you're interested in Tantra, there's great value in applying this attitude to your sexual encounters.

Sometimes everything seems like it will go smoothly, and then something goes awry. Any number of things can conspire to derail even the best orchestrated tryst—a ringing telephone, a child with a nightmare, an ill-chosen word, a random intrusive thought; you can undoubtedly think of your own examples. If you're treating sex as an exploration, a shared adventure, and your only goal is to see what happens, you won't think of these less than optimal encounters as failures. Instead, you may see them as comical or, even better, as instructive.

From another perspective, if you think about sex as an endless exploration, you may find that you're a lot less prone to falling into a totally habitual pattern of activity, and similarly will be less focused on performance or concerned about recreating a past peak experience. Be on the lookout for new sensations, and be open to the unexpected. If you can nurture this way of thinking, it will be easier to notice more subtle textures in your sexual encounters—from the intensely orgasmic to the gentler and less dramatic and everything in between—and you'll be less prone to the normal human impulse to evaluate your experiences in hierarchical terms.

Chances are that when you were first falling in love, you somewhat greedily enjoyed the process of exploring sex as a couple. Treating your lovemaking as an exploration, thinking of yourselves as Lewis and Clark, setting out to discover unknown territory, having the awareness that you never know what lies around the next bend: all this will help you keep some of that initial intensity and innocence alive for many years to come. Having this attitude will also help you be more collaborative in your lovemaking. You don't have to change anything about what you actually do. All it takes is a slight change in the way you think.

BE FLEXIBLE

Humans are creatures of habit, and in many respects there is nothing wrong with behaving habitually. Most of us would not be able to function without some form of daily routine, and doing things like getting regular exercise generally requires developing a consistent pattern of activity. Habits are often labeled "bad," so much so that addictions are referred to as "habits." Of course, most habits are not addictions at all; they're simply the way we're accustomed to doing things—and frequently we're accustomed to acting in certain ways because it is functional to do so. What habits share with addictions is that they can be very hard to alter.

We learned just how hard some years ago when visiting our Tantra teacher, Dr. Jonn Mumford, in Sydney, Australia. We were talking about awareness and how to avoid habitual behavior. He gave us a challenge designed to illustrate just how difficult making a change can be. The exercise was simple. He asked Mark which way he dried himself after showering, from head down or feet up. Mark replied, "Feet up", and our teacher said, "Okay, next time, do it in the opposite direction." We went home, and Mark had a shower before we headed out to dinner. Within seconds of drying himself, he realized that he had completely forgotten the exercise. Of course, there's no correct way to dry yourself after a shower or bath. We offer this story to illustrate that much of our behavior is habitual; it can be very hard to modify; that's the reality of being human; and for the most part, there's absolutely nothing wrong with it.

All of that said, this tendency to behave habitually can sometimes be a problem in the context of relationships and sexuality. In life, it may not matter much to others if your habit means you either go to the gym before 9:30 or you skip it that day, but if you're in the habit of having sex in the morning before leaving for work, and your partner is put on a midnight-to-8:00-a.m. shift, your sex life is going to suffer unless you can alter your pattern and adapt to the change in circumstances.

Of course, this is a rather crude example, but the more flexible we can be, the better equipped we will be to handle the vicissitudes of life with ease and grace. There are many changes that take place over the course of a long-term relationship. Children, aging, and illness are the most obvious among them, but the changes are frequently subtler. You and your partner may go through periods when your interest in sexual activity is equally high or equally low, or there may be times when one of you is more interested than the other. In terms of the relationship in general, you may experience varying degrees of satisfaction or dissatisfaction over time. Unless the trend is consistently one of diminished sex drive and satisfaction, it is much healthier to realize that these changes are just fluctuations and to be flexible enough to accept and roll with them. There are many different ways to do so.

In a more explicitly sexual context, being flexible is akin to moving beyond goal orientation. In other words, sex is unpredictable, and people's responses can vary from day to day. If stimulating your partner in a familiar way doesn't seem to be turning him on and you keep on doing it anyway, you're not responding to the current reality. If one (or both) of you is not getting highly aroused in a given encounter, the answer may be to stop and try again later, but it may also mean you should shift your mental focus, change positions, or switch to some other form of erotic engagement.

This plays out frequently in men. The belief that not getting an erection means that the encounter has ended in "failure" is still very common. In a situation like this, it is better not to beat yourself up. Instead, be flexible, recognize and accept that the absence of "wood" is just a function of blood flow; shift your focus, and ask yourself, *What would my partner respond to right now?* This often reduces the absence of an erection to insignificance. Moreover, there is a greater chance that the erection will return if you can approach its absence with a flexible attitude.

Being flexible also applies to your beliefs about yourself and your self-definition. Even if you have a strong sense of self, there's great value in recognizing that identities are not iron-clad. Flexibility is liberating; it can open you to delights and erotic possibilities that may not entirely match your self-image.

ABOVE ALL, HAVE FUN

This is a very brief section of a very serious book, but it may be the most important one of all. We have a healthy appreciation for the absurdity of writing so seriously about something that is a natural function that virtually anyone can enjoy. While we recognize the importance of sharing what we've learned over the years, we also realize that sex is often funny and sometimes can be hilarious, something that authors of sex comedies and tellers of ribald jokes have understood for millennia. In fact, sexual humor seems to exist in virtually all societies, though what people find funny is often culturally specific.

There are a multitude of reasons for having sex, but the simplest one is the mere fact that it's enjoyable, and we wouldn't want our suggestions to take the spontaneity, the fun, and, let's face it, the silliness out of the experience. If you're like a lot of people, your earliest sensual explorations were innocent and childlike—playing doctor in early childhood or spin the bottle in later years. It's also likely that when you were first dating, you brought some of this childlike quality to your encounters. Some of the playfulness may have faded as sex became more familiar. If so, there's nothing to stop you from reintroducing it into your erotic life.

We've taught at a number of events that were geared for the most part to the BDSM/Kink community, and if you're unfamiliar with that scene, you may have some preconceptions and judgments about it. (See Chapter 10: Kink.) We certainly did before we were exposed to it. One of the things we soon discovered is that many seasoned kinksters actually have a far more playful and fun-loving attitude toward sex than most so-called vanilla people do. This playfulness manifested itself in many ways—in outrageous dress, in carefully orchestrated scenes involving role play, in the delight that some people find in tickling, teasing, or tormenting their partners. A sexual way of life that many assume is frightening and primarily dark revealed itself as having a surprisingly playful and light-hearted dimension.

Later, we'll go into more detail about the value of incorporating some kinky play into even a fairly conventional sex life. For now, we'll just point to this aspect of kink as an example of how to rediscover the childlike and playful dimension that you may feel you have lost. Perhaps the easiest way to do this is to engage in some mild and somewhat ridiculous role play—

the naughty student being disciplined, the inept servant and master/mistress, or the captured spy being questioned. Come up with your own scenarios, keep it simple, keep it silly, and let your shared laughter at the silliness function as a turn-on.

5

GREAT SEX: CONCEPTS

WHAT IS SEX?

Let's examine the meaning of the word *sex* itself before getting into what makes for "great" sex. While the definition may seem to be self-evident, at least on the surface, the reality is more complex and nuanced. Different people define sex differently, depending on individual points of view and various cultural biases. For some, sex means genital intercourse, and anything short of that isn't really sex. Indeed, the *Random House Dictionary* defines sex in this context as "coitus,"[29] a word that usually refers to genital intercourse.

---

29 *Random House Unabridged Dictionary,* 2nd ed. (New York: Random House, 1993), 1754.

HOW DO YOU DEFINE SEX?

We posed this question on Facebook, and the post generated some interesting discussion.

I would say anytime there is penetration with anything IN anywhere as well as oral sex on a woman without penetration ... but then when people ask me how many people I've had sex with in my lifetime I never count people that I've just had oral sex with (giving or receiving), and for sure not when only hands were used, even if there's penetration. I'm not quite sure why I think one way about others but when it's about me I think another way. LOL. It's not that I worry about looking like I've been with too many people or anything, so I'm not sure.

I would tentatively say that sex happens whenever one's internal sexual energy is engaged. Or, to better define it in the way you ask: "sex" is when our sexual energy is activated past a minimum threshold, that point which brings it to our attention.

I totally understand what you mean, but there can be a very noticeable arousal when you read some erotica or talk to someone online who attracts you (without ever mentioning anything sexual), and when I'm ovulating I get highly aroused by all sorts of seemingly benign things. Surely I am not partaking in sex at those times.

I have a pretty pedestrian answer to that and it involves at least one set of genitalia.

Intimate and sacred!!!

"I you he she we... In the garden of mystic lovers, these are not true distinctions." —Rumi

AH! The best question is one that creates more questions!

As Master Winnie the Pooh might say, I don't define it; I feel it. Ha-ha.

At the same time, in the New Testament, Jesus tells us that feeling lust in the heart is equivalent to acting on those lustful feelings.[30]

We don't endorse the sex-negativity that accompanies the New Testament view—and we don't think feeling lust or enjoying sex, for that matter, is a sin. Defining sex as genital intercourse is also a limiting and basically sex-negative way of thinking. Sex is whatever you decide it is. We like to define it as any consensual activity that produces sexual arousal, with or without genital intercourse or orgasm. Some people consider themselves pansexual and have refined their abilities to recognize the erotic dimension in a wide variety of experiences. Renowned sex educator Annie Sprinkle defines herself as being "eco-sexual," a term that implies not only a respect for the environment but a view of the natural world as vibrant and erotic. The more deeply you can recognize and embrace the erotic in every aspect of life, the more fulfilled you are likely to be. We'll leave the exact parameters up to you, but we suggest that by defining sex in expansive terms, you're not only liberating yourself from convention, you're developing a deeper understanding of sex and sexuality. As Dr. Ruth Neustifter says, "People who have broad definitions of what sex is tend to report higher sexual satisfaction."[31]

---

30 Matthew 5:27–29.
31 Dr. Ruth Neustifter pointed this out in a talk she gave at Momentum Con 2012. Her observation is supported by Dr. Gina Ogden's ISIS research. Gina Ogden, *The Heart and Soul of Sex* (Boston: Trumpeter Books, 2006).

"GOOD-ENOUGH" SEX IS GOOD ENOUGH

We suggest you forget about trying to have great sex or even striving to improve your sex life. We say this in part because seeking the great can leave you feeling unsatisfied with the good, and also because for people who are already getting some enjoyment out of their sex lives, the secret of great sex has more to do with focusing on what is already pleasurable than on trying to learn new tricks and techniques.

Modern American culture places a strong emphasis on making comparisons, and this can lead to entirely unwarranted feelings of dissatisfaction. Ever since the advent of consumer culture and especially since World War II, virtually all of us have been conditioned both to compete with our neighbors in terms of what we acquire and to seek new possessions and experiences with an avidity that would have baffled our ancestors of even just a few generations ago. In the realm of sex, we are bombarded with information that can easily lead us to feel inadequate. Much has been written about body image and how commercial representations of beauty set a standard that most people cannot meet. Similarly, we've already talked about how cinematic depictions of sex, both mainstream and pornographic, depart from reality, sometimes leaving viewers feeling inadequate.

It is somewhat less obvious but equally important to recognize that much of what gets reported in popular media can have the same effect. Statistics and studies can be informative and often make for great sound bites; however, they can't give you any specific information about your own life.

For example, it's been widely asserted that between 15 and 20 percent of American couples are in "sexless marriages" (defined as having sex fewer than 10 times per year), and there has been a good deal of media hype about this growing "problem."[32] There are a few obvious issues with this statistic. First, some people in these so-called sexless marriages may be quite happy with the arrangement and the infrequency of their sexual activity, but even more importantly, the quoted statistic does not account for age, health, commuter relationships, and an array of other factors that might contribute. Similarly, the oft-quoted figure of 68.5 as the average number of sexual encounters per year for married couples[33] is just an average—it is not a standard against which to measure yourselves. There may be times when you have sex far more frequently than every six days and times when you have it less often, and the reasons for this can vary. The issue is not what other people are doing or how you measure up compared to the national average; it's about whether or not *you're* enjoying what you're doing and whether you're making the most of it.

Some sex and couples therapists are now advocating for what they call the "good-enough sex" model.[34] They argue

---

32 Elena Donovan Mauer, "The Big No: The Truth About Sexless Marriage," MSNBC, September 8, 2009, http://today.msnbc.msn.com/id/32735936/ns/today-relationships/.

33 Ava Cadell, "Mismatched Sex Drive," http://www.loveologyuniversity.com/DrAvaPages/Mismatched_Sex_Drive.html. The study cited was conducted by the University of Chicago's National Opinion Research Center.

34 Barry W. McCarthy and Michael E. Metz, "The Cognitive-Behavioral 'Good-Enough Sex' Model: A Case Illustration," *Sexual and Relationship Therapy* 2, no. 3 (August 2008), 227–234, full text available at http://www.michael-metzphd.com/20071112/INCLUDES/IsGESenough%20-%20website%20abstract.pdf.

that the prevailing emphasis in most forms of treatment is on performance rather than on satisfaction and enjoyment. Conventional sex and couples therapy approaches tend to focus on male erection, performance, and genital intercourse as the standard to which all should aspire. The "good-enough sex" approach is more holistic and flexible, with an emphasis on interaction, shared pleasure, and enjoyment. The term "good enough sex" was inspired by the psychoanalyst D. W. Winnicott, who coined the phrase "good-enough mother" to illustrate that a perfect infant–mother bond was not essential to psychological health, and that ordinary loving care is sufficient.[35] In our performance-driven culture, with its excessive focus on financial success, external achievements, and goal-orientation, it seems deeply sensible to apply the "good enough" concept to sex as well as to parenting.

So, the key to having great sex lies in how you define that term for yourselves and in what's good enough for you at any given moment. You can write your own rules and change them any time. The word *great* is a superlative. It tends to suggest that sex is a performance, that it needs to be spectacular, better than the last time, and better than anybody else's. As long as you're enjoying the sex you're having, we think that's great.

---

35 Donald W. Winnicott, "Transitional Objects and Transitional Phenomena— A Study of the First Not-Me Possession," *International Journal of Psychoanalysis* 34, no. 2 (1953), 89–97, abstract available at http://www.pep-web. org/document.php?id=ijp.034.0089a.

TIP: Good-Enough Sex Is Great

When we're on the road, we tend not to have sex as frequently as we'd like, or as often and intensely as others may assume. We like to remind ourselves that the quality is still great by asking:

Was it relaxing?

Was it enjoyable?

Did we feel happier afterward?

Did one of us feel a little dirty and degraded, and did it feel good?

Did we feel desired?

Did we feel connected?

Did we fall into a deep sleep?

Did we feel energized?

We know we're having great sex if we can answer yes to one or more of these questions. Feel free to use our list, or better yet, create your own.

It's not easy to block out the cultural messages we all receive, whether they pertain to sex or any other aspect of life. Nevertheless, if you can strive to live by your own standards and refrain from measuring yourself against external or self-imposed ideals, you'll make it more likely that your sex will be much better than "good enough."

QUALITY OF TOUCH

In working with couples, we've often encountered a dynamic in which the woman wants more touch but conveys her feelings about the quantity and quality of touch in a way that leaves the man baffled about what she wants from him. In other words, she complains about the lack of touch while criticizing the quality of whatever touch is being offered.

When Sunny and Charles came to study with us, the sense of sexual disappointment was palpable. When we tried to guide them through a very basic exercise involving touch, his hands trembled, leading Sunny to exclaim, "This is how it always goes. I want him to be gentle and slow, and I keep telling him, but he doesn't listen. He's clumsy and shaky, and I can't stand the way it feels." A dynamic like this one places the man in a bind, since earnest attempts to fulfill the desire for more contact and better touch are met with more criticism. A negative spiral often ensues.

We suspect the reason for this gender imbalance has to do, at least in part, with the way boys are brought up. Studies suggest that this may begin in infancy. While mothers tend to be more physically engaged with their infant sons than with infant daughters, it appears that boys more often receive stimulating rather than comforting touch.[36] As they get older, boys generally experience physical contact in the context of rough-housing and sports but are never schooled in tender touch.

While some of this may well be rooted in biology, the role of culture cannot be minimized, and many men have simply never been educated about touch and body awareness. In many segments of our society, it is still unacceptable for men to hug each other. (This component is clearly cultural; in

---

36 Matthew H. McIntyre and Carolyn P. Edwards, "The Early Development of Gender Differences," *Annual Review of Anthropology* 38 (October 2009), 83–97, full text available at http://digitalcommons.unl.edu/cgi/viewcontent.cgi?article=1401&context=psychfacpub. The research also indicates that whether the source of these issues is nature, culture, or a combination of the two, men pay a very heavy price for this lack of physical connection.

many countries it is both commonplace and accepted for men to hold hands in public, and such displays of affection are not treated as an indicator of sexual orientation.) While body awareness and touching well are skills that can be learned, it can take time if they have not been acquired through life experience; they cannot be developed on demand, and feeling both pressured to perform and utterly inadequate to the task frequently leads to emotional and physical withdrawal.

In many cases, people only seek help when the situation has deteriorated to the point where one party is furious and the other feels incompetent. If you feel even the slightest hint of this dynamic, it is very important to act promptly and change direction. This way of engaging is very counterproductive, and demanding more and better touch isn't the way to get what you want; instead, it is sure to create more distance.

An experience we had as we were writing this chapter should help to illustrate just how sensitive the subject of the quality of touch can be. Nan Wise, a PhD candidate in Cognitive Neuroscience, invited us to serve as preliminary test subjects for her dissertation project at Rutgers University, a functional magnetic resonance imaging (fMRI) study of the brain during partner-induced female orgasm. Nan was just starting to develop her study protocol, and wanted work with us, since Patricia had participated in an earlier fMRI study on self-induced orgasm. This was likely the first partner-induced orgasm to be recorded in this manner.

We did our best to practice and replicate the conditions we'd be facing using a massage table, but that did little to prepare us for the experience. The machine is at about chest height, and in order for the scans to produce clear images, the subject has to lie still, with head restrained and only the lower legs and feet outside the machine. This makes access to the genitals extremely awkward; the angle is poor for digital stimulation, and the only way to maintain contact with the clitoris was to rest the palm on the mons and use the thumb, which was something that had to be figured out on the spot.

The conditions also made it impossible for us to interact as we usually do; there was no way to communicate verbally, nor was it possible to make eye contact or rely on our normal, nonverbal cues. Despite these difficulties, we succeeded, but the debriefing was somewhat challenging. As Patricia wrote Nan the following day:

> It was difficult for me to give a less than stellar report on the partnered stimulation in front of Mark. Even though we are fine with feedback and are not performance junkies, giving a less than 10 on "satisfaction" in front of people was not easy ... I told Mark not to feel bad and likened his experience to giving a hand-job with mittens on.
>
> Mark's comment was that he expected that it was a 2 out of 10, but it still didn't feel great to be told it was a 5. In some ways, I agree with his number because I couldn't look into his eyes. There was so much of what we do in our normal partnered love-making (or giving-receiving sessions) that couldn't come into play because I had to focus on coming to the exclusion of everything else ... Mark didn't

discover that the thumb would work until later, and
we were mindful of the time and equipment.

We share this story to illustrate that even people who are very experienced sexually, who talk about sex a great deal, and who are comfortable in situations that most would consider unusual can be vulnerable when it comes to questions of competence, skill, and quality of touch.

The vulnerability exists even when the person receiving the feedback is fully aware that it is not intended in a negative way and that conditions were less than optimal. So, if one of you is starting to feel frustrated by the quantity and/or quality of touch, do not let resentments build. Bring the issue into the open, and do so in a way that supports your partner's efforts to reach out to you. If you can tell your partner in an unthreatening way that you'd love to have more physical contact, you're likely to get what you want. Try saying something like this: "Remember how we used to hold hands when we were dating? I really loved that, and it would be great if we could do more of it."

Do your best to avoid letting any sincere effort pass without acknowledgement and appreciation. This is a way of rewarding your partner and will build good feelings. If you want to give feedback, be sure to be constructive and frame things in a supportive way. Instead of saying, "Why can't you just let your hand rest on mine?" focus on whatever feels good, and reinforce what is working. It's much better to say, "I love it when you hold my hand. When you stay still, it really feels wonderful. Does it feel good to you too?"

One of the best ways to make this work is to agree to

increase the frequency and duration of physical contact. We've long maintained that physical contact is a core element of sustaining an erotic connection, though this is a complex subject. Excessive cuddling, to the exclusion of other types of touching, is sometimes related to a decline in sexual connection. Nevertheless, if you've lost touch with each other, it's important to renew your physical relationship, and this is something you can do deliberately.

You'll have to do some talking in order to agree to touch each other more frequently. If you can decide to have physical contact in low-pressure situations, it will reduce anxiety as well as the chance that one of you will feel compelled to give the other feedback. This will make it easier to converse about quality of touch when the time is right. It's probably easiest to start by taking a walk and holding hands or finding ways to touch each other in contexts that are not going to lead to a sexual encounter and are not emotionally charged.

As a next step, you might try what we think is a delightful exercise for exploring touch in a deliberate, methodical, and unthreatening way. It comes from *Touching for Pleasure: A 12 Step Program for Sexual Enhancement*, by Adele P. Kennedy and Susan Dean, PhD (first published in 1986), and it reflects a sensibility that has fallen out of favor. The authors describe an incident one of them observed in which two small children were doing an exercise they had learned in class.

TIP: Invited Touch

The exercise is as useful for adults as it is for children. Sit facing each other, about a foot apart. Begin by asking your partner, "Please look at my nose." After a moment, thank your partner. Your partner can then ask you, "Please look at my mouth." (Any part of the face will do.) After looking at several parts of the face, you can shift to asking to be touched. "Please touch my lips." "Thank you very much."

This may feel awkward at first, but you will grow more comfortable with practice. When you first try it, limit yourselves to the face, head, and neck, but you may find it interesting and worthwhile to expand to other parts of the body once you've fully explored your faces. Even when you touch each other's body parts, don't treat this as a kind of foreplay—maintain an exploratory and playful attitude.

Touching well and with awareness is easier if you bring as much of your mind into the body part that is doing the touching as you possibly can. The invited touch technique can be a very good way to begin touching more consciously. Here's a way to explore the concept a little more deeply.

TIP: Bringing Awareness to Your Fingertips

Bring as much awareness as you can to the tip of the index finger on your dominant hand. You may find it helpful to close your eyes. Spend a minute or so focusing on your fingertip, then move your consciousness to the middle finger, and do the same. Repeat this process with each finger and your thumb. Finally, bring all of your attention to the palm of your hand. It may help to imagine that your palm is getting warmer and warmer. Keep focusing on your palm, and see if you can notice any changes as you do so. Next, try holding your hands together and bringing as much attention to the points of contact between your palms as you possibly can. This is likely to change the way you use your hands during lovemaking as you discover that touch involves far more than skin-to-skin contact.

People who are well trained in massage therapy learn how to be very conscious of the way they touch, in part through exercises like this one. Good massage therapists have mastered this skill; if you have had a bad massage, chances are that the therapist was not focused and not sufficiently aware of the quality of touch. While some of us are undoubtedly more gifted than others when it comes to this kind of sensitivity, for the most part it is a skill that can be learned, and bad massages are more likely the result of distraction or poor training than lack of innate ability.

If quality of touch is this important in the context of massage, it is even more so in sensual and erotic situations when you need to alternate between observing how your touch is received and focusing on your physical and emotional state. This can be somewhat daunting. We suspect that many complaints about quality of touch during lovemaking stem from the fact that arousal can be so intense that thought processes get clouded. Nevertheless, you can refine your skills, in part by altering the way you think and focusing on what is happening in the moment not on the delights that are yet to come.

TIP: Quality of Touch

Ask yourself:

How is my touch being received?

Does my partner seem to melt with each caress?

Is he leaning into me?

Does she seem to be tensing up or pulling away?

Is she turning to meet my gaze?

Has his facial expression changed?

Are my motions overly repetitive? (Some people find this irritating except in the context of building toward orgasm.)

AGENDA-FREE TOUCH

One way that sex therapists and others have tried to address touch-related issues has been to define certain kinds of touch as "nonsexual" and to encourage couples to spend time engaging in "nonsexual" touch, as a way of building intimacy while avoiding conflict around clumsy sexual overtures. This seems to be, in large part, a somewhat misguided attempt to deal with the way men and women are socialized. Teenagers sometimes use baseball as a metaphor for sex, and the emphasis on hitting a home run is illustrative; boys often talk about how far girls will "let" them go—to second base, for example—and for the most part they try to get as far as they can. In adult life, this kind of conditioning can create a sense of urgency about initiating a sexual encounter and an inability to be present in the experience of giving and receiving touch. In these instances, the focus is on the need to "score," even with a long-term partner. This model does not always conform to conventional gender roles. Women can certainly be aggressive initiators and feel urgency too. Whatever your gender, it is much healthier to embrace the erotic element that resides in human contact.

All consensual touch has an erotic element, and it's up to us to recognize it and enjoy the experience for its own sake, without pushing for more or worrying about whether a sexual encounter will ensue. Denying the innate pleasure and eroticism of touch may result in a reflexive shutdown and limit your capacity for enjoyment.

The attempt to draw a bright-line distinction between sexual and nonsexual touch is troubling for several reasons. First, there's an implicit denigration of the erotic in the distinction, a tacit suggestion that "nonsexual" touch is good and "sexual touch" is bad. Secondly, for couples, overemphasizing nonsexual touch can serve to dampen the erotic ardor between the partners by devaluing the sexual and favoring the comfortable or comforting.

We feel it is better to think about touch in terms of whether or not there is an agenda. People are uncomfortable being sexually aroused while touching or being touched in what are commonly deemed to be nonsexual situations. Massage therapists, for example, go to great lengths to negate or deny the erotic component of their work. This is understandable, in part, because it is so commonly assumed that massage therapy is a form of sex work. Nevertheless, it is unfortunate and also reflects the widespread and mistaken belief that getting aroused or even enjoying a mildly erotic charge must lead to genital sex, that being turned on means somehow that you need to push for an orgasm. This is a by-product of both the idea that sex and coitus are synonymous and the biblical notion that lusting in the heart is the same as acting on that lust. Just allow yourself to feel lust, to feel turned on, to recognize the erotic current in your consensual interactions, and revel in whatever you feel, whether or not the physical contact leads to what people conventionally call "sex."

AWARENESS AND ATTUNEMENT

In many communities, being aware when having sex is a rarity, if not a taboo. From college students to adult singles to couples who go to swinger or lifestyle events, heavy drinking is often a precursor to sexual encounters. We have no moral objection to this kind of behavior, and we often say in our lectures on Tantra that the quickie you have after a couple of cocktails is just as sacred as any formal, ritualized lovemaking session. This is, of course, a somewhat provocative statement to puritanical practitioners of sacred sex, but our point is that making distinctions between sex that is good and sex that is bad, whether or not you're using spiritual terminology, is sex-negative. If intoxicants are not a problem for you, there's nothing wrong with sharing an encounter while you're under the influence from time to time, though you should never make decisions about safer sex practices under the disinhibiting effects of alcohol or other substances.

People enjoy drunken sex because intoxicants tend to lower inhibitions and make it easier to lose oneself. The problem is that many intoxicants, alcohol in particular, dull awareness, especially when they are consumed in excess. For the most part, the best sexual encounters take place when our faculties are not impaired and we can pay close attention to what's going on.

Awareness involves not only paying attention to what's happening with your partner and monitoring how he or she is responding to your touch; it also means tuning in to your own body. We'll discuss sexual dysfunction in Chapter 11: Dealing with Discrepancies, Distractions, and Disruptions, but for now we'll observe that many sexual problems seem to have their roots in a lack of awareness or an inability to pay attention. For preorgasmic women, distraction is often the issue; a number of factors may contribute to premature ejaculation, but one of the most significant elements is difficulty with monitoring one's own physiological state.

Being aware of your own state while recognizing what's going on with your partner and moving back and forth between the two are skills that you can develop. It is usually easiest to begin by exploring the interplay between inner and outer observation in nonsexual and pressure-free circumstances. You can practice this in virtually any context, and with or without a partner. For example, if you're out walking in the woods, you can move your attention back and forth between what you're observing in nature and what you are feeling in your body.

ABANDON, ENTHUSIASM, AND LACK OF INHIBITION

At first glance, this section may seem contradictory in light of the previous one, which focuses on the importance of awareness. But in certain ways, making love is like creating art or being an athlete; it requires the ability to be highly aware and focused while also surrendering and releasing control, allowing yourself to get into the flow and be fully submerged in the experience. On a physiological level, this paradox is reflected in the fact that both the sympathetic nervous system (which is responsible for arousal and the fight-or-flight response) and the parasympathetic nervous system (which governs relaxation) must be engaged in a balanced way. Each of these aspects of sex presents its own set of challenges.

"Imagination is more important than knowledge" is one of Albert Einstein's most often quoted aphorisms.[37] A similar principle applies in the realm of sex: abandon is more important than skill. Sexual knowledge, including sexual self-knowledge, is very important if you want to be a good lover; our society as a whole suffers from a severe lack of sexual knowledge and information. Similarly, there's absolutely nothing wrong with being a skillful lover and having a variety of techniques at your disposal, but bringing your partner to the height of ecstasy is a mutual undertaking, and skilled but unenthusiastic ministrations are not likely to lead to much fulfillment for either one of you.

---

37 Albert Einstein and George Bernard Shaw, *Cosmic Religion: With Other Opinions and Aphorisms* (New York: Dover Publications, 2009), 97.

Similarly, in some communities, extended, nonejaculatory sex for men is held up as an ideal, often for health and sometimes for ostensibly spiritual reasons. We will discuss nonejaculatory sex and what we see as its appropriate place in the sexual repertoire in Chapter 7: Tantra and Neo-Tantra. For now, we'll point out that refraining from ejaculation, especially if it becomes a predominant mode of engaging sexually or a point of pride, can be a way of maintaining control and refusing to give over fully to the experience. When this is so, it may function as a distancing mechanism. Orgasms, and especially ejaculatory orgasms in men, are a form of surrender, of allowing the body and nonrational parts of the brain to take over. These moments are some of the most purely experiential and completely absorbing states that are available to us as human beings. To refuse to surrender to them is to deny not only your own pleasure but also your partner's ability to see you and join you in that state. Compulsively holding back and maintaining control can be a way of avoiding this surrender, perhaps because it is overwhelming or because many men equate control with prowess.

This is not to say that becoming skilled at regulating and delaying the ejaculatory response is valueless. Lasting longer, within reason, is generally a good thing; prolonged states of sexual arousal produce delightful alterations of consciousness, but this is endurance as a means to an end, not an end in itself. In this context, endurance is used in service of the abandon that follows. If endurance is the goal, total immersion is not possible.

Enthusiasm is closely related to abandon and is in many

ways the state of mind that makes abandon possible. Enthusiasm is not something that can be learned in the conventional sense. We are keenly aware of the irony in writing a sex book with this kind of advice. Most sex books focus on techniques, because techniques can be taught and described specifically. Enthusiasm is more complicated and elusive. The word implies not only that you are enjoying the experience, but also that you are giving yourself over to it.

You can train yourself to be enthusiastic by acting enthusiastic. Suppose, for example, that you don't particularly enjoy giving oral sex. (If you actively find it unpleasant, what we're suggesting may be too challenging.) If you get little pleasure from this particular act but do it out of a sense of obligation, chances are your partner will pick up on your mental state and will get less pleasure from receiving it. After all, partnered sex is a feedback loop, and this particular loop is more of a downward spiral.

In order to reverse the direction, you can choose to display enthusiasm, whether you feel it or not. Some people, especially trained surrogates, skilled sex workers, and top-level porn performers, are capable of finding the beauty, attractiveness, and desirability in every person with whom they interact. This is a rare gift, and the people we are describing are extraordinary; they truly enjoy their work and are very good at it. For more ordinary people, this is a skill set that can be cultivated.

FINDING ENJOYMENT IN THE MOMENT BY FOCUSING ON PLEASURE

Tamar Reilly is an IPSA (International Professional Surrogates Association) -trained sex surrogate. She told us how she developed the ability to take pleasure in every encounter.

I developed this skill by learning how to stay in the moment. It takes a lot of practice, but if you focus on sensation, something positive or pleasurable in any given moment, you can extract enjoyment. For example, when I do a hand caress exercise, I tell my client we are to touch and explore for our own pleasure and not concern ourselves with giving the other person pleasure. I know it sounds selfish, but take the focus off of giving pleasure and bring awareness to what gives you pleasure instead; it's a win–win. Realize that it's difficult at first. It's like breaking a habit. I've had a lot of sensory practice working in the sex field through the years, and I'm so fortunate to enjoy my work.

WHAT IS THE DIFFERENCE BETWEEN A SEX SURROGATE AND A SEX THERAPIST?

The most reliable surrogates are IPSA credentialed, but most surrogates are not qualified therapists.

A sex surrogate works in collaboration with a therapist.

A sex therapist never engages physically with a client.

A sex therapist has an advanced degree and may be certified by the American Association of Sexuality Educators, Counselors, and Therapists (AASECT).

If you can focus on a kernel of enjoyment in whatever you're doing and can express your pleasure authentically and enthusiastically, your partner is likely to get caught up in your enthusiasm and respond accordingly. This kernel of enjoyment may be nothing more than delighting in your partner's delight. If you can do this, you will have reversed the spiral, and over time, the rewards you receive should make the activity increasingly pleasurable for you too. In some respects, this is simple Pavlovian conditioning, and it is likely you will gradually train yourself to enjoy and perhaps look forward to the act itself.

This approach can even impact activities about which you feel even less interest. We're not suggesting that you force yourself to like something you find very unpleasant, just that you may be surprised by the degree to which you can train yourself to take pleasure in things you might think you don't like. For example, enjoyment of G-spot or prostate massage can be an acquired taste. Because of past associations, insufficient arousal, and unfamiliarity, these forms of sexual stimulation can be uncomfortable at first. It takes time for some people to forge neural pathways and create an association between the sensation and pleasure. Contemporary scientific research is revealing that the brain is considerably more plastic (responsive to experience, malleable, and capable of development, even late in life) than anyone imagined a generation ago.

We will be discussing orgasm, the brain, and current scientific research in more depth in the next chapter. For now, it's sufficient to point out that some people have the capacity to induce orgasm by thinking themselves off, but even in those who do not have this ability, thinking about orgasm activates some of the same brain regions as actually having one. This highlights what is possible if you can make a concerted effort to create or reinforce pleasurable associations and more specifically erotic or orgasmic ones.

Generally speaking, women seem to have a greater capacity in this realm than men, perhaps because of innate physiological differences, not just in genital anatomy but also because they seem to have a greater variety of pathways to orgasm. For example, it is not all that unusual for women to be able to train themselves to have real orgasms when viewing erotic material or performing oral sex. To some degree, this may be social and cultural; most men believe that orgasm and ejaculation are the same and that erection is a prerequisite; and for most men, spontaneous ejaculation is not desirable. Recognizing that orgasm is possible without ejaculation may make it easier to start experiencing orgasmic sensations in the same context as women who can think themselves off or orgasm through giving head.

Regardless of your gender and whether you ever develop the capacity to orgasm without any direct genital stimulation, associating pleasurable or orgasmic sensations with giving your partner pleasure will deepen your pleasure as well. It will help you move beyond your self-imposed boundaries, lower your inhibitions, and make you freer. This freeing up and lowering of inhibitions will make it easier for you to surrender to the experience.

TIP: Focus on and Communicate Enjoyment

Focus on whatever you can find that's enjoyable in any given act or sexual encounter, and keep it in mind as you're interacting. Convey this enjoyment to your partner, with your eyes, your body, and your vocalizations; just don't be artificial. This is a great way to manage distraction during a sexual encounter. In any given moment, you can ask yourself, *Where am I experiencing the most pleasure in my body?*

Authenticity in this context is important because your partner is likely to pick up on it if your enjoyment isn't genuine. There is some value in faking it, as we will discuss in more detail in the context of Tantra (see Chapter 7), but if you are going to fake it, fake it authentically. Don't try to imitate what you've seen in porn or what you imagine someone enjoying an act would do. Instead, make the sounds you would make when you are in the throes of pleasure, and do your best to imagine yourself having an orgasm through whatever you're doing. This too will affect you deeply and forge neural pathways, creating associations with those things that are truly pleasurable for you. Chances are that, before long, you will be able to throw yourself into the experience and surrender to it fully. You will have trained yourself to make love with abandon.

DON'T WAIT TO FEEL DESIRE

Back in the days of Masters and Johnson, the sexual response cycle was described in a fairly mechanistic way: arousal, plateau, orgasm, and resolution. While the Masters and Johnson model remains something of the standard even now, more recent models have added additional elements in an effort to incorporate sex's more mental and emotional components.[38] Helen Singer Kaplan proposed a three-stage cycle that involved desire, arousal, and release.[39] Another approach, developed by Rosemary Basson, is based on the idea that women respond differently than men and that their interest in sex is influenced by a need for intimacy, among other factors. Basson also recognized that sexual desire in women frequently is experienced concurrently with arousal not as a precursor to it.[40] While there is no need to delve into the details of these various models, it is worth considering the role of desire, which is popularly accorded far more significance than it should be. In long-term relationships, waiting to have sex until you feel desire is a very bad idea.

Humans can choose when to be sexual. We don't have to feel desire before we make love. You can use whatever works to keep the choice to be sexual foremost in your mind, whether

---

38 "Your Guide to the Sexual Response Cycle," http://www.webmd.com/sex-relationships/guide/sexual-health-your-guide-to-sexual-response-cycle, for example, reflects how popular the Masters and Johnson model remains.

39 Helen Singer Kaplan, "Hypoactive Sexual Desire," *Journal of Sex and Marital Therapy* 3, no. 1 (1977), 3–9, abstract and preview available at http://www.tandfonline.com/doi/abs/10.1080/00926237708405343#preview.

40 Rosemary Basson, "The Female Sexual Response: A Different Model," *Journal of Sex and Marital Therapy* 26, no. 1 (2000), 51–65, abstract available at http://www.tandfonline.com/doi/abs/10.1080/009262300278641.

it's your interest in being close to your partner, a decision to make sex a priority in your life, or just the recognition that sex is a great tool for reducing stress. This is a way to transform desire from a bodily need or a vague emotional state into a more conscious process, something over which you have greater control. This will enable you to choose erotic activities even when you do not actively desire sex. Unless there's a serious physical or emotional disruption, having sex when you're not in the mood is likely to leave you feeling just as satisfied as having it when you are.

Overall sex drive or libido is probably influenced by a variety of factors that are beyond our control: genetics, childhood environment, culture, and hormones. There is clearly a spectrum, just as there's a spectrum when it comes to orientation. In fact, there's currently an active effort to define asexuality (meaning a lack of interest in or desire to have sex) as an orientation, and it seems likely that many of the people who identify as asexual are born with a considerably lower basic sex drive than the vast majority of the population. Given all the mixed messages people receive about sex, those who are on the lower end of the sex drive spectrum often feel marginalized. Since you're reading this book, however, chances are your basic sex drive is moderate to high. Maybe you're interested in having better sex, but there's a good chance you'd like to have more of it too.

To return to desire, in most males, it is at its strongest during the teenage years. This form of desire is hormonally driven, and it is a very intense, physically charged state, characterized by spontaneous erections, wet dreams, and frequent masturbation. As adolescence gives way to adulthood, this dramatic form of desire starts to recede, and while interest in sex may continue to be strong, it has a more mental quality. Hormones also play an important role in shaping female sexuality. By now it is well documented that female desire is profoundly influenced by the menstrual cycle and is usually at its peak around the time of ovulation. Stress and other emotional factors also come into play, as can medications.

There wouldn't be much to worry about if the human life span were only thirty years, and if we were only interested in sex for procreation. In our society, people often live into their nineties, and most of our sex is nonprocreative. For this reason, it is very limiting to rely on hormones alone to make sex happen. Not only that, but many hormonally driven encounters are not very well thought through beforehand and often lead to less than pleasurable experiences, or worse, fiascos.

6

ANATOMY: A LITTLE TECHNICAL KNOWLEDGE GOES A LONG WAY

Freud claimed, "Anatomy is destiny" (he was referring to gender-determined differences in human psychology), and George Santayana wrote, "Those who cannot remember history are condemned to repeat it."[41] We'll borrow a little from each of these observations, while taking them entirely

---

41 For Freud, see Sigmund Freud, "The Dissolution of the Oedipus Complex," in Peter Gay, ed., *The Freud Reader* (New York: W.W. Norton, 1989), 665. Some scholars suggest that the statement does not relate to gender but to the issue of nature vs. nurture; however, the language in this essay is unambiguously gendered. Freud wrote, "The little girl's clitoris behaves just like a penis to begin with; but, when she makes a comparison with her playfellow of the other sex, she perceives that she has 'come off badly' and she feels this as a wrong done to her and as a ground for inferiority." For Santayana, see George Santayana, *The Life of Reason; or the Phases of Human Progress,* Vol. 1. (New York: Scribner's, 1905), 284. Variants of this statement are often mistakenly attributed to Edmund Burke.

out of context, and state that those who don't have a basic understanding of anatomy and physiology are destined to have less than optimal sex lives. While you can certainly function adequately, and perhaps even well, without this knowledge, knowing something about these subjects will make you a more skillful lover. You may be surprised to discover that even the experts still have a lot to learn.

We encourage you to think broadly when it comes to sexual activity and to expand your definition of sex to include far more than "penis-vagina intercourse" or "penis-in-vagina" sex (PVI or PIV). At the same time, human physiology is such that a majority of people experience the most pleasurable sexual sensations in their genitals. There's certainly nothing wrong with being genitally focused; PVI sex is a central part of our personal repertoire. This is probably true for most heterosexual couples, and for this and other reasons, it's valuable to have a good knowledge of sexual anatomy. Many people who lack anatomical knowledge focus almost exclusively on what is visible: the external parts of the clitoris, the labia, the penis, and the testicles. The vagina is an exception; it is well known but not very well understood. There is more to the genitals than meets the eye, and keeping these unseen parts in mind and knowing what to do with them can enrich your sexual encounters.

Similarly, surprisingly little is known about orgasm. The experience has a highly subjective component, especially for women, who don't have the obvious, albeit somewhat limiting, feedback loop of erection and ejaculation as an indicator. Of course, male orgasm can happen without one or both of these elements, but from early adolescence on, boys and men have access to physical evidence of their orgasms. This is one of the reasons why "cum shots" are so prevalent in pornography. Even though they can be faked, they represent a kind of proof that an orgasm has happened; female performers can fool most of the public by pretending to orgasm, though knowledgeable and careful observers can usually recognize the real thing. Understanding what constitutes an orgasm, developing an expanded definition of the term, and knowing something about the physiological processes related to orgasmic release will enable you to stay present and focus on the signals your partner is giving.

There are different kinds of orgasms, probably a greater variety in women than in men, and they involve different neural pathways. Many people are only familiar with one or two forms, so there is likely more to orgasm than you think. You can define the experience in any way you choose.

BARBARA CARRELLAS'S MULTIGASMS

Tantra teacher and author Barbara Carrellas has a great gift for recognizing the orgasmic potential in a wide variety of experiences. She has come up with quite a catalog: gigglegasms, angergasms, crygasms, emotiongasms, breath and energy orgasms, to name a few.[42]

42 Barbara Carrellas, *Urban Tantra: Sacred Sex for the Twenty-first Century* (Berkeley, CA: Celestial Arts/Ten Speed Press, 2007), 80–110.

There is no single accepted, scientific definition of orgasm. Considering how much is known about many other aspects of human functioning, it's surprising that such a fundamental aspect of our lives remains so poorly understood. While there's excellent, pioneering research being done on what happens in the brain during orgasm (and thus far most of that research has been on women), the question of what happens in the body remains to a large extent unanswered, as do questions about how the brain and the body interact during sexual arousal and orgasm.

Similarly, it's somewhat astounding that even today there is so little understanding when it comes to female genitalia, and that certain questions about female sexual anatomy remain highly contested in the scientific and sexological communities. Some of the uncertainty is no doubt because having sex under laboratory conditions is challenging and is likely to result in distortions of the data. The fact that many studies rely on self-reporting is another complicating factor. Perhaps more importantly, scientific research is impeded by cultural attitudes toward sex and by the persistent discomfort the subject inspires in many people.

The debate over sex education in public schools has been going on for decades, and sex-negative attitudes are still embedded in American culture, so it shouldn't come as a surprise that the study of sex is not a priority higher up in the educational system. Even today, sexology remains, for the most part, outside the mainstream in the scientific community, and there are only a handful of universities that offer graduate programs specifically focused on the study of human sexuality, sex education, or sex research.[43] This lack of academic interest (or perhaps this academic unease is more accurate) in human sexuality also manifests itself in the therapeutic and medical communities. Many couples therapists are not adequately trained to address sexual issues because human sexuality courses are generally electives in graduate psychology and psychiatry programs.

Doctors often seem uncomfortable and not particularly well informed when asked questions of a sexual nature. To provide a few specific examples: Patricia once asked her (female) gynecologist a general question about ejaculation, and the doctor responded with concern, "Do you think you're voiding during sex?" thus betraying her ignorance of the G-spot and the ejaculatory orgasmic response. Debby, a patient facing a hysterectomy, inquired about having anal sex post-surgery; her doctor seemed taken aback and struggled to come up with an answer. Ed's doctor placed him on high blood pressure medication without informing him that the side effects might include erectile problems. This level of discomfort about and ignorance of human sexuality serves no one and can often be damaging. In recent years, it has become fashionable to complain that young people are getting their sexual education from pornography, but those who are so concerned rarely ask

43 According to the American Association of Sexuality Educators, Counselors, and Therapists (AASECT), http://www.aasect.org/profession.asp, as of March 19, 2013, there were only three major graduate programs that offer degrees in human sexuality. On the same page, AASECT offers a partial list of other institutions that provide advanced training in human sexuality and sex research, in the context of other degree, postdoctoral, or other educational programs. There are only twenty-one graduate or higher level programs listed.

the more important question: why is it necessary for them to do so?

We are not experts on anatomy, physiology, or neuroscience. Nor are we trained sexologists or couples therapists. Our teacher, Dr. Mumford, is a chiropractor-osteopath who taught anatomy and also has a background in psychology. He has always emphasized the importance of becoming familiar with anatomy and educating oneself about the science of human sexuality, and we have done our best to follow his example and inform ourselves about these subjects. Nevertheless, others are far more knowledgeable than we are, and what we're offering here is a very basic overview.

THE PELVIC FLOOR: CRUCIBLE OF YOUR SEXUALITY

Let's start by looking at the parts of the body that men and women have in common and that lie at the very core of our sexual beings. These body parts all play a role in sexual functioning and orgasmic response, regardless of your gender. Remember that thinking about the sexes as "opposites" is often counterproductive and also that human sexuality varies a great deal from individual to individual, so talking about male sexuality or female sexuality will inevitably be overly general. What you discover about your own mind and body is far more relevant to your life than broad statements about human sexual response or behavior.

The pelvic floor

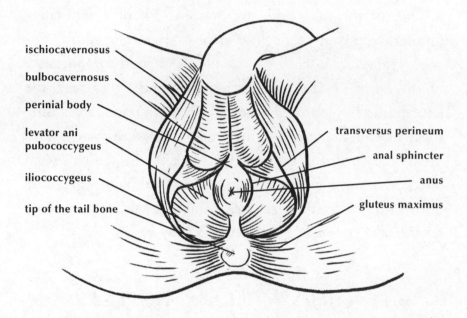

ischiocavernosus

bulbocavernosus

perinial body

levator ani
pubococcygeus

iliococcygeus

tip of the tail bone

transversus perineum

anal sphincter

anus

gluteus maximus

As we've already indicated, your sexual anatomy is not limited to what's on the outside of your body. In both sexes, the entire pelvic bowl, especially the pelvic floor—the area that runs from the tip of your tailbone to the top of your pubic bone—is part of your sexual apparatus. It is suffused with nerve endings, erectile tissue, and the organs that are responsible for sexual function. For example, the anus is connected to the sex organs, and shares a neural pathway via the pudendal nerve. The anus frequently pulses during orgasm, especially an intense orgasm, and this is an involuntary response. Beyond that, virtually any point in the area surrounding your genitals will be responsive in some way, provided it's receiving the right kind of stimulation.

One of the most effective ways to become intimately familiar with your pelvic floor involves exercising your pubococcygeal (PC) muscles. We cannot overstate the importance of this form of exercise. It stimulates and strengthens the entire pelvic region. It also stimulates your mind. Exercising these muscles compels you to bring attention to your genital area. People are often mentally disconnected from their sexual parts, even those who enjoy sex a great deal. Becoming more aware of and attentive to your whole genital area can, by itself, make you more responsive sexually.

FINDING YOUR PC MUSCLES

To find your PC muscles, do the following:
  Drink at least sixteen ounces of a beverage of your choice.
  Wait until you have the urge to urinate.
  Gently release your urine in pulses.
  Make a mental note of which specific muscles you engaged to do this.

Blood flow plays an extremely important role, since the engorgement of erectile tissue (which exists in equal amounts in both men and women) is a key component of sexual arousal. Pulsing your PC muscles not only increases their strength and focuses your attention on your genitals; it also increases blood flow and hence responsiveness. Women with strong pelvic muscles generally have stronger contractions during orgasm, which suggests that they are likely to experience more pleasure, and men often find that exercising the muscles leads to firmer erections and more powerful orgasms.[44]

ISOLATING AND EXERCISING YOUR PC MUSCLES

There are many different ways to exercise your PCs. (There are fourteen muscles in all.) This method will not only strengthen them, it will make it easier to isolate specific parts of the pelvic floor and increase your control over the muscles.

Begin by clenching all the muscles you can in this part of your body, including your lower abdomen and butt cheeks.

Gradually move your attention toward the center, and focus on your anus, while allowing the outer muscles to relax.

Try to isolate and pulse your anal muscles gently.

Bring your attention forward to the perineum, and imagine that you are pulling your perineum up toward your lower abdomen. Squeeze, release, and bear down gently, focusing your mind on the exact point where the pulsing is taking place.

In time, you'll become skilled at isolating specific locations and pulsing them at will.

---

44 Talli Rosenbaum, "Pelvic Floor Involvement in Male and Female Sexual Dysfunction and the Role of Pelvic Floor Rehabilitation in Treatment: A Literature Review," *Journal of Sexual Medicine* 4, no. 8 (January 2007), 4–13, abstract available at http://www.ncbi.nlm.nih.gov/m/pubmed/17233772/.

Working your PCs is also helpful if you want to learn to delay ejaculation, but not because tightening them increases control. Some people advocate tensing the muscles to impede ejaculation. This can sometimes work, but it can also backfire. If you want to avoid ejaculating, the better approach is to relax (as the song of that title advocated[45]). Increased awareness of and skill at isolating the PC muscles makes it much easier to relax them in high states of arousal. Reducing tension, as opposed to increasing it, is the most effective way to delay and regulate ejaculation, since ejaculatory orgasms involve the spasmodic release of tension.

We have been teaching people to exercise these muscles for years and have long emphasized the three-step process: squeezing, releasing, and bearing down slightly. We think this final element is important because it makes the muscles more flexible, and bearing down is part of the female ejaculatory response. We have recently learned that some who teach the technique advise against bearing down because they say it may lead to incontinence or to vaginal or uterine prolapse. While we still prefer the three-step process, provided the bearing down is done gently, we want to alert you to the potential downside.

---

45 Frankie Goes to Hollywood, "Relax," *Welcome to the Pleasuredome*, ZTT Records, 1983.

TIP: Pulsing Your PCs to Build Arousal or Trigger Orgasm

Women may find that pulsing the PC muscles when they are highly aroused is an effective way to trigger an orgasm. Start pulsing as you get very turned on while masturbating or during intercourse. In addition to pulsing, you can experiment with squeezing and holding for several seconds as you approach your climax. You may find that the quality of the experience differs depending on which technique you use. Men can try this too, but if you do, be sure to refrain from forcing yourself to come. This skill set will make it easier for you to time your own orgasms and enhance your ability to have more varied orgasmic experiences.

Becoming adept at using these muscles can be a great addition to your sexual repertoire. The female version of the technique is sometimes known as *pompoir, Singapore grip,* or *kabazzah* (a more advanced form that also involves the abdominal muscles), and a skilled practitioner can bring her partner to orgasm while remaining externally motionless. Whether or not you're interested in mastering the technique to such an extent, you can still have a lot of fun with it. Men too can bring their partners a lot of pleasure by remaining motionless and pumping their PC muscles during penetrative sex.

The anus, the rectum, and the perineum all benefit from working the PC muscles. The perineum is technically defined as the entire pelvic floor but is more commonly thought of as the area between the genitals and the anus. These parts of the body are not always associated with sexual function, especially the anus and rectum, since people tend to think of them as organs of excretion. In popular culture, anal sex is often associated with violence and domination. (Doggy-style genital intercourse has similar, if not such dramatic, cultural connotations.) Although the taboos related to anal sex are weakening, there's still an association between anal play and homosexuality in the minds of many men. Pornographic depictions of women receiving anal sex often emphasize the perceived humiliation and degradation associated with being "fucked in the ass," as if anal sex were all about power and domination, not pleasure.

Whatever your gender, the anus and rectum are part of your sexual apparatus; the nerves and musculature are connected, and anal, rectal, and perineal stimulation all affect the genitals, both directly and indirectly. In women, anal penetration stimulates the erectile tissue in the lower part of the vagina and the G-spot.[46] In men, vigorous perineal stimulation can be felt in the prostate.[47]

Stimulation of the anus, perineum, and rectum can engage the pelvic and pudendal nerves, which are implicated in the orgasmic response. The pudendal nerve also innervates the genitals and is thought to be most central to orgasm. The pelvic nerve connects the cervix, uterus, and prostate to the brain, and the hypogastric nerve relates to the vagina, cervix,

---

46 Tristan Taormino, *The Ultimate Guide to Anal Sex for Women,* 2nd ed. (San Francisco: Cleis Press, 2006), 15–16.

47 Charlie Glickman and Aislinn Emirzian, *The Ultimate Guide to Prostate Pleasure: Erotic Exploration for Men and Their Partners* (Berkeley, CA: Cleis Press, 2013), 187–197.

and rectum. The role of the vagus nerve is less well understood, though research over the past decade has shown that some women with completely severed spinal cords can still experience orgasm and that the vagus nerve is the pathway.[48] It is not clear whether the same is possible in men.

48 B. R. Komisaruk, B. Whipple, A. Crawford, S. Grimes, W. C. Liu, A. Kalnin, and K. Mosier, "Brain Activation During Vaginocervical Self-Stimulation and Orgasm in Women with Complete Spinal Cord Injury: fMRI Evidence of Mediation by the Vagus Nerves," *Brain Research* 1024 (2004), 77–88, abstract online at http://www.ncbi.nlm.nih.gov/pubmed/15451368.

Neural pathways and the related body parts. Based on a graphic by B. R. Komisaruk et al. in *The Science of Orgasm*.[49]

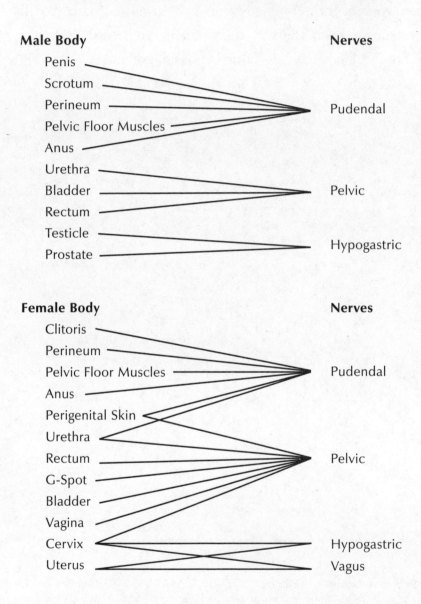

49 Barry R. Komisaruk, Carlos Beyer-Flores, and Beverly Whipple, *The Science of Orgasm* (Baltimore: Johns Hopkins University Press, 2006), 228.

Thus, while the role of each of these nerves in orgasmic response is known in general, many of the details remain unresolved, especially with regard to how the neural pathways to orgasm in men and women may resemble each other or differ. For our purposes, it's sufficient to recognize that there are multiple pathways, and that orgasms vary depending on what nerves are engaged. This may help explain why, for example, some women experience their most intense and satisfying orgasms through anal sex, while others prefer direct clitoral stimulation. That said, unless there is some kind of physiological impairment or damage to one of these nerves, they can provide anyone with sexual pleasure and can all be brought into play.[50]

ADDITIONAL PATHS TO ORGASM

While we're on the subject of the role of neural pathways, we should move to another part of the body that can produce orgasm: the breasts. The nipples in both men and women are comprised of erectile tissue, just like the genitals. The breasts swell during sexual excitement, and a substantial number of

---

50 Ibid., 7–15, 226–239. For the role of the pudendal nerve, see S. Hamdy, P. Enck, Q. Aziz, S. Uengoergil, A. Hobson, and D. G. Thompson, "Laterality Effects of Human Pudendal Nerve Stimulation on Corticoanal Pathways: Evidence for Functional Asymmetry," *Gut 45* (1999), 58–63, full text online at http://www.ncbi.nlm.nih.gov/pmc/articles/PMC1727586/pdf/v045p00058. pdf; and Noelani M. Guaderrama, Jianmin Liu, Charles W. Nager, Dolores Pretorius, Geoff Sheean, Ghada Kassab, and Ravinder K. Mittal, "Evidence for the Innervation of Pelvic Floor Muscles by the Pudendal Nerve," *Obstetrics and Gynecology* 106, no. 4 (October 2005), 774–781, abstract online at http://journals.lww.com/greenjournal/Abstract/2005/10000/Evidence_for_ the_Innervation_of_Pelvic_Floor.18.aspx.

women can have orgasms through nipple stimulation alone. (It seems a small minority of men also have this ability.) Although it is somewhat of a taboo to say so, this can (and often does) happen during breast-feeding.

The reasons are interesting. The connection between nipple stimulation and orgasm is not purely neurological; it also has a substantial hormonal component (something that does not appear to have been very well studied in men). Oxytocin is one contributing element to this largely hormonal orgasmic response. It is commonly referred to as the "love" hormone and is responsible for uterine contractions and the release of milk; it also plays a role in male ejaculatory response. It is widely believed that oxytocin is responsible for bonding between nursing mother and infant and for postcoital feelings of connection, but as yet there is no scientific evidence that this is the case in humans.[51]

In terms of orgasm, stimulation of the nipples triggers the sensory receptors for the genitals that are located in the part of the brain known as the hypothalamus. This is what leads to the release of oxytocin and produces uterine contractions. If you're eager to learn how to have orgasms that originate in parts of the body other than the genitals, you may find it easiest to begin with the breasts because the basic hormonal and neurological wiring is already in place, just waiting to be activated. That said, everyone's a little different, and some people simply don't enjoy nipple stimulation. If you're one of those people, wait until you are highly aroused before you try

---

51   B. R. Komisaruk, pers. comm., October 29, 2012.

it. This may lead to recognizing the sensations as pleasurable, though it may not happen on the first try. If you become more sensitized, that's great. If not, don't worry, and keep focusing on other parts of the body that are responsive.

The process underlying nipple orgasms[52]

Nipples

↓

Trigger neurons in hypothalamus and sensory cortex

↓

Neurons are the sensory receptors for the genitals

↓

Trigger a release of oxytocin

↓

Uterine contractions

---

52 B. R. Komisaruk, N. Wise, E. Frangos, W. C. Liu, B. Whipple, and S. Brody, "Women's Clitoris, Vagina and Cervix Mapped on the Sensory Cortex: fMRI Evidence," *Journal of Sexual Medicine* 8 (2011), 2822–2830, full text available online at http://www.ncbi.nlm.nih.gov/pmc/articles/PMC3186818/. Dr. Komisaruk explained that "nipple stimulation also activates the sensory cortex overlapping with the region of the sensory cortex that is activated by genital stimulation. This could create a conscious, pleasurable 'confusion' with genital sensation." B. R. Komisaruk, pers. comm., October 29, 2012.

FEMALE ANATOMY
External female genitalia

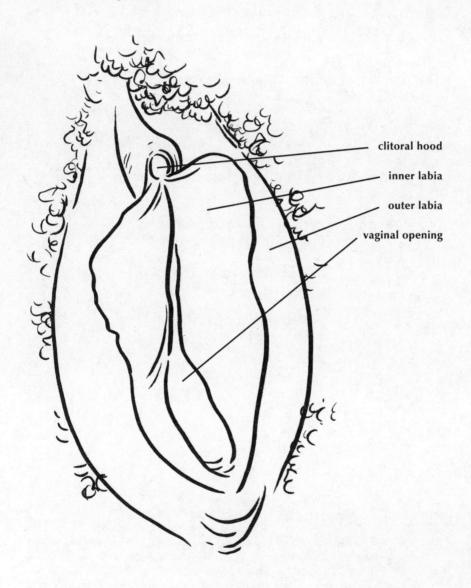

clitoral hood

inner labia

outer labia

vaginal opening

Internal female genitalia

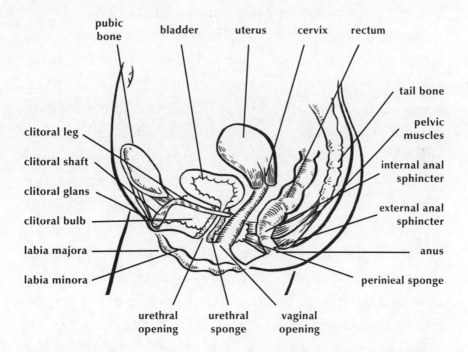

Now let's look at the less obvious components of a woman's sexual anatomy. Figures 4 and 5 depict the external and internal female genitalia, showing the most significant and relevant components. In this context, it may be useful to become familiar with some of the technical terminology. The word vulva is used for the external genitalia, including the head, shaft, and hood of the clitoris, the labia majora (outer lips) and labia minora (inner lips), and the vaginal vestibule (the external area between the labia, including the vaginal and urethral openings). People often mistakenly use the word vagina when they are actually referring to the vulva. Vagina applies only to the internal structure, between the vestibule and the cervix.

The Clitoris

It is well known that the head or glans of the clitoris is highly sensitive. It is said that the clitoris is the only part of the human body that has only one function—pleasure. It is the most densely innervated organ in the body.[53] But it is a much larger organ than most people realize, comprising more than just the glans, hood, and shaft. Even Masters and Johnson failed to depict this in their groundbreaking book *Human Sexual Response*. (They also seem to have been unaware of the G-spot.) In addition to the glans and the shaft, the clitoris has legs that extend downward around the vaginal opening and under the labia, forming a wishbone shape. These legs can be accessed if you stimulate your partner between her inner and outer labia. Of course, the labia themselves contain erectile tissue and are highly sensitive in their own right.

People tend to focus exclusively on the clitoral glans, but the legs too are usually sensitive, so it can be highly arousing to stimulate this area. One effective approach is to slide two well-lubricated fingers up and down between the inner and outer labia. This has the added benefit of affecting both the labia and the clitoral legs. Applying gentle pressure can make this even more pleasurable.

---

53 N. S. Crouch, C. L. Minto, L. M. Laio, C .R. J. Woodhouse, and S. M. Creighton, "Genital Sensation After Feminizing Genitoplasty for Congenital Adrenal Hyperplasia: A Pilot Study," *British Journal of Urology International* 93 (2004), 135–138, abstract online at http://www.ncbi.nlm.nih.gov/pubmed/14678385.

Stimulating the legs of the clitoris can be very erotic.

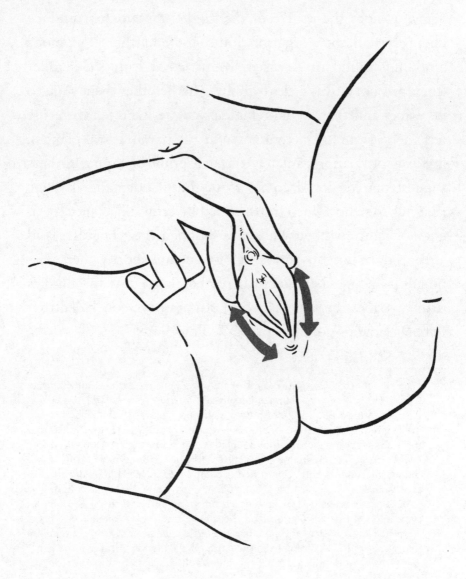

The G-spot

The existence of the G-spot remains the subject of controversy, as does the source of the fluid some women produce
during ejaculatory orgasm. Some contend that if copious
amounts of fluid are released, it must come from the bladder
(they are not always clear about whether they believe it to
be urine) and that actual female ejaculate, secreted from the
female prostate (formerly known as the paraurethral glands),
involves only approximately one teaspoon of liquid. Others
suggest that the fluid comes from the bladder and is urine
that has somehow been transformed by arousal.[54] The experience of many women who have emptied their bladders and
still produce copious amounts of ejaculate shortly thereafter
makes us somewhat skeptical of the claim that the fluid is
urine, as does the fact that some studies have concluded that
female ejaculate contains prostatic fluid.[55]

---

54   Gary Schubach, "Urethral Expulsions During Sensual Arousal and Bladder
     Catheterization in Seven Human Females," *Electronic Journal of Human Sex-
     uality* 4 (August 25, 2001), http://www.ejhs.org/volume4/Schubach/abstract.
     html. Schubach's paper includes a review of other studies. He concluded that
     the fluid he observed came from the bladder but had characteristics—reduced
     levels of urea and creatinine—that differentiated it from typical urine. In ad-
     dition, the subjects had been catheterized and had their bladders drained be-
     fore their ejaculatory sessions, which continued for an hour and a half. The
     paper doesn't make it clear how much time elapsed between the draining of
     urine and the first ejaculation, and the sample size was very small. Schubach
     suggested that most of the ejaculatory fluid emanates from the bladder but
     that some could be coming from the paraurethral glands. Although the paper
     was written more than a decade ago, the whole subject remains controversial
     and unresolved.
55   F. Wimpissinger, K. Stifter, W. Grin, W. Stackl, "The Female Prostate Revisit-
     ed: Perineal Ultrasound and Biochemical Studies of Female Ejaculate," *Jour-
     nal of Sexual Medicine* 4, no. 5 (2007), 1388–93, abstract available at http://
     www.ncbi.nlm.nih.gov/pubmed/17634056. As with the Schubach study, the
     sample size is probably too small to be conclusive.

All controversy aside, many women find G-spot stimulation to be very pleasurable, whether or not they ejaculate. Some ejaculate and feel little or no pleasure, and others neither ejaculate nor enjoy having the G-spot stimulated. Questions about the nature and source of the fluid are interesting and worthy of scientific inquiry, but it should not be a concern if the fluid is urine, as long as the experience associated with squirting is pleasurable. Whatever the case and contrary to some popular myths, the G-spot is not very hard to find.

Part of the reason people may be confused or have difficulty locating the G-spot stems from the fact that the name is misleading. The G-spot is not a spot at all. It is a band of erectile tissue that surrounds the female urethra.[56] Like all erectile tissue, the G-spot becomes engorged during sexual arousal, and this engorgement makes it easy to find the spot, provided the person receiving stimulation is sufficiently excited. In the absence of arousal, it may be difficult to locate, or the attempt may cause discomfort.

To find the G-spot, stimulate your partner (or yourself) externally until she's very turned on. Those who are multi-orgasmic will probably want to have one or more orgasms to start. Once a high state of arousal is reached, insert a

---

56 Adam Ostrzenski, "G-spot Anatomy: A New Discovery," *Journal of Sexual Medicine* 9, no. 5 (2012), 1355–1359, abstract available at http://onlinelibrary. wiley.com/doi/10.1111/j.1743-6109.2012.02668.x/abstract. The author, a cosmetic gynecologist, and his claim to have identified a specific structure as the G-spot, were widely criticized and challenged by some of the world's foremost sex researchers, who argued that the G-spot encompasses more than one structure; B. R. Komisaruk, B. Whipple, and E. Jannini, "Commentary on the Paper by Dr. A. Ostrzenski: 'G-spot Anatomy: A New Discovery,'" *Journal of Sexual Medicine*, 9 (2012): 1954–1958.

well-lubricated finger into the vagina and feel around on the front wall between two-thirds and a full finger-length inside. If you're stimulating yourself, it's probably easiest to do this while squatting. You should be able to find an area of tissue that has a somewhat rougher texture than anywhere else in the vagina. That's the G-spot. Over time, you may notice that it varies somewhat in size and sensitivity. Most of these changes are due to the menstrual cycle.

It's easiest to stimulate your own G-spot while in a squatting position.

The most effective way to stimulate the G-spot is with a come-hither gesture (or pressing forward toward the head of your clitoris, if you are self-stimulating from inside). This area is more sensitive to pressure than it is to thrusting. Some of the difficulty that people have in finding it may stem from a tendency to use the finger as if it were a penis, forgetting that it has joints. As we've indicated, sensitivity can vary a great deal, so there will be times when applying just a little pressure is all it takes and other times when you may find that using a lot of upper-body strength is necessary.

It's important to keep the human capacity to form new neural pathways in mind when deciding to experiment with G-spot stimulation. Initially, some people may find the experience unpleasant. Sometimes the stimulation can create a sensation that's similar to the need to urinate. Other forms of discomfort may be due to insufficient arousal. Applying pressure when the erectile tissue is not engorged squeezes the urethra up against the pubic bone, which most people find uncomfortable if not painful. While inattentiveness or poor technique can be a factor, it is more often a matter of associating a new sensation with pleasure; our brains often code the unfamiliar as unpleasant, and many of our greatest pleasures are acquired tastes. Thus, it's worth giving your brain the time it needs to form the needed connections. (The same applies to receiving prostate massage for men.) If, after eight or ten attempts, you're finding that it still isn't pleasurable, then you may not be built for this particular way of interacting sexually. Just be sure that you've found the G-spot and have been stimulating it properly. If you're more visual, and you haven't been able to find it based on our written description, there are numerous instructional videos available. (See the Resource Guide for sources: Tantra.com, Tristan Taormino, Nina Hartley, and the Alexander Institute.)

There's another aspect of female sexual structures that's worth mentioning. A good way to think of sexual anatomy—male and female—is to focus on erectile tissue. This is perhaps more relevant in women than in men, which may seem counterintuitive, since the penis is so obvious. Men and women are made out of the same basic materials, and during the early fetal stages the sex organs are undifferentiated. Differentiation begins at eight weeks *in utero*. The process is not always completed, which is why some individuals are deemed to be intersexed, an important reminder that gender is a continuum, not a fixed and polar opposition. Differentiation determines, among many other things, how the erectile tissue will be distributed in the body. In men, it concentrates in the penis, and in women it is diffused among the clitoris, the labia, the G-spot, and the perineal sponge, between the floor of the vagina and the rectum. All of these areas are interconnected, and the fact that the erectile tissue is diffuse may make it easier for many women to experience a broader range of sexual pleasure and to be more sensitive to different forms of stimulation.

In the Modern era, women have been at once commodified as sex objects and desexualized. As we've already noted, pre-Modern Europeans believed that men were by nature sexually restrained and women were by nature wanton seductresses. By contrast, most contemporary Westerners tend to think of women as basically monogamous, as interested in nesting more than in fucking, and of men as essentially philanderers, whose randiness and barely controllable desire to spread their seed to as many women as possible must be reined in. Contemporary preconceptions about sexuality reveal themselves in numerous ways of thinking that are taken for granted in our society—from the way that sex addiction is constructed in some branches of the therapeutic community to the popular (albeit oversimplified) forms of evolutionary psychology that treat the mid-twentieth-century ideal of man as breadwinner and woman as nester as biologically determined outcomes of the evolutionary process.

Contemporary ideas about female sexual anatomy and response have been heavily influenced by this set of cultural beliefs—from the persistence of the Freudian notion that vaginal orgasms are superior to clitoral ones to the increasingly common belief that women store sexual trauma in their genitals and need healing massage to release their pain. All of this thinking takes the focus away from sexual pleasure, preventing women from owning their bodies and responses and leaving men mystified by the complexities of female anatomy. The truth is that the greater complexity of female sexual anatomy provides women with a more varied menu of pleasures than are readily available to men.

MALE ANATOMY
Male sexual anatomy

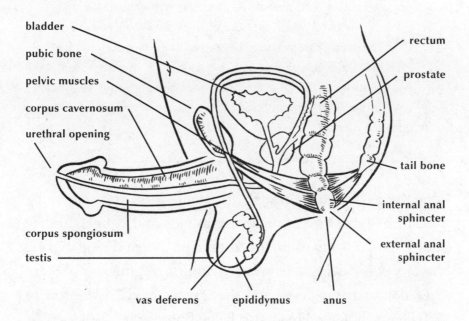

The Penis

If women's sexual anatomy is frequently characterized as mysterious and confusing, male sexual anatomy is often assumed to be simple. So much of it is externally visible that many people fail to realize it has its hidden aspects as well. Thus, men are often surprised to learn that the penis includes an internal structure, called the root, which culminates near the prostate gland. Even if it is not being directly stimulated, this internal structure is no less important; the prostate, while not absolutely essential to sexual functioning, plays an important role in arousal and orgasm, and not just because it is the source of 20–30 percent of the fluid component of ejaculate.

TIP: Stimulate the Hidden Penis

Even though you can't see the root of the penis, you can incorporate it into your lovemaking. Find the hidden parts of the penis by applying gentle pressure at the base when he's hard. Vibrating gently can increase the sensation for him and can be especially enjoyable during oral sex. As he gets more aroused, you can focus on this area, which will help him enjoy the heightened erotic state without having to worry about going over the edge too rapidly.

One theme that runs through all of our work, and something that bears repeating, is the fact that men and women are far more similar than they are different. When Freud wrote, "anatomy is destiny," he meant that girls feel inferior because they don't have penises, and that "penis envy" is central to female psychology. Freud also helped propagate the idea that women are somehow radically different and utterly impenetrable (pun intended) when he asked, "What does a woman want?"[57]

The truth is: what men and women want is not all that different. Beyond food and shelter, most humans want love, appreciation, and acceptance. Most want good sex too, and if people could get past cultural prejudices and social condi-

---

57 This last, well-known question was posed to his student Marie Bonaparte. Freud wrote: "The great question that has never been answered, and which I have not yet been able to answer, despite my thirty years of research into the feminine soul, is 'What does a woman want?'" Sigmund Freud quoted in Ernest Jones, *Sigmund Freud: Life and Work*, Vol. 2 (New York, Basic Books: 1981), 377.

tioning, the differences between "male" and "female" desire would likely seem a lot less significant. And when it comes to anatomy, men and women are not really so different either. Much of the clitoris is hidden, and so is much of the penis. The clitoris has a glans, and so does the penis.

This is not to say there are no differences at all. The glans or head of the clitoris is much smaller than the glans of the penis, and the nerve endings are considerably more concentrated in the clitoris. Some contend that stimulation of the upper left quadrant is optimal, but in our experience as teachers, excessive focus on one specific location is misguided; sensitivity and the ideal place to stimulate vary a great deal. By contrast, the glans of the penis not only has far more erectile tissue, it is also bisected by the urethra and has the urethral opening at the tip; and guys, if you've ever gotten a little soap in your urethra, you know how sensitive the area can be, even though the nerves are more concentrated in the clit.

If the glans as a whole is not quite as sensitive as the clit, part of it comes very close. The frenulum is the area on the underside of the glans, between the urethral opening and the point where the foreskin attaches (or formerly attached). It is the slightly less sensitive male equivalent to the glans of the clitoris, and if you focus all of your attention on stimulating this point when your partner's highly aroused, there's a good chance he'll have an ejaculatory orgasm in very short order, even if he's skilled in delaying that response. It's also a spot that is often hypersensitive after orgasm, so when he asks you to stop after you've given him a blow job, it's probably because there's too much stimulation in this little area. If you can position your mouth to avoid contact with the glans, he'll probably enjoy your holding him there for a while.

The Foreskin

Perhaps no part of the male body is the subject of such intense debate as the foreskin. There have been some recent attempts to outlaw circumcision, but because it is mandated in Judaism and is a widespread Islamic practice with religious implications, these efforts have not gained much traction. Beyond the religious aspects, advocates have long contended that the practice has health benefits, and there is a sizable body of research (albeit contested) suggesting that, at least in Africa, circumcision significantly reduces the risk of HIV transmission. Data for the United States are considerably more ambiguous, but since August 2012 the Centers for Disease Control and Prevention have taken the position that circumcision reduces the risk that heterosexual men will contract HIV and certain other STIs and also the risk that men will transmit some STIs to their female partners.[58] Although there is more controversy around the practice than there was a few decades ago and circumcision rates have declined, it remains common in the United States, with in-hospital circumcision still performed on over 50 percent of newborn males. This is down from the rate of over 60 percent that prevailed in the 1990s.[59]

---

58 CDC Fact Sheet, "Male Circumcision," http://www.cdc.gov/hiv/malecircumcision/.

59 "Trends in In-Hospital Newborn Male Circumcision—United States, 1999-2010," *Morbidity and Mortality Weekly Report* (MMWR), http://www.cdc.gov/mmwr/preview/mmwrhtml/mm6034a4.htm?s_cid=mm6034a4_w. These figures are based on hospital records and thus do not include many observant Jews, since ritual circumcision is done outside the hospital.

Thus, the odds are that if you're an American male reading this book, you have been circumcised. We are hesitant to wade into the controversy on this subject, except to say that one of the objections to circumcision has to do with the loss of or decrease in erotic pleasure, for both men and their partners. This is yet another area where there has not been sufficient research, and there is no way to draw any firm conclusions, but anecdotally, many women express a preference for uncircumcised men, and one study suggests that for men, the foreskin is the seventh most erotically sensitive component of the genitals, though the number of uncircumcised men in the study was small.[60]

Virtually all of the studies seem to have been subjected to harsh criticism from the opposing side. It is very difficult to find good research on the subject that is devoid of an agenda. Science aside, it seems like common sense to point out that while circumcised men can obviously function and get plenty of enjoyment out of sex, and the impacts of male circumcision are nowhere near as severe as those of its female counterpart, it is still the removal of a body part that plays a role in sexual pleasure and function.

Would we recommend circumcising a newborn in the United States? No. Any health benefits are modest, and there may actually be some risk because the foreskin provides protection to the glans. Moreover, we would never advocate

---

60 J. M. Schober, H. F. Meyer-Bahlburg, and C. Dolezal, "Self-Ratings of Genital Anatomy, Sexual Sensitivity and Function in Men Using the 'Self-Assessment of Genital Anatomy and Sexual Function, Male' Questionnaire," *British Journal of Urology* 103, no. 8 (April 2009), 1096–103, abstract available at http://www.ncbi.nlm.nih.gov/pubmed/19245445.

surgery that diminishes sexual pleasure absent compelling scientific evidence that it is beneficial. One key component of the foreskin's role in sex is that it represents a large percentage of the movable skin on the penis, which can contribute to both partners' pleasure. It is also suffused with nerve endings and is connected to the frenulum. Most men who don't have foreskins probably don't give it very much thought, and the minority of American males who still have them are probably familiar with their erotic sensitivity.

The Prostate Gland

The prostate is the male analogue to the G-spot. This is apt in terms of anatomy, and from a more practical standpoint, the prostate resembles the G-spot because it is very sensitive to direct stimulation when a person is highly aroused, but in most cases, stimulating it prematurely is unpleasant at best. With proper buildup, prostate massage can lead to very powerful orgasms because it is the most direct way to stimulate the nerves surrounding the gland.

The prostate feels like a walnut-sized organ at the base of the internal part of the penis. Not only is it responsible for producing one of the main fluid components of the ejaculate, the surrounding nerves play a very important role in both erection and orgasm. The prostatic nerves are directly attached to the gland, and the cavernous nerves connect it to the nerves of the pelvic plexus, which are involved in both sexual and excretory functioning.

Thus, before pharmaceutical interventions such as Viagra were available, prostate cancer treatments often meant the end of genital intercourse for survivors. Surgical techniques have also improved, and nerve-sparing surgery is an option in many cases. Although the prostatic nerves themselves are not saved during this type of surgery, the cavernous nerves are, and in 95 percent of cases, normal urinary function returns after a few months. It usually takes longer for erections to return, whether chemically assisted or not.[61] Chemical and mechanical interventions also make it possible for some of those who have not had nerve-saving surgery to regain erectile function.

SEXUAL PLEASURE AFTER PROSTATE SURGERY

Aviator attended one of our workshops in 2012. Despite having had a radical prostatectomy more than a decade ago, his enjoyment of sex is undiminished.

At the age of 49 (I'm 59 now) I was diagnosed with prostate cancer. I elected to have a radical prostatectomy via a minimally invasive procedure. Fortunately I do not suffer from incontinence, and with the help of Viagra and a cock ring, I have no problems with erection. This past year I remarried, and two years ago, Aviatrix and I started swinging; no one (including her) has ever raised any concerns. Orgasms are like before, just without any ejaculate. I maintain your sex life is 90% in your mind. You can compensate for your physical limitations by remaining positive and focused!

---

61 Johns Hopkins Medicine, "Erectile Dysfunction Following Radical Prostatectomy," http://urology.jhu.edu/prostate/erectyle_dyssfunction.php.

This illustrates the interconnectedness of the urogenital tract, which is a fact regardless of gender. Maintaining prostate health is thus very important for male sexual function. While we are not aware of any research on the subject, it makes sense to suggest that exercising the PC muscles provides stimulation to the prostate and may be useful in keeping it healthy. More significantly, the correlation between ejaculation and prostate health, specifically lower rates of cancer, is well documented.[62] While correlation is not causation, the association between frequent ejaculation (a lifetime average of twenty-one per month in one study) and a reduced risk of prostate cancer is strong, so contrary to the beliefs of some that it's healthier to practice seminal retention, there are health reasons for ejaculating and for doing so frequently.

The Testicles and Scrotum

Although we have suggested that sexual response in women is considerably more varied than it is in men, the way men react to having their balls and scrotums stimulated is highly individual. Where women's ovaries are internal, their male counterpart evolved to be external so that the optimal temperature for sperm production could be maintained. This makes men vulnerable in a way that is recognized all too infrequently. The caricature has it that men are all about their cocks, but as any high school athlete can tell you, the balls are a very sensitive part of the body, and men are very concerned about

---

62 Shaoni Bhattacharya, "Frequent Ejaculation May Protect Against Cancer," *New Scientist*, April 6, 2004, http://www.newscientist.com/article/dn4861-frequent-ejaculation-may-protect-against-cancer.html.

protecting them. While "having a set of brass balls" can be interpreted in a number of ways, on one level at least, it implies the replacement of a very fragile body part with something indestructible.

For some men, the balls are an absolute no-go zone in terms of erotic play. Others may enjoy having the scrotum gently caressed, stroked, and licked, but only when they're turned on. Still others may enjoy having their balls actively sucked, and there are those who like fairly hard tugging just before orgasm. Because of this wide variety of sensitivity and diversity of preferences, there's no single recommended way to stimulate this part of the body. You'll have to figure out what works for you.

This discussion of sexual anatomy and the science of orgasm is just a general overview. You may wish to explore some of these subjects in more depth. The ongoing research on orgasm and the brain is fascinating, and much of it is fairly easy to understand. We hope that what we've shared here will give you new ways of thinking about pleasuring each other and some tools for becoming more sexually creative.

TANTRA AND NEO-TANTRA: TECHNIQUES FOR ENHANCED LOVEMAKING

We've already alluded to Tantra and our background as practitioners and initiates. While this is not a book on Tantra, we feel that employing even a few Tantric techniques and principles can be beneficial for virtually anyone. For those who are interested in exploring the sexual aspects of Tantra in more detail, our first three books, *Great Sex Made Simple* (Llewellyn, 2012), *Tantra for Erotic Empowerment* (Llewellyn, 2008), and *The Essence of Tantric Sexuality* (Llewellyn, 2006), cover this subject in depth, each from a somewhat different angle.

The subject of Tantra is complicated, contested, and potentially confusing. Add in the abundance of bad information and media hype surrounding the popular Western form of Tantric practice, and the mere use of the word becomes off-putting for many. This is unfortunate, because the tradition is vast, diverse, and very rich. If you want to better your sex life, developing even a slightly Tantric approach is likely to be very helpful. If you want to go deeper, practicing Tantra can be transformational and may even become a way of life.

So, what is Tantra, anyway? We've been asked that question numerous times, and there is no simple answer. Nevertheless, we often say that "Tantra is an ancient Indian tradition that recognizes sexual energy as a source of personal and spiritual empowerment." This may seem a little confusing, especially if you're not interested in Eastern traditions or take a dim view of "spirituality" in either its conventional or alternative forms. You don't need to adhere to any belief system to understand that the Tantric approach involves working with and harnessing the life force that exists within all of us, whether or not we think of it in spiritual terms. Tantra encompasses far more than just sexual activity. People are often surprised to learn that the vast majority of Tantric practices don't involve sex at all, and Tantric practitioners are often celibate.

THE ROOTS OF TANTRA

From a historical perspective, Tantra emerged as a distinct tradition in the early Common Era. It partakes of beliefs and philosophical perspectives that had long existed in South Asian culture, and Tantric currents exist within, at least, Hinduism, Buddhism, Jainism, the Tibetan Bön religion, and arguably the Sikh and Sufi traditions as well. In addition, a modern, Westernized form—usually called Neo-Tantra—took shape in the twentieth century.

In some schools of classical Tantra, sexual ritual plays an important role. It has been argued that sex is what sets Tantra apart from other related traditions and that the sexual ritual was even more central in Tantra's earliest manifestation.[63] These historical facts have inspired many Westerners seeking to resacralize sex to embrace Tantra, because it is one of the only living spiritual traditions in the world in which sexuality and spirituality are seen not only as compatible but as deeply intertwined. This concept is finding validation in contemporary research on brain function during sexual, meditative, and mystical experiences.[64]

Neo-Tantric teachers and practitioners have fused various forms of human potential movement psychology with ideas borrowed from Wilhelm Reich, Masters and Johnson, some vaguely Eastern elements, putatively Native American and Egyptian concepts and practices, as well as aspects of neo-paganism, and even Christianity. This synthesis often bears little resemblance to any form of traditional practice and raises some troubling questions about cultural appropriation.

---

63 David Gordon White, *Kiss of the Yogini: "Tantric Sex" in its South Asian Contexts* (Chicago: University of Chicago Press, 2006).

64 Kayt Sukel, "Sex on the Brain: Orgasms Unlock Altered Consciousness," *New Scientist* 2812: 6-7 (May 2011), http://www.newscientist.com/article/mg21028124.600-sex-on-the-brain-orgasms-unlock-altered-consciousness.html?full=true; John Horgan, "The God Experiments: Five Researchers Take Science Where it's Never Gone Before," *Discover,* December 2006, http://discovermagazine.com/2006/dec/god-experiments/article_view?b_start:int=1&-C; Nadia Webb, "The Neurobiology of Bliss—Sacred and Profane: Sex in the Brain, and What It Reveals about the Neuroscience of Deep Pleasure," *Scientific American,* July 12, 2011, http://www.scientificamerican.com/article.cfm?id=the-neurobiology-of-bliss-sacred-and-profane. These articles offer an accessible introduction to recent scientific research on sex, the brain, and altered states of consciousness.

We think anyone who claims to practice "Tantra" should, at the very least, be mindful of the complexities surrounding this issue. Some think of Tantra as couples therapy or a sexual skill set. Others have emphasized "sexual healing" and have even espoused the idea that women store sexual trauma in the G-spot and men store it in the prostate, and that massaging these body parts will lead to emotional release and thus to enhanced well-being. After one of our lectures, a professional escort approached us to say that in her business the word *Tantra* is commonly a euphemism for prostate massage. Thus, Tantra means different things to different people.

There is a great deal more to Tantric practice than sex, and those contemporary approaches that reduce it to something that is only sexual (with or without the emphasis on healing) tend to diminish this remarkable and profound tradition. Notwithstanding these observations, we were both drawn to Tantra due to our interest in sex. Each of us had experienced something extraordinary in some of our sexual encounters, and each of us wanted to make those extraordinary experiences something that we could have at will, as opposed to at random. Neo-Tantra seemed to offer techniques for fulfilling this wish. As it turned out, we were right, and our decision to explore a more traditional approach evolved over time. Notwithstanding our critique, we recognize that Neo-Tantric practices can be very beneficial, and much of what we'll be discussing in this chapter can more properly be called Neo-Tantra, albeit informed by our more traditional background.

As an aside, it's worth mentioning that there are a wide variety of teachers and workshops on Tantra in the United

States and around the world. If you have an interest in taking a workshop or working with a teacher, we strongly encourage you to evaluate that person very carefully, with regard to both qualifications and ethics. It's worth waiting to find someone who is grounded and well qualified, and settling for less can be risky. We've listed some teachers we respect and materials that we think are useful in the Resource Guide, which is a good place to start, but even if you rely on the guide, do your own due diligence and be sure you feel a personal resonance with whomever you choose.

HOW TO EVALUATE A POTENTIAL TEACHER

Look closely at the person's resume—a clear statement about training and background, including the name of one or more of that person's teachers is a good starting point.

Does the cost of private or public workshops seem exorbitant?

Is there a promise or a hint that secret teachings will be revealed, but only if you sign up for more classes?

Does the teacher seem grounded and present?

Do you have a good gut feeling about working with this individual?

We'd like to introduce you to a few important Tantric concepts that pertain to sex. These concepts have significant implications for contemporary relationships and sexual encounters. Tantra is, ultimately, a very pragmatic tradition, and it's up to every practitioner to discover and employ what works. It's unusual for those of us who grew up in a culture so heavily shaped by Christianity, and especially Protestant Christianity, to be exposed to something some would call a "religion" in which faith has so little relevance. It's what you do, not what you believe, that matters. Thus, you can explore these Tantric concepts and use them in ways that work for you, whether you believe in them or not, and without regard to whether you delve more deeply into what Tantra may have to offer. We've already indicated that subtle shifts in thinking can often be the key to enhancing relationships and improving sex, so even if you think of this as a mental game or thought exercise, you may still find it beneficial.

- In Hindu Tantra, the universe itself is seen as an ongoing process of sexual union between two deities known as *Shiva* and *Shakti*.

- Shiva represents the masculine principle, consciousness. Shakti represents the feminine principle, energy. This has nothing to do with contemporary Western ideas about gender roles, and it is not related to human biology.

- In Tantric sexual ritual, the practitioners engage in a form of role play in which one embodies Shiva and the other embodies Shakti. Classically, the genders of the participants would match the "genders" of the deities, but this is not essential.

• In the context of the ritual, the practitioners worship each other as Shiva and Shakti, making offerings of food, wine, possibly flowers, and other items. Perhaps more importantly, the attitude of each practitioner is one of service, a focus on the other for the purpose of facilitating that person's experience in the ritual.

• The great insight of the early Tantric practitioners is that the moment of orgasm is when most ordinary people can have access to mystical experiences, with very little effort.

• Most sexual encounters are brief, and most orgasms last only a few seconds. In Tantric sexual ritual, arousal is built and extended for the purpose of producing altered states of consciousness. By prolonging arousal, it is possible to reach these states well before orgasm and for them to last far longer.

• In Tantra, there is a focus on what many people call energy. While this is a term that tends to get shrouded in mystification, it can be helpful to think about energy as something that's pulsing within you at all times. If you can develop the ability to focus on the subtlest physical sensations, you are actually attuning yourself to this energetic aspect.

• You can also use the imagination, visualization, and conscious breathing to direct energy within the body. This is crucial for men who want to learn how to experience full-body, nonejaculatory orgasms. (These can be delightful, even though they are not "Tantric" per se.) Of course, the techniques are valuable regardless of gender.

• The Tantric notion of worshipping one's partner as an embodiment of a god or goddess in a ritual setting is something that can be applied in all aspects of everyday life and can be useful for contemporary couples. It takes very little to remember that the person you love is someone worthy of being honored and respected. This can be particularly valuable when things are a little rough. We like to say that an especially rich and fruitful time to do this is when one or the other of us is "being a butt."

• Tantra is not about separating yourself from the world; it's not about world peace or lofty notions of love; it's not about your emotions, or your needs. The practices are a technology for accessing blissful or altered states of consciousness at will.

• Don't stop doing what you already enjoy. Use the techniques and concepts to give your sex life new textures. Just add what works for you.

• Avoid goal orientation. Don't worry about the orgasm. Try to experience each moment as fully as you can, and treat every sexual encounter as an exploration.

This list is by no means exhaustive, but it should give you a basic overview of what underlies Tantric sex as we understand it. It should also give you a general idea of how some rather traditional and at least superficially alien concepts can be relevant for contemporary Westerners.

If you are interested in becoming more sexually adventurous, attending a Neo-Tantric workshop can be a good place to start. Whether or not you have any interest in exploring Tantra in a workshop setting, you may find that the techniques we discuss below are valuable.

BREAKING OUT OF UNCONSCIOUS AND HABITUAL PATTERNS

Typically, when people make love, there are numerous unspoken, unexamined, and unconscious behaviors that are central to the interaction. As with so much else in life, there's nothing intrinsically wrong with unconscious and habitual behavior. To reiterate, habitual, unconscious behaviors are essential for our survival, and anyone who suggests you should strive to free yourself from all your habits is either delusional or is trying to manipulate you.

At the same time, it is a good idea to recognize that while habits are necessary, they need not govern us at every moment. This is highly relevant when it comes to sex. Sex is a realm in which many assumptions are made and in which people tend to operate by rote, basing their actions on these tacit assumptions. There is a strong tendency to think about sex in roughly the following terms: "I'll do you for a while. Then you can do me. And if we're both fortunate, everything will work out fine, and we'll both get off."

This can be OK; many people are perfectly happy to function in this mode, but it is limiting. If you're well matched sexually, you might never have considered a different way of interacting. If you're not so well matched, you probably feel less satisfied. If you've had some good encounters but not as consistently as you'd like, it's possible that your overall experience has been one of groping for that intangible element that elevates some over others. Regardless of how satisfied you are, changing these rote behaviors is likely to make things even better.

Modern Neo-Tantric teachers have developed a very effective technique for breaking out of habitual lovemaking patterns and bringing consciousness to activities that are usually engaged in without a lot of thought. This method involves separating giving and receiving pleasure, so that the "you do me for a while, and then I'll do you" formula is broken down, and the "maybe we'll both get off" component is eliminated altogether. This is done in the context of what are sometimes called "giving and receiving sessions." In these sessions, one partner simply gives, and the other simply receives. By interrupting the typical lovemaking pattern with its tacit understandings about give-and-take, you will create an opportunity to discover more about each other.

Most commonly, giving and receiving sessions are structured in a way that resembles conventional bodywork. The process usually begins with a full-body massage, with the giver gradually working toward the receiver's genitals. Different teachers have somewhat different views about how much eye contact to maintain and how much verbal communication is appropriate. Some advise using these sessions for the purpose of sexual healing. We suggest you focus on pleasure rather than on past traumas. In addition, many teachers discourage men from ejaculating in this context, while suggesting that G-spot (which some call "Goddess Spot") orgasms should be the goal for women.

SEXUAL TRAUMA AND TANTRA

Sexual abuse and trauma and their aftereffects can be devastating. Some people find that Neo-Tantric practices are an effective way of reclaiming their sexuality; however, we think there is a tendency in some circles to overemphasize trauma and encourage people to dig into the past to find evidence of and then to reexperience painful events. If sexual trauma is an issue and you are interested in exploring Tantra (or if it comes up in the course of your exploration), it's probably best to address the issue with a qualified professional. Only a small minority of Tantra teachers are trained therapists, and while lovers can certainly facilitate each other's healing, relationships are not therapy and conflating the two is probably unwise.

Sexual abuse and trauma are all too common in our society, and the consequences can manifest themselves in a variety of different ways. There's no real basis for assuming that they must be stored in the G-Spot or anywhere else; the value of cathartic modalities has been questioned, especially if the trauma is revisited repeatedly. In fact, dissociation is one of the most common ways of coping with trauma, so developing the capacity to be present is a particularly valuable part of the healing process. Of course, many Tantric practices emphasize developing and refining the ability to be present, and we suspect that this, not catharsis, is one reason why Tantra can be healing. For more on dealing with trauma, see *Healing Sex*, by Staci Haines.

As we see it, the real value in these giving and receiving sessions lies in the opportunity they provide to learn about and expand your sexual response. We encourage you to set your own parameters and time limits. See what it's like to make a decision not to ejaculate and to receive direct genital massage for a half hour; explore what G-spot or prostate stimulation feels like; pay close attention to the differences between closing your eyes and meeting your partner's gaze. Keeping your eyes closed for too long will limit your ability to feel connected, but if you spend the entire time looking at your partner, you'll miss out on the subtle information about your sexual response that can only be grasped by turning inward. Don't bind yourselves to any hard and fast rules about what should or should not happen. These sessions can be very intense and profound, regardless of your belief system or how sexually knowledgeable you are. Even very seasoned members of the swinging community have told us that experiencing a giving and receiving session was something new, utterly surprising, and delightful.

There are only a few guidelines. One is that you should not treat the session as foreplay; don't segue from a session into a more conventional form of lovemaking. In addition, if you set an intention, for example to refrain from ejaculating, stick with it. Perhaps most important, maintain the clearest possible boundary between giving and receiving. This is not always easy, since most people are somewhat more comfortable in one role or the other. The person who is receiving may feel a desire to reach out, caress, or otherwise offer some form of reciprocation. The person giving may experience a strong desire to get something back, so that an outstretched hand may seem very alluring. Try to resist this kind of temptation. Giving in to it can defeat the purpose of the exercise. It may be helpful to think of it as you would a professional massage and to maintain the kind of boundaries (excluding sexual boundaries) that would be appropriate in that context. In addition to interrupting habitual patterns of interacting, this exercise is designed to help people explore and expand their capacities to give and receive. Maintaining a clear separation between the two roles is the only way to experience each one in real depth. There will be plenty of time to go back to behaving as you typically do after the end of the session.

The standard giving and receiving session involves sensual and erotic massage and ends there. We're not familiar with any contemporary Neo-Tantra teachers who encourage taking the sessions a step or two further, but we'd suggest that doing so is very much in keeping with the spirit of the Tantric tradition because each partner is in service to the other. Thus, you may find it very interesting to move the concept of giving and receiving beyond the realm of massage, once you've spent some time with the more conventional form. Too often, long-term couples engage in oral sex as a precursor to intercourse, not as an erotic activity in its own right, so try applying the concept to cunnilingus or fellatio, and give your partner a long slow session during which your goal is to give pleasure, and your partner's is to receive it.

You can even experiment with applying the concept to genital intercourse. This is a little more difficult, since it's very hard to receive completely in this context. Nevertheless, it can be delightful and deeply moving to begin with the intention that one of you will make love to the other, and the other will be made love to. Just remember to maintain a balance and be sure that you're giving and receiving in approximately equal measure. We don't generally recommend keeping score, whether it's the number of orgasms or how often one of you does the dishes, but this is one context in which being sure that things are fair is a good idea.

MAKING ENERGY CONCRETE

In Tantra, there is a very strong emphasis on becoming aware of energy and working with it deliberately. The meaning of the word *energy* is not intrinsically obvious, and it is sometimes used in ways that are more confusing than illuminating, so let's do what we can to make the meaning clear. The term *energy* refers not only to something esoteric and mystical (in Tantra this is called *Kundalini* and is represented as a coiled serpent that resides at the base of the spine); it also refers to phenomena that people generally recognize as physical. There's no need to believe that a coiled serpent dwells at the base of the spine, waiting to be awakened, so that she can journey upward and open our divine consciousness. It's sufficient to say that sexual energy is our life force—the impulse to make love is what brought us into the world—and that the more attuned we are to this energy, and the more skillfully we work with it, the more attuned to ourselves we can become.

TANTRA AND ENERGY: A PRACTITIONER'S PERSPECTIVE

Kyle Applegate is a New York area Tantra teacher. He has some uniquely valuable insights into Tantra, energy, gender, and intimacy.

When I started studying Tantra several years ago, I realized that I had been having Tantric sex for a good decade before I ever took a course or cracked a book on the subject. Learning about Shiva and Shakti energy made perfect sense to me, as I realized I had been inhabiting them both, interchangeably and at times indistinguishably, from the core of my being.

Fast-forward 10 years … I am finally at home in my two-spirit, trans-sexual identity. Tantra has taught me to honor and incorporate the many sides of my being, physically, mentally, energetically, and spiritually, with reverence. Having walked in both worlds of female and male, I don't have to work as hard as my non-trans counterparts to "understand" or "figure out" the dance of intimacy between partners. I have more compassion toward gender differences and see more similarities too.

Tantra works beyond the trappings of gender, where we can call upon and explore an infinite variety and combination of energy. I think exploring Tantra was a natural evolution of my gender transitioning and fluidity. As my body shape-shifted hormonally and I recuperated from surgeries, I found I vibrated on a different sexual frequency, and I had to relearn how to interact with it. Tantra is great for anyone who may have had a major health event and is learning to be intimate again.

For me a Tantric union is one established through mutual emotional and spiritual safety and respect. With that understanding, we can start to drop our neuroses and egos and begin to merge energetically. In an energetic merge it is normal to lose track of time, place, and gendered bodies, while maintaining a high level of conscious connection and heightened sensitivity.

Becoming skilled at working with energy is really nothing more than honing our ability to notice the phenomena taking place within our bodies, in the environment around us, and as we interact with others. It's thus important to develop the capacity to focus on and notice very subtle sensations. This means being aware that when you touch your partner, the intention behind the touch will alter its quality. It also means tuning in and focusing on aspects of your encounter that you might not otherwise notice. For example, during penetrative genital intercourse, it can be very profound to stop and pay close attention to what you feel in your genitals and what sensations may be flowing between you.

To have a more concrete experience of what we mean by energy, try this simple exercise. It's not particularly subtle, but it's a pretty good place to start. You probably did this as a kid without giving much thought to the implications. Stand in a narrow doorframe with your arms at your sides; next, press the back of each hand against the frame; use as much strength as you can and try to raise your arms. (The doorframe will make this impossible.) Continue to press for at least thirty seconds. Step away from the frame and observe what happens.

If you're like almost everyone, when you stepped away your arms seemed to levitate, to rise spontaneously. You may want to try the experiment again (after a rest) and see if you can resist this movement. Chances are your ability to do so will be very limited. There are undoubtedly multiple scientific explanations for why this happens, but the key point is that we've invested energy in trying to push against the doorframe, and when the obstacle to raising our arms is removed, the energy of the body simply takes over, whether we want it to or not.

Once you begin to think in energetic terms, sex can be a lot more interesting and varied. Giving and receiving sessions are a great place for both of you to start focusing on and recognizing energetic sensations. For example, you may find that you can drive your partner to new heights of ecstasy just by resting your finger on the prostate or G-spot. So, start thinking about lovemaking as an energetic act, an exchange that involves your minds and bodies, not just your genitals.

ORGASM AS AN ENERGETIC PHENOMENON

The Neo-Tantric movement has contributed a very important concept to the body of sexual knowledge: sex is more than a strictly physical phenomenon or a way of expressing emotion. It includes both physical and emotional elements, but it is also an energetic experience. This understanding can open us to an array of new possibilities.

For most people, orgasm is primarily or exclusively genital. One unfortunate consequence of the sex-positive feminist movement and views that became current during the 1960s and '70s, and that remain influential today, was the elevation of the clitoral orgasm above all others. While this was a much-needed corrective to the Freudian insistence that "vaginal orgasm" was not just an ideal, but also a sign of well-adjusted and "mature" sexuality, it has proved to be somewhat limiting. This has led many people to focus on the glans of the clitoris to the near exclusion of the erectile tissue and nerve endings that make the entire vulva an erogenous zone.

Men face a somewhat analogous situation, though its origins are not so recent and are more deeply entwined with anatomy, biology, and the way men experience sex. Erection and ejaculation are visible phenomena in men, and from adolescence on, people generally fixate on these external signs. Thus, erection equals arousal, and ejaculation equals orgasm. In reality, erection makes penetration easier and it is necessary for active, thrusting intercourse, but arousal can exist without erection. Similarly, male orgasms can take many forms; ejaculation can take place with minimal or no erection, and with or without orgasmic sensations; and orgasm can happen with or without ejaculation and with or without erection.

It is often said that the brain is the most important sex organ of them all, and research on sex and the brain is revealing this to be truer than anyone imagined even a decade or two ago. There are people who are capable of having hands-free orgasms; this talent is certainly more common in women than it is in men, but the French writer Jean Cocteau was reputed to have shown off this rare gift at parties. We're not suggesting that developing the ability to think yourself off is essential, but if you can allow yourself to accept that a wider variety of orgasmic experiences are possible—ejaculatory, nonejaculatory, G-spot, clitoral, genital, anal, nipple, full-bodied, or from having your toes sucked—you'll be creating the mental climate that will give you a chance to start experiencing a more varied orgasmic palette.

You may be wondering how this relates to energy. If you can accept that orgasm is more than what you have always believed it to be, the next step is to think about it as energetic and not strictly physical. This will enable you to bring your imagination to bear on your experience. If you want your orgasms to be more than genital phenomena, you can start by imagining or pretending that they are. This may seem a little silly, but it can be a very effective way of retraining yourself. To give a concrete example, one of the easiest ways for men to learn to separate orgasm from ejaculation is to go to the edge repeatedly (whether alone or with a partner), stop the stimulation at the last possible moment, and then imagine drawing the energy that was about to be ejaculated back into and through the body. With practice, many men will have an orgasm—one that includes pulsing in the genitals and prostate—without ejaculating. The sensation is likely to be less localized, and while the experience is not exactly the same as if ejaculation took place, it is still likely to be orgasmic in quality and can often be intense.

The way to imagine moving energy is highly individual. For some, it is easiest to visualize white light concentrating at the head of the penis and then imagine that light flooding back up into the body instead of spurting out the urethra. For others, it may not take anything more than an inhalation accompanied by the idea of breathing the orgasm back in. Another approach is to use the hands to stroke from the genitals upward, a gesture that suggests moving and spreading this energy from one part of the body to the next. This can be done during self-pleasuring or partnered sex.

Gesture for spreading orgasmic energy through the body

We've already discussed the PC muscles in some detail, but not in this specific context. (See Chapter 6: Anatomy.) In recent years, some men's magazines have started popularizing Kegel exercises as beneficial for male sexual health and performance. Although this is a relatively new development in American society, claims about the general health (as well as spiritual) benefits of these practices can be found in some classical Tantric and Yogic texts. To reiterate: the most obvious benefits of working the PC muscles regularly include improved prostate health, firmer erections, and an increased potential for having G-spot orgasms. You are also likely to experience a general enhancement of both libido and sexual responsiveness simply by focusing on and actively engaging the area that includes your genitals. In addition, by bringing your attention to something that can also be understood as an energetic phenomenon, you are taking steps to activate, build, and recognize sexual energy.

ORGASM AS AN ENERGETIC PHENOMENON: PART II

There are some obscure and advanced Yogic practices that are designed to drive sexual energy from the genital region into the rest of the body. These techniques include pulsing the PC muscles, and in their most difficult and elaborate forms they involve pressing the heels into the perineum while standing on your head. We are not going to suggest that you engage in such gymnastics. These postures can take years of training to master, and contemporary Tantra teachers employ a simpler and effective way to move sexual energy from the genitals to the rest of the body. This technique, sometimes called "Streaming" or "Fire Breath Orgasm," should help you arrive at a more expansive understanding of what an orgasm can be and provide you with the skills for having a full-body orgasmic response without directly engaging your genitals.

Many people find it difficult to accept that it's possible to experience full-body orgasm without any direct stimulation whatsoever, and in the case of men, without erection or ejaculation. Personal experience tells us otherwise, and before we describe the mechanics of the practice, we'd like to share a story that reveals just how profound and intense streaming can be. Here's Mark's description of his first experience with the technique.

MARK'S INTRODUCTION TO TANTRA

Back in the mid-1990s, I decided to start exploring Neo-Tantra, a subject that had intrigued me for years. I was at a very difficult point in my life. I had gone through an unhappy marriage and a very painful divorce, followed by several less than optimal dating experiences, among other early midlife crises. As a consequence, I was on antidepressants, medications for attention deficit disorder, and other drugs to make it easier for me to sleep. This was well before I met Patricia, and at the time, there were very few people teaching Tantra in New York.

I had done some reading about Tantra, and in those early days of the Internet, I started doing online research. I discovered that California, and especially the San Francisco Bay Area, was a hotbed of what I later learned was Neo-Tantra. I wasn't ready for a full-on retreat, so I decided to do a weekend workshop that had a Tantric component, among other elements. Since my interest was in Tantra, I also booked a private session before the workshop with Satya, the woman who was teaching the Tantric material that weekend.

My visit to her was transformational. She demonstrated the streaming practice and appeared to experience an orgasm without any direct physical stimulation within a minute or two. Her next words were "Now you try it." I got down on the floor and tried to mimic her movements, breathing, and vocalizations. It took much longer to achieve the state that Satya had reached—she was far more experienced, after all— but after a time, I had a nonejaculatory orgasm, although the phrase does not do full justice to the experience. The sensations were indeed orgasmic, but they were also life-changing. I was so transported that I had to walk around the block and take about a half hour before I felt comfortable driving back to my hotel. I was in an uninterruptedly blissful state for several days, and the effects of the experience remained visceral for many months thereafter.

I knew immediately that I could go off my medications, and I stopped taking some right away. It took a few months more to wean myself off the antidepressants, but I was able to do so, and have not had to go back on any such medications since then. There is a technical term for this type of experience in the Tantric and Yogic traditions, and it has gained currency among a small number of psychotherapists in the West. It is called a Kundalini awakening, a reference to the energy that is said to reside at the base of the spine, and the purpose of many practices is to awaken and work with this energy, which is believed to be crucial for spiritual evolution.

We told a truncated version of this story in *Tantra for Erotic Empowerment* but didn't reveal all the details. We have been hesitant to share it in its entirety because we don't want to participate in hyping "Kundalini awakenings," set up unrealistic expectations, or encourage people to think that such an experience is an ideal treatment for depression or attention deficit disorder. (And if you are on medication of any kind, you should consult your physician before making any changes to your regimen.) We share it here to illustrate that orgasms can be transformational and, more importantly, to make it very clear that there is far more to coming than the ejaculation of semen or a series of genital pulses. Your experience may never be as intense or transformational as Mark's, but your capacity for orgasmic response is probably far richer than you've imagined, and streaming is one way to develop a more varied set of orgasmic skills.

Streaming

Streaming can be done alone or with a partner. You can use it to build sexual energy before an encounter or to have an intense, erotic experience in just a few minutes, while keeping your clothes on. You may find watching a demonstration to be more helpful than reading a written description, so if you are having a hard time understanding what to do, you can check out our segment in Tristan Taormino's film *Chemistry IV,* in which we taught the cast the partnered form, or find a very instructive demonstration in *Ancient Secrets of Sexual Ecstasy* (a comprehensive DVD dealing with Neo-Tantric sexual practices, available from Tantra.com and elsewhere).

There are a variety of different approaches to the technique, and some are more complicated than others, often involving the movement of energy and awareness from one part of the body to the next, from the genitals up to the crown of the head. We prefer to keep it simple and focus on three basic elements.

In solo streaming, you start by lying on your back, with your knees bent and your feet flat on the floor. (Uncarpeted is best.) The only external movement involved is rocking your pelvis. Your lower back will arch slightly, and the upper back, neck, and shoulders should remain in contact with the floor. Be sure not to elevate your hips. (This seems to be the most common mistake beginners make.) The hips and the lower part of your spine should remain in contact with the floor as you rock. Moving your pelvis in this way should cause your head and shoulders to slide up and down. It may take some practice to isolate the pelvis and to rock rather than elevate it, but becoming adept at this is likely to make you a better lover. Even if your experience with this practice is not particularly interesting, learning to isolate your hips and rock them is worth the effort.

The next element is somewhat difficult for many people because it requires a certain kind of coordination that may be unfamiliar. Pulse your PC muscles as you rock. Some who teach this technique suggest a set pattern of rocking, pulsing, and breathing. We think it's more effective to work out your own rhythm, so just focus on rocking your hips and pulsing your PCs in a way that feels natural. Being overly concerned with when and how to pulse can distract you from the pure feeling of the practice. If you stay with it, you're likely to experience something.

The third element presents a different set of challenges, especially if you're not accustomed to being vocal during sex (or if you have children in the house). It may also feel silly or phony, especially at first. Combine orgasmic moans with your pelvic rocking and PC pulsing. Think of the famous faked orgasm scene in *When Harry Met Sally,* and make your sounds as dramatic as you possibly can.

We've heard the third element described as "faking it until you make it," and while there's some truth in this description—at first you are making orgasmic sounds to simulate an orgasm—there are deeper elements to the vocalizing. By making noises, you're creating an unconscious association between what you are doing and an actual orgasm and connecting the technique with past orgasmic experiences. From a somewhat more esoteric perspective, you're using the voice to amp up your sexual energy and change your physical and mental state, so it's not so much faking it as it is using sound as a kind of aphrodisiac. We strongly encourage vocalizing during sex; people often restrain themselves. It may take some effort to be big and loud, but doing so is sure to bring greater intensity to your lovemaking.

Solo streaming

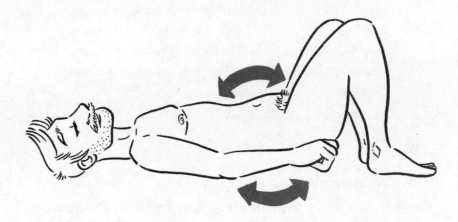

This practice is not always easy to master, and it may take several sessions before you get the hang of it. It often feels awkward at first, but give it a chance and stay with it. Allow yourself at least five minutes of rocking, pulsing, and moaning per session. If you feel that you're hyperventilating, stop until the feeling subsides and try again; don't push yourself. You obviously shouldn't try this technique if you have any significant health issues, such as uncontrolled high blood pressure or back trouble, but for those who are basically fit, there shouldn't be any problems.

TIP: Streaming Step by Step

Lie flat on your back, knees bent, with your arms at your sides.
Rock your pelvis.
Pulse your PC muscles in your own rhythm as you rock.
Take deep breaths and make orgasmic sounds as you exhale.
Continue for five minutes or more, and enjoy the ride.

Partnered Streaming

Whether or not solo streaming works for you, the next step is to try the partnered form. The basic elements are the same: pelvic rocking, PC pulses, and orgasmic vocalizations. There are some differences and additions, since this is no longer a solo practice; the two of you will be working mutually to build the energy, draw it up through your bodies, exchange it, and then allow it to flow back down. This can be great as foreplay or for those occasions when you don't have the time or inclination for a more conventional sexual encounter. Because it involves two people and requires you to both observe each other and time your actions, it may take longer to master, but with a little practice you're likely to discover the joys of nongenital simultaneous orgasms.

In solo streaming, you lie on the floor. By contrast, in partnered streaming, you are in a modified version of a Tantric sexual position called Yab Yum. In this position, one partner sits cross-legged on the floor or on a cushion. If this is uncomfortable, you can also do it seated on the edge of a bed or in a chair. The other partner sits astride the first, in an embrace. If you're on the bottom, you can provide support by holding your partner's lower back. Conventionally, the man sits beneath and the woman is on top, but there's no need to be bound by this convention, and it can be very interesting to explore reversing the roles.

Variation on Yab Yum seated on the edge of a bed

Just sitting in Yab Yum, gazing into each other's eyes, and breathing together can be very powerful. It's an intimate posture, one that inspires a calm and quiet harmony, and it can enhance the eye-gazing practice. Sitting silently in Yab Yum can be an effective way to defuse conflict and bring you back into balance.

As a sex position, Yab Yum has a couple of big advantages. It's great for less vigorous lovemaking that incorporates periods of stillness as well as motion. It's also one of the more effective postures for both clitoral and G-spot stimulation. Partnered streaming is very active and doesn't involve direct genital interaction, but Yab Yum is still the optimal position for doing it, since you're both free to move, and it enables you to stay in sync.

Once you're seated in Yab Yum, begin rocking your pelvises (this may feel somewhat closer to conventional intercourse than what you experience in solo streaming), pulsing your PC muscles, and moaning. Follow your own pattern, and in time you are likely to find a rhythm that suits you both. Keep your eyes open and watch each other carefully. Continue rocking, pulsing, and making sounds, while imagining that you are raising energy together. One way to visualize this is to think of a Ping-Pong ball being carried upward, from the genitals to the head, by a jet of compressed air or a fountain. With every breath or exhalation, the ball is lifted a little higher. At a certain point (with practice and careful observation you can perfect the timing), you will both wordlessly agree that it's time for the next step. When you're just starting out, you may find it useful to set a timer—try three minutes. This will provide an external cue. Once you're comfortable with the technique, you can dispense with the timer.

When you feel you are ready or the alarm goes off, stop rocking, take a deep, controlled inhalation, bring your foreheads together, and hold your breath. As you hold your breath imagine that the Ping-Pong ball is suspended between you, or that the energy is passing back and forth through your foreheads. To prolong your retention of breath, take a sniff or two of air. Hold the breath for as long as is comfortable and then exhale in a way that lets your partner know the time has come to do so. Allow the exhalation to be audible, and pay close attention to the sensations as you release. We often feel as if something is cascading down from our heads through our bodies, landing in the genitals, producing a strong series of aftershocks. This is an orgasmic sensation, sometimes just as intense as a more conventional orgasm would be.

TIP: Partnered Streaming

Sit in Yab Yum.

Rock your pelvises.

Pulse your PC muscles.

Inhale deeply and make orgasmic sounds as you exhale.

Gaze into each other's eyes and monitor each other.

When you are both ready, take a long, slow inhalation and hold your breath.

Bring your foreheads together. Take a sniff or two of air.

Imagine that you are exchanging energy through your foreheads.

Exhale and allow the sensations to cascade down through your bodies.

Even if you understand the instructions and can apply them easily, watching someone else do any technique, whether on film or in person, can be very valuable, so we strongly encourage you to check out the films we've referenced so you can see for yourself.

At first, streaming may feel a little foreign; it requires a certain lack of inhibition and even a willingness to make fools of yourselves. And there is something quite silly and strange about it. The same can be said about virtually any kind of sexual activity. When you were prepubescent, the very idea of sex may well have seemed ridiculous or odd. We can only suggest that you shed any inhibitions about how you might appear to others. This is a good idea not only when it comes to streaming but for your sex life in general. Mark will certainly never forget the delighted look of anticipation on Satya's face when she was preparing to demonstrate the technique. With a little practice and enough willingness to give yourself over to the experience completely, you too may understand just why she was smiling.

KAREZZA: A DIFFERENT WAY OF MAKING LOVE

People tend to think of genital sex as a very active affair, one that involves hard cocks, wet pussies, aggressive thrusting, some moaning and groaning, culminating in an explosive orgasmic release. Encounters of this type are often very brief, though in their pornographic version they can appear to be prolonged and gymnastic. The classical form of Tantric sex, which takes place in a highly ritualized context, is far slower, encompasses only a couple of female-superior positions (basically forms of Yab Yum or the man lying supine with the woman atop), and is characterized by periods of stillness interspersed with periods of motion.

The purpose of this is twofold. On one level, as we've explained, prolonging the arousal stage is crucial for inducing mystical states, and if you are going to be making love for hours (the ritual can go on for that long), rapid and intense thrusting is not exactly optimal. While some men are naturally slow to reach orgasm and others have become very skilled at delaying, for most, rapid and intense sex usually means the encounter will be of limited duration. For those who are skilled at pounding away, chances are the focus is, at some level, on damping down excitement, not building it up. Doing mental tricks to damp down excitement defeats the purpose of Tantric sex, as does being fixated on performance or striving to set endurance records.

Perhaps even more important than building and prolonging arousal, being still and even doing some form of meditation during genital intercourse can allow you to experience all the accompanying sensations in a much more subtle way. In the more spiritualized form of Tantric sex, these periods of stillness and meditation are seen as crucial for creating the *bhava* or spiritual mood of the ritual, which depends on each partner having an attitude of love for and service to the other. Some would describe this as "sharing energy." In some forms of Taoist and Tantric practice this notion of sharing energy gets taken to extremes and used for a purpose that is quite different, a kind of sexual vampirism in which it is believed that older men can obtain the vital energy of younger women by having intercourse with them, while refraining from ejaculating.

In the late nineteenth and early twentieth centuries, Tantric and Taoist ideas about prolonging arousal and nonorgasmic sex began to filter into American culture. Members of the Oneida Community, a group of nineteenth-century utopians renowned for what was then called "free love," were encouraged to be sexually open, but the men were expected to be "continent," to refrain from ejaculating.[65] Later in the nineteenth century, the feminist gynecologist Alice Bunker Stockham (the fifth woman to become an MD in the United States) wrote a book titled *Karezza: Ethics of Marriage (1896)*. While Stockham was inspired by John Humphrey Noyes, founder of the Oneida Community, she had also traveled to India and had likely been exposed to Tantric ideas. She advocated monogamy and nonorgasmic sex for both men and women.

Stockham's description of karezza is somewhat vague, as might be expected of someone writing in 1896. She was no doubt mindful of the risk of being prosecuted for obscenity that publishing might engender. She wrote:

> At the appointed time, without fatigue of body or unrest of mind, accompany general bodily contact with expressions of endearment and affection, followed by the complete but quiet union of the

---

65 In later years this rule was modified, and the group engaged in a selective breeding program, one of the first experiments in human eugenics.

sexual organs. During a lengthy period of perfect control, the whole being of each is merged into the other, and an exquisite exaltation experienced. This may be accompanied by a quiet motion, entirely under subordination of the will, so that the thrill of passion for either may not go beyond a pleasurable exchange. Unless procreation is desired, let the final propagative orgasm be entirely avoided.[66]

Thus, her beliefs about erotic passion were very much a product of the nineteenth-century American sensibility. For Stockham, as for many of her contemporaries, achieving control over basic human urges, up to and including the orgasmic response, was an indicator of triumph over the debased, animalistic essence of human existence. For all her bravery and professional accomplishment, Stockham's basic attitudes were quite conventional.

From her perspective, human behavior could either be "higher" or "lower," and she saw friction sex and orgasm as outward expressions of this lower aspect of humanity. The main thrust of her book was transcendence, getting beyond the "degrading" aspects of sex, and she imagined that karezza would diminish the overall sex drive. According to Stockham, the karezza practitioner would discover that "it is far more satisfactory to have at least an interval of two to four weeks [between sexual contacts], and many find that even three or four months afford greater impetus to power and growth as

66   Alice Bunker Stockham, *Karezza: Ethics of Marriage* (Chicago: Stockham Press, 2nd ed., 1903), 25.

well as more personal satisfaction."[67] It's very easy to divorce Stockham from her time and brand her as sex-negative. This is not entirely wrong, but given the cultural context, she deserves credit for bringing attention to aspects of sex that otherwise would have been neglected and for developing and popularizing a sexual technique that can be immensely valuable, irrespective of whether you accept the ideology that undergirded it.

Some modern Tantra teachers have encouraged their students to practice a variant of Stockham's technique on a regular, indeed daily basis. The underlying concept is that by connecting genitally for five or ten minutes a day, without engaging in friction sex or seeking any of the less subtle pleasures of conventional intercourse, people can experience a different kind of sex—one that is goalless and energetic—and build intimacy and connection in the process. Popular Australian Tantra teachers Diane and Kerry Riley have even taken the practice and renamed it "Daily Devotion." The Rileys' term points to a purpose that is similar to Stockham's while highlighting a very different attitude about frequency, and hence about sex in general.

We have done this practice on a daily basis at various points in our relationship and recommend that you try it. There's no need to worry about refraining from having friction sex or orgasms at another time, but bear in mind that when you're doing karezza or daily devotion, the practice should be kept separate from conventional sex. Erections may come and go,

---

67 Ibid., 29.

but the presence of an erection is not a reason for either one of you to start thrusting. You should both remain still, though some pumping of PC muscles back and forth is OK, in our opinion, and can be very interesting.

The process itself is simple, and it can be a great way to start your day. The penis should be inserted when flaccid. This means using a lot of lube and finding a position that minimizes the risk of slipping out; missionary and scissors are among the easiest, both for insertion and remaining connected. Once he's inside, you both should remain still and pay attention to what you feel. You may combine this soft form of penetrative sex with eye-gazing. Your breathing is likely to sync up, and you may feel a deep and perhaps surprising sense of bonded-ness. Remain united in this way for as long as is comfortable, but not less than five minutes. Again, you should do your best to refrain from moving, except with your internal muscles. Conclude by expressing love and appreciation for each other in a way that feels right to you.

Practicing karezza can create feelings of connection and bondedness.

Unlike Stockham, we're not going to suggest that karezza will diminish or eliminate your desire to have conventional sex, and we wouldn't recommend the practice if we thought it could. What it can do is give you access to a whole range of sensations that are far outside what is conventionally recognized as erotic. It's also a great technique for moving beyond goal orientation and being focused on orgasm. Doing so is likely to make orgasms more enjoyable, not less. Beyond that, if you have any kind of performance anxiety, practicing karezza can help reduce it, since performance is not an issue. It can also be a great way to stay sexually engaged when erections are not possible. At the very least, we encourage you to try the practice, following the Rileys' model, every day for a week. It may not feel like the sex you're used to at first, but it's worth seeing what happens.

This discussion of Tantra and Neo-Tantra is just an introduction. If any of the material in this chapter resonates with you, it is worth exploring the subject in more depth.

8

BASIC SEXUAL ADVENTURING

By now, you should have a very clear understanding of the elements we think are central to building a strong and enduring relationship. We've stressed the value of treating your sex life and your relationship as collaborations and have highlighted the importance of being flexible. We also believe that every sexual experience has the potential to be revelatory, but this is only one side of the equation. It's equally important to keep your mind on the erotic, to be imaginative and open. To do otherwise would be to limit yourselves erotically. In long-term relationships, the erotic intensity almost always starts to diminish with time. One of the most effective ways to stay passionate is to explore your sexuality consciously, to start pushing your boundaries a little bit, and to become sexual adventurers together.

Before we address how to make this happen, let's examine the concept of sexual adventuring in general terms. Sexual adventuring, as we define it, has little to do with thrill seeking. You may experience thrills, but the objective is more complex than achieving the momentary rush that accompanies a thrill. In our definition, sexual adventuring is a shared undertaking with a clear set of purposes—generally, to build sexual self-awareness, find new sources of pleasure, and bring you closer. As we'll explain, the more specific purposes are for you to determine together. This approach to sex has been central to our relationship since our first date, and we are convinced that it has kept things vibrant for us.

It's up you to define sexual adventuring for yourselves. Adventuring may or may not include other people (as we discuss in Chapter 9: Advanced Sexual Adventuring); it may or may not include various forms of kinky interactions (Chapter 10: Kink); it may include things that look entirely "vanilla" to people in alternative sexual communities; or it may involve things that would shock your neighbors. It's about expanding your boundaries together, about mutually exploring new sexual possibilities, while respecting each other's limits, and building intimacy and trust by thinking of each other as comrades on an exciting journey. While we certainly don't encourage criminal behavior, we often describe ourselves as "partners in crime," and we can't think of better words for the attitude because they imply a certain impish mischievous-ness. After all, sex should be fun!

SEXUAL TRUST

"The currency of intimacy is trust."

—SIMON HAY

We love our friend Simon Hay's insight into the nature of intimacy. We've already scoffed at some of the popular ways in which intimacy is characterized and celebrated. The popular model of intimacy overemphasizes closeness, safety, and sharing. While sharing is wonderful, excessive closeness can often work against maintaining a vibrant erotic connection and end up being both stifling and infantilizing. It is important to feel a certain degree of safety in a relationship, but an excessive focus on assuring and reassuring each other that you are safe means that the messiness, complexity, dangerousness, and potentially transgressive aspects of sex, which are key components of what most people find erotic, will of necessity be diminished. When this happens, sex can become bland and routine, and both desire and intensity can start to fade.

If instead you think of trust as more central to intimacy than closeness, safety, and sharing, you can start to develop a more nuanced understanding of intimacy and recognize it as something that's liberating rather than potentially stifling. Trusting a person includes feeling safe, but the kind of safety that exists in a trusting relationship is not what people generally mean when they use the word. In common parlance, especially pertaining to relationships and sex, "safety" implies a certain power dynamic—protector and protected. Trust has more mature and egalitarian implications. In contrast to safety, trust is not an amorphous feeling or an emotional state that the other person is responsible for preserving. It is mutual, dynamic, and it is built up over time. At its core, trust means knowing that your partner cares deeply about you and will take care to treat you with respect and avoid causing you undue pain. Unlike safety, trust makes it possible to be more flexible when your partner lets you down, as will inevitably happen from time to time. Trust can be rebuilt, even after a severe betrayal. If you require your partner to make you feel safe and your partner somehow fails you, the sense of safety can be very difficult to restore.

Perhaps more importantly, trust is the foundation for sexual adventuring. The more you trust each other, the more fully you can know that your partner will take you into consideration and will not act in a way that is disrespectful, uncaring, or unmindful of you, and the more freely you can support each other as you adventure. This is true even if your sexual explorations involve activities that might be defined as monogamous. If anything, the importance of trust is amplified in the context of nonmonogamous explorations and kink. Whatever your style, trust is central, and with greater trust comes greater freedom and flexibility.

To turn more specifically to sexual exploration and expansion: deliberately exploring and expanding your sexuality together will place you in situations that are optimal for growth, both as a couple and individually. When this is done well and intelligently, it can strengthen your partnership and build deeper, more enduring trust, especially since trust is not only built but also earned.

We have stressed that relationships are dynamic and that we don't buy into the myth of signing a contract and living happily ever after. This is highly relevant to the question of trust and what it really means. Trust is not based on a commitment or a promise. Commitments and promises may have their allure, but sexual adventuring is not about maintaining the status quo; it is about venturing into the unknown. There is much to be said for comfort, and there are many times in life when taking the easier course is a very good idea. Nevertheless, deep trust gets built in a more dynamic way.

To return to betrayal for a moment, when people believe that trust is based on a commitment or a promise, they may feel badly betrayed if that promise is broken. Feeling betrayed is painful and can be very damaging to a relationship, but in some situations we'd suggest that the betrayal may not be real, especially if what is being betrayed is an expectation that was never clearly agreed upon in the first place. We think it is a far healthier and much deeper way of relating to be specific about your agreements, to recognize that they can be modified if circumstances change, and to actively build trust together. This will make trust something that grows over time, is organic to the relationship, and is not just a set of abstract ideas that may not have the same meaning for both of you.

If you plan to become sexual co-adventurers or partners in crime, it is very important to build sexual trust. This is not always easy because sex can be so emotionally fraught and people bring their personal histories into their relationships. We all have some vulnerabilities around sex—we have been taught to be less than open about it and probably to feel ashamed of at least some of our desires. Thus, sexual trust implies more than just being mindful of and honoring your agreements. It also means being aware of each other's vulnerabilities and striving always to be supportive and understanding.

With sexual trust comes the knowledge that your partner treasures your erotic development for its own sake. This means you are reasonably confident your partner will not be judgmental, will never risk your physical safety, and will support you in your explorations or be open to compromise. You can't just say these things and make them so. In time, experience will teach you that your partner values you as a person, will always be careful with your feelings, desires, and sexuality, and will actively display that respect.

This is not to suggest that things will always go smoothly or that nothing will ever go wrong, but having the repeated experience of navigating challenging circumstances with kindness and mutual respect will make these disruptions and missteps seem less consequential. Trust is like putting money in the bank. You can draw on it when things go awry. Better yet, when there is deep and abiding trust, even the missteps can enrich your relationship; the conversations about what didn't quite work are often opportunities to grow together. And if you both can laugh at the missteps, you'll be even better off.

Let's take a look at sexual trust from a different angle, and consider secretiveness in relationships, specifically in the context of viewing pornography. As we've already observed, for some people, a partner's looking at porn is a betrayal, a form of infidelity. The belief that this is so has been fueled in the popular media. Thus, in many couples there is a tacit or explicit understanding that viewing porn is tantamount to cheating. This idea may originate with the nonviewing partner or both may subscribe to it, even if the interest in porn predates the relationship. The person who enjoys porn is often forced into the role of betrayer, even if she doesn't start out thinking of the activity as at all problematic.

Whatever the starting point, it is often the case that pursuing this sexual interest (or any forbidden sexual interest) and needing to be clandestine about it can snowball, generating more and more secretive behavior. Diana and Bill came to us with an expressed desire to feel more connected. In our early conversations, there were some vague references to sexual problems, but they were reluctant to discuss these issues openly, and we preferred to focus on techniques that would deepen their emotional intimacy. After a few months, it emerged that Bill enjoyed watching and masturbating to porn, both straight and gay, that included scenes of bondage and humiliation. Diana had been aware of this interest for years and had told him that she was disgusted by it. Despite his repeated efforts to reassure her that his interest was purely about fantasy and that he had no desire to do anything other than watch and masturbate (we believe he was being truthful), she was never able to make peace with his interests. He never promised to stop and had continued to view the material in secret.

Diana had caught him several times over the years, and with each incident, her feelings of disgust intensified, as did her anger. By the time they came to us, the dynamic of secretive behavior, discovery, and recrimination had become a very destructive cycle. Bill could not be open about his activities, and Diana was unable to refrain from describing his interests with disgust, taking his watching personally, and feeling deeply betrayed, even though no promises had been broken. There was thus no room for negotiation. In the end, we advised them that their issues were too deeply entrenched and that they should seek therapy. In this dynamic, the secretive behavior was a violation of Diana's expectations but not explicitly of her trust, because no agreement was in place.

By contrast, if you have built trust, you may still keep some activities to yourself. Remember that privacy and secrecy are two different things and that it is OK to keep some aspects of your sexuality private; your partner is not your confessor, so you don't have to tell her every time you masturbate or let him know that you enjoy watching gay porn from time to time. In fact, requiring total disclosure in this way is usually counterproductive because it fosters excessive entanglement. There is a big difference between sharing the details of a sexual adventure with your partner because you want to and doing the same because "I have to tell him everything." Keeping little secrets in the context of a trusting relationship can be benign and even beneficial because the secrecy is not driven by the need to hide something, by feelings of shame, or by the desire to avoid terrible consequences. For this reason, it doesn't have the same intensity and power as compulsive secrecy.

We've already stressed the importance of collaboration in any sexual relationship, and we've hinted at its role in building sexual trust by proposing that you think of yourselves as partners in crime. This is an active and engaged form of partnership, and when the team takes priority (but not when someone is "taking one for the team") you are likely to find that your emotional bond deepens, regardless of how adventurous you become.

This can be somewhat delicate and complex, and it does require a good deal of attention and awareness. Adventurers of all kinds have to remain aware, since the very nature of adventuring involves leaving the comfortable, moving into the unknown, and taking some risks—but doing so intelligently. There are many dangers in mountaineering, and sometimes avalanches happen, but climbers get to see natural beauty and experience a kind of elation that isn't available to most of us. The best mountaineers reap the rewards without taking foolish risks, and more often than not, accidents are caused by fatigue, lack of oxygen, and inattentiveness.

In the context of sexual adventuring, inattentiveness often takes the form of forgetting that the relationship is central. This can lead to pursuing a personal agenda without regard to your partner's feelings. There is nothing wrong with having a personal agenda; we all do, and even in the best and most collaborative relationships, there may be times when you get carried away and lose awareness of what your partner may be feeling or wanting. When ample sexual trust exists, these incidents are of little consequence, and it's easy to restore relational equilibrium. It is incumbent on each of you to self-monitor, and to recognize when personal agenda is becoming an issue. It's also incumbent on each of you to make gentle corrections to the course when the other is headed in the wrong direction.

Sexual adventuring carries some risks, both physical and emotional, but so does everything else in life. Ultimately, being a sexual adventurer means living authentically and having the opportunity to experience what the more conventional among us will never know. Skilled sexual adventurers are like the best mountaineers, roped together for their mutual protection, not bound but connected, functioning as a team, trading off between leading and following when necessary, and finding new routes to the high peaks of pleasure.

How to Build Sexual Trust

We have discussed the importance of trust in all relationships. Now we'll provide you with some tools for building sexual trust together. This will involve establishing some clear boundaries and hard rules, some of which may be negotiable in the future or may change over time. The essence of sexual trust is not rule-based, so some aspects will be more ambiguous, depending on time, circumstances, and your knowledge of and instincts about each other. As you gain more experience, you will be able to be more flexible and make judgments in the moment. As you start out, however, rules will be more important, and we recommend that you talk them through, agree on them, and stick to them.

Having rules is a way of ensuring your emotional alignment while establishing a foundation for exploring more freely. This is because the recognition that your partner knows the boundaries and respects them will be reinforced over time, and having this awareness deepens trust. If you follow the rules at the beginning, you will be creating the conditions for being more flexible in the future.

Your sexuality is shaped by an array of forces, many of which function entirely or almost entirely at an unconscious level. Being truly open and connected with your partner involves taking significant emotional risks. When people start exploring new ways of being sexual, more open ways of relating, or even just sharing long-held fantasies, unexpected things can happen; all sorts of repressed or unrecognized material can emerge. There may be feelings of urgency, the sense that a previously unknown or unacknowledged desire needs to be met and needs to be met now. At the same time, expressing these newly discovered desires or ones that have been kept secret for years can lead to feelings of vulnerability. Rules make it much easier to manage both the urgency and the vulnerability, and knowing that the rules have been honored builds confidence and trust.

While we don't believe in radical or promiscuous honesty, in the context of sexual adventuring being honest is essential. (See the section "Build Trust and Create Goodwill" in Chapter 4.) If you are exploring together, you must be truthful and kind. Being transparent will reinforce your partner's sense that you are worthy of being trusted, that you are not like that former lover who was deceitful, and that your explorations are truly a joint venture.

TIP: Ground Rules for Sexual Adventuring

The details of your ground rules may vary a good deal, but some basic elements should be in place for everyone (in addition to safer sex agreements). These include:

I will be as honest with you as I can.

I will strive to express myself kindly.

I will not shame you for your fantasies or sexual desires and will never use them against you, even if we encounter difficulties or our relationship ends.

I will not push you to engage in activities that do not feel right to you.

I will always look for some sexual common ground, even if what you're proposing seems unappealing or odd at first.

I will check in with you before I do something.

CREATE AN EROTIC STATEMENT OF PURPOSE

While having rules and sticking to them is a good idea, especially at the start, having clarity about why you are adventuring and what form that adventuring is going to take is more central to building trust. Thus, it's valuable to spend time talking about and thinking through your motivations and coming to a mutual understanding of your purposes.

Some people suggest drafting a contract to establish your intentions and guidelines, an approach that is fairly common in some BDSM circles. (See Chapter 10: Kink.) Contracts have their uses, but we have some reservations about them, except in very special circumstances. They are legal documents that are based to some degree on an adversarial as opposed to a collaborative model. While there are, of course, collaboration agreements and partnership contracts, they are still documents that are predicated on an exchange, on calculating how benefits and burdens are allocated, with the potential for litigation in the event of a breach. None of these elements are conducive to fostering a sense of collaboration and mutuality, nor do they necessarily keep the intention behind your activity in mind. Thus, we suggest limiting contractual thinking to the narrowest possible category— for example, in discussing rules like the ones listed in Tip 22 and your agreements about safer sex practices. It can be helpful to put these agreements in writing, just so there's no confusion.

Composing a Statement of Purpose together can be far more valuable than signing a contract. It can help to reinforce the sense that your explorations are collaborative and co-created. It can also provide you with greater clarity about your motivations, intentions, and aspirations in pursuing a more sexually adventurous way of life. Be clear—whether your motivation is simply to have more fun or greater pleasure, whether you're seeking to deepen your relationship, know yourselves more fully, or are exploring the spiritual aspects of sex. Instead of thinking of this as a negotiation, think of it as an exchange of ideas, hopes, and desires for the future, while keeping in mind that you are seeking common ground, areas where your sense of purpose is shared or congruent. This will help build feelings of mutuality and will keep the idea that this is a joint adventure at the fore. Remember that your purposes may change over time, and you can craft and recraft your understandings to suit your circumstances, so think of it as work in progress, something that can be modified and amended.

───────────────────●───────────────────

TIP: Things to Consider When Crafting a Statement of Purpose

As you create your statement of purpose, it should be helpful to answer some or all of the following questions:

What do we love about our erotic relationship?

Which of these qualities would we like to enhance?

What values will we keep in mind as we explore?

What do we hope to gain by doing this?

How will we know that we are acting in accordance with our ideals?

What are the things that make us uneasy about this exploration?

How can we as a couple be sure that these concerns are not neglected?

What steps will we take to recognize and manage discrepancies, feelings of being out of balance, and individual interests that the other does not share?

───────────────────●───────────────────

SAMPLE STATEMENT OF PURPOSE

Below is a sample statement of purpose. Take it as just that, a sample. We hope it will inspire you to create your own.

We enjoy a rich and diverse sexual life together, and it is a priority for us. We are also committed to personal growth and development.

We recognize that sexual exploration is a particularly rich avenue for gaining deeper insights into our relationship and ourselves. We want to continue to grow in this way and to facilitate each other.

I love the way that you are so sexually responsive; your ability to be transported during lovemaking is delightful for me, and it is beautiful to see you grow as a sexual being.

I love your character, integrity, and passion. I know you have been wounded in the past, and that some aspects of your sexuality have been a challenge for you. I am in awe of your courage in addressing and moving past these issues and in transforming what once brought feelings of shame into a source of delight.

We have not made any decisions about opening our relationship, but we recognize that this may be something we want to explore in the future. We will discuss it when and if the time comes. Whatever degree of openness we decide on must help us stay focused on our sexuality as a couple; must keep us talking to each other; thinking about sex, love, and relating; and must stimulate and inspire us to go deeper together.

Throughout our explorations, we will strive to hold mutual respect, emotional/physical safety, honesty, curiosity, and fun in the forefront of our minds. We will also strive to be creative and inventive.

We'll know that we are succeeding when we are enthusiastically engaged, have a wider variety of sexual pleasures available to us, and are eager to have more shared adventures.

We recognize that there may be times when one of us feels an intense need for an experience. We will strive to be honest when these feelings emerge and to resist them. We do not want to act out of feelings of need, or even worse, desperation. Thus, we will act only when we are feeling full, perhaps with anticipation of having a great time, but also with the recognition that if a good time is not had, nothing has been lost.

One concern we share is that these explorations could interfere with our primary connection. We recognize that if one of us expresses an interest in having new experiences or an attraction to another person, it may lead the other to have some fears—perhaps of loss and abandonment, being replaced, or being compared unfavorably to someone else. Similarly, being the object of another person's desire can be very alluring and receiving attention can be intoxicating. We recognize that this is a potential peril, even if we decide never to engage sexually with others.

We will do our utmost not to lose sight of each other, to avoid these potential pitfalls, by always taking time to debrief after any experience, by promising not to make on-the-spot decisions when the other cannot fully agree, and by valuing our partnership more highly than our individual gratification. If at any moment either one of us needs to stop an activity and talk, or feels uneasy (regardless of whether it is something that was agreed to in the past), we will immediately take steps to understand each other's feelings.

We will always strive to be kind to each other, to cultivate empathy, mutual understanding, and respect. We will look out for each other and do our best to be open, transparent, and accountable, to ourselves, to each other, and to everyone we encounter along the way. While we may not always be able to live up to these ideals in full, they are our intentions and reflect our core purposes in undertaking a more exploratory sexual relationship.

ADVENTURING AS A COUPLE

While we will be discussing various forms of sexual exploration that we're calling monogamous, we think that the dichotomy between monogamy and nonmonogamy is a false one, at least as the terms are commonly understood. Let's begin by reiterating some basic features of human sexual behavior. It has been fairly well established that most people have a strong biological and psychological need to form pair-bonds. Most people also seem to have a strong biological urge for variety—at the very least to feel attracted by and attractive to others. While monogamy may mean different things to different people, unconscious monogamy usually entails either denying or thoroughly suppressing this basic urge for variety. Ironically, this insistence that feeling desire is tantamount to acting on it can often erode the pair-bond.

As a general rule, being open about your desire for others, talking about those feelings, and acknowledging any fantasies about acting them out is a healthy way to relate. This is true regardless of your relationship style. Contrary to conventional wisdom, being open about feeling desire for others is likely to strengthen your relationship not weaken it.

This is not a small shift in thinking, and for many, it requires throwing away decades of conditioning. This may be difficult and scary at first; it is not entirely risk-free, since desire can be complicated, which is one of the reasons people go to such lengths to squelch it. It may also be risky to tell your partner about your feelings, since we've all been taught to think that desire for another means betrayal and loss of interest. (This is frequently untrue, even in the context of affairs.) And as you start giving voice to these feelings, there is a chance that jealousy may arise, especially at first. In time, however, jealousy is likely to become less of an issue. You will have built trust and will have had many experiences that reinforce the awareness that your desires are not a reflection on either of you and will not necessarily put your bond in jeopardy.

It may be helpful to treat this recognition and expression of desire for others as the first form of sexual adventuring you undertake. Perhaps you work out at a gym, there's someone there, a trainer or another member, and you think he's hot. Instead of just ignoring the feeling, or hiding it, make a point of telling your partner about it—what you find appealing and maybe even what you'd like to do with or to the object of your desire. If you don't belong to a gym, you can pick someone at the grocery store, the mall, or the beach. We're not very interested in celebrity culture, but we've sometimes made a game of listing the movie stars with whom we'd have sex if the opportunity presented itself. Making a game of it can help take the pressure off and reduce both the discomfort and the potential for jealousy to arise.

CHOOSING YOUR ADVENTURES

Now that you've given some thought to your statement of purpose and perhaps have been a little more forthright about your desires, you can start thinking about and planning some specific adventures to undertake together. In the early stages, it's especially important to be deliberate. Your statement of purpose or whatever conversations you've had about your objectives will provide you with a foundation for making good mutual choices. While it's optimal to find something that appeals equally to both of you, that may not be possible, at least not initially. If one of you is more interested in something and the other is content to go along for the ride, that's fine. Just be clear about that from the start. Sometimes the one who is going along for the ride may be surprised to discover that it is a lot more enjoyable than anticipated.

We've described how conventional lovemaking often operates, with one partner giving something with the hope of getting something in return, and we've explained why we think this way of interacting is not optimal. The same is true in the context of adventuring. When you're just starting out, you may find it easier to take turns—this will keep things clear and relatively balanced. But over the longer term, we encourage you to develop a more flexible approach and refrain from thinking, let alone saying, "You got what you wanted last time, so now it's my turn." If you can manage it, the best approach is to use emotional intelligence rather than economic calculations. Don't treat your exploration as a form of commerce. It is even more important to avoid falling into a dynamic in which one person is always asking permission and the other is always granting it or at best going along. Taking turns is preferable to one person's repeatedly "taking one for the team."

HOW TO TALK ABOUT TRYING SOMETHING NEW

Talking about your purpose and openly discussing your sexual desires takes courage, especially since many people don't do very well when it comes to talking about sex. In a recent online survey, *Wall Street Journal* readers were asked, "How well do you communicate with your partner about sex?" At the time of writing, 1,815 people had responded. Of those, 31.9 percent said "never, but we need to," 29.3 percent said "not badly, could improve," 19.1 percent said "easy to discuss when necessary," and only 19.7 percent said "We're great at talking about sex."[68] This is not a scientific sample, so it's not unreasonable to suspect that the number of people who claim they're great at talking about sex is inflated, and the percentage of people who have difficulty is substantially higher than what is reflected in the survey. Express your appreciation for your partner's courage in exploring sexuality more openly. This will make it much easier to have mutually reinforcing conversations about sex.

Next, reiterate the things you enjoy most about your sexual life together. Convey your interest in a particular adventure in terms that refer back to what's strongest and most satisfying in your relationship. Rather than saying, "I want to go to a nude beach," try, "I've been intrigued by the idea of being naked in front of other people, and I think your body is gorgeous. It would be kind of hot for other people to see it. I'd like to visit a nudist resort—would that interest you?"

---

68 "How Well Do You Communicate with Your Partner About Sex?," *Wall Street Journal*, May 31, 2012, http://online.wsj.com/community/groups/general-forum/topics/how-well-do-you-communicate.

If you're the one who is listening to the suggestion, it is important not to express a knee-jerk "no" if something seems unappealing, not very interesting, a little scary, or even shocking. Instead of rejecting the proposal outright, it can be very valuable to have a conversation about why this idea appeals to your partner and whatever thoughts and fantasies may underlie it. If it is something you can't accommodate, you may be able to arrive at an alternative that partakes of some of the same ideas and interests but that isn't beyond your comfort zone. Thus, if you're not quite ready to go to that nudist resort for the weekend, it is better to say, "I'm not sure I would like that, but how about we go to a local clothing-optional beach for an afternoon? I may not be ready to take my clothes off, but I can be there with you."

Even if you are feeling uncomfortable and a little threatened, try not to take your partner's erotic interests as a negative reflection on you or your sex life. We all have a tendency to think that if a partner has a certain attraction, it means that something is missing from the relationship or that it is a sign of some shortcoming or dissatisfaction. Many predispositions are formed at an early age and have nothing to do with the dynamics of your relationship. While it is very easy to take these expressions of sexual interest personally, it is wise to resist the impulse to do so and to remember that your partner is sharing these interests openly, not trying to keep them from you. That should make it clear that the interest does not present a threat.

On the other hand, if one of you feels you have a desire that's being denied or feels pressured into doing something, it is a sign that as a couple you are off track and have lost your sense of collaboration. For some, erotic desires can be very primal, especially if they have been denied or kept secret for many years. Sometimes when these urges are brought into the open and discussed at last, it can seem like a life-or-death situation. When listening to your beloved's first expression of a deep desire, it is important to be as supportive as possible. We've encountered this often in people who are in the early stages of sexual adventuring. One partner expresses a long and deeply held fantasy, and the other may be amenable to exploring it, but because the fantasy has gone so long without being mentioned, let alone fulfilled, a sense of desperation can take over.

To minimize this problem, recognize that the feeling of urgency is not coming from an emergency. It is just the by-product of bringing something long suppressed to the surface. In many cases, that desire can be fulfilled, perhaps not right away, but eventually, if you are patient and open. Applying more pressure will actually make it much less likely that the desired outcome ever happens.

Just as the person who is giving voice to some new fantasy or unexpressed desire is taking a big risk emotionally and may have to contend with unexpected repercussions, it takes courage to be the one who is listening. It requires a good deal of flexibility, and the capacity to accommodate, adjust, and embrace new insights into your partner's inner world. There can be a real vulnerability on both sides.

If your discussions seem to be going off track, step back and try to connect nonverbally; eye-gazing is probably the quickest and most effective technique. You should do your best to take a time-out at the earliest hint of a disruption, before you get too far out of sync. This will make it much easier for you to keep your shared sense of purpose in mind and get back to being a team.

You can also use an approach drawn from Occupy Wall Street and other groups that emphasize consensus-based decision making. In this approach, the listener's first step is to ask questions for the purpose of developing a clear understanding. When employing this method, do your best to resist the tendency to form and express reflexive opinions. Continue posing your questions until you feel you fully understand the suggested activity. If you react too quickly, the reaction may well be based on your own unfounded assumptions or anxieties, and that can end the conversation.

Focus on what is being said, and remain calm. If you find yourself getting excited or irritated, ask your partner to slow down or take a short break before continuing. Stay with the discussion, and avoid walking away. This can be difficult if your emotions are being triggered. Of course, this is generally good advice for any challenging conversation, and it's all the more important when talking about sexual matters.

Finally, take some time to let the idea settle in. At this stage, you are just discussing a desire or a fantasy, and there's no need to start planning the activity. For now, your task is to understand as fully as you can. Take a few days before returning to the subject and trying to make a plan. This approach should be helpful whether you're talking about watching porn together or doing something a bit more adventurous, such as having sex outdoors or trying out a new sex toy, and whether you're a newbie or a seasoned player.

TIP: Steps for Building Erotic Consensus

Ask questions until you fully understand what's being proposed.
Don't make assumptions or snap judgments.
Remain calm.
Allow the idea to settle in.
Take as much time as is necessary before deciding on a course of action.

EROTIC IMAGINATION

Now that we have gone over how to talk about erotic adventuring, we can start to explore some more specific ways to keep your adventures and your sex life creative. Couples may feel that they are reasonably adventurous without recognizing the subtle ways in which they limit themselves. Being creative and coming up with new ideas can keep you from getting into a sexual rut, something that can happen all too easily in long-term relationships.

People generally buy how-to books and instructional films to develop skills, and sometimes for titillation. Developing skills is a valuable and important part of the process. At the same time, becoming a masterful lover involves far more than just knowing which strokes to use and where and how to touch. It requires being tuned in to your partner, as well as creativity and imagination. There's no road map. Being creative and imaginative ultimately involves being able to use whatever is at hand to enhance the erotic dimension of your lives. There are numerous ways to stimulate your sexual creativity.

Fantasy

Fantasies can involve scenarios, elaborate stories, specific activities, and, of course, particular people. There is considerable variation in the way people fantasize. Some rely on actual experiences, perhaps with some embellishment; others prefer imaginary scenes. Whatever the nature of your inner erotic life, fantasizing is an act of imagination, and it will keep you sexually engaged and vital. We've been surprised to learn that some people just don't fantasize and don't know that they can make an active choice to do so as means to increase libido.

For some, the erotic element in fantasy is all about the narrative. If the story is a good one, with the right elements, it will be a turn-on. (This may or may not involve actual role play.) Using this type of narrative, story-based fantasy, even something as simple and clichéd as seducing the pizza delivery person, can function as a tool for staying focused on the erotic and curtailing intrusive thoughts and outside distractions. It may seem strange and perhaps counterintuitive, but using a narrative as an erotic enhancer is similar to meditation. Some Tantric practices, eye-gazing for example, give the mind a task, thereby blocking out intrusive thoughts and allowing the person to become immersed in the experience, without being either distracted or overwhelmed. Ironically, some Tantra teachers frown on fantasy, claiming that it keeps people from being present. This is true if fantasy is being used to escape or to avoid a real connection with your partner, but if used skillfully, fantasy can actually make it easier to be present during sex. If you find it helpful to have a story (and perhaps to act one out), just make sure you're being the best pizza boy or French maid ever.

Similarly, fantasy can be very useful for taking you beyond self-consciousness. If you are enacting a story and playing a role, you may find that you're freed not only from intrusive thoughts but also from other concerns and inhibitions. Just as some performers are charismatic and flamboyant on stage but shy and introverted in their offstage lives, some people may be sexually reserved and inhibited until they are set free by having a role to play.

STAGE NIGHT

Don and Eve have been married for nineteen years. They enjoy enacting very elaborate scenarios. They do so on a regular basis and have made this a major feature of their erotic life together. Even if you don't go to the same lengths as Don and Eve, bringing just a little more imagination to your erotic encounters can heat things up. Here is Eve's account:

My husband and I plan and schedule our play nights, which we call "Stage Nights."

We have a foyer at the entrance to our home, and two steps below the foyer is a sunken living room. We didn't realize it at the time we were designing our home, but the foyer made a perfect a stage! I love to sing and love to wear sexy clothes for my husband, and so it began. My husband, a cabinetmaker by trade and all-around handy guy, came up with a backdrop for the stage, strobe lighting and black light, and a power board to control it all. It takes him about an hour to set up for stage night. I pick out a bunch of outfits, some club attire, some lingerie, all my great sexy shoes, and they become the outfits I perform in. He sits in his recliner and controls all the lighting on his board.

Don is extremely complimentary about how I look, and what woman doesn't want to hear how hot she looks all night long! Some nights, we have "strip night"; I sing and lose a few articles of clothing along the way until I am naked on stage when the song is over. Of course, there's lots of touching, kissing, feeling, licking, etc. throughout the evening. The champagne flows all night. There is something about the little bubbles that make us especially horny. I have several wigs, and will sometimes come out of the bedroom as "another" woman. We role-play and pretend I am a friend he hasn't met or perhaps a complete stranger. At some point we make our way to the bedroom. I usually have lots of candles lit, Don and I pick out the toys of choice for the evening and we begin amazing sexual play.

These evenings allow us to really connect sexually and emotionally. We wake up the next day with what we call "residuals." This amazing feeling of closeness, crazy in love, don't wanna let you out of my arms kinda feelings. Sometimes we feel like we really NEED a play night, not just want, but really need one, because of the connection we make. It rejuvenates us!

Engaging in this kind of narrative fantasy and role play is also very valuable because it can remind us that sex is powerful and profound and also profoundly silly. Playing the French maid may feel forced and goofy, especially at first, but that is perfectly fine. Enacting your fantasies, which is what Don and Eve are doing on "Stage Night," is different from acting out a fantasy—actually stripping in a club or having a sexual encounter with a stranger. You don't have to go to deep, dark places and explore forbidden, repressed desires. There's ample room for childlike enjoyment. Fantasy can be a goof, and goofiness can be a turn-on.

Since many people feel some measure of embarrassment about their fantasies, we have suggested making a game of it and coming up with scenarios or playing roles that are by now cultural clichés. This takes some of the pressure off and creates a kind of neutral ground where you can both participate without taking huge emotional risks. Nevertheless, even this approach may be challenging for some, either because it feels too silly or because it still feels a little too personal in some way.

If this is the case and you don't feel ready to invent your own fantasies, you can try reading an excerpt of erotica aloud and talking about what you found interesting and exciting. You can then explore playing out the scene described in the excerpt, if it turns you both on. This creates an added buffer, since neither one of you is responsible for the story, and although you do have to acknowledge finding it erotic, it's the product of someone else's imagination, not yours. This makes it less personal, and you may feel less vulnerable in using it as erotic fuel. There are many excellent anthologies of contemporary erotica available, and Cleis Press is one of the leading publishers in this genre. We're sure you'll find something that works for you in these books, and the act of reading to each other is itself a way of building intimacy.

Visual Erotica and Porn

"Pornography is a vibrator for the mind."

—SEX HACKER, EROTIC ARTIST, PORN PRODUCER,
AND WRITER MAGGIE MAYHEM

Pornography is at least as popular in our society as it is despised. It has been the subject of an intensifying moral panic ever since the 1970s, when the adult entertainment industry started to become a big business and a part of the mainstream. Some find it intrinsically offensive. Some are troubled by the industry and its often exploitive nature. Some say pornography is addictive and that viewing it even once produces "eroto-toxins" that forever alter a person's sexual proclivities.[69] Some argue that it does a poor job of educating people about sex. Others express concern that we're in the midst of a huge social experiment, that the quantity, variety, and availability of all kinds of erotic material, including some that is extreme, may have a significant impact on human sexuality.

There is certainly room for criticism of the commercial porn industry. Much of what is available is of poor quality, and most of the sex portrayed in porn is not the kind of sex you should be having in real life, starting with the absence of condoms and lube. It also seems possible that the abundance of porn, some of it truly extreme, and the ease with which adolescents have access to it could have some undesirable

---

69 Mark Pilkington, "Sex on The Brain," *Guardian*, July 13, 2005, http://www.guardian.co.uk/science/2005/jul/14/farout.

impacts. Nonetheless, many of these criticisms are simplistic, and some of them are absolute nonsense. Erototoxins indeed!

Like reading erotic literature aloud, watching porn can function both as a general erotic enhancer and as a tool for creating fantasies together. The popular notion that men are more responsive to visual imagery is both a gross overgeneralization and scientifically questionable. We both enjoy visual erotica, and if anything, the reverse is the case for us. Some research suggests that women get equally aroused by porn, and in fact get aroused by more varied forms of visual erotica, but are less willing to acknowledge it.[70] The truth is that if you are sighted, some form of visual erotic material will turn you on, regardless of your gender. This is part of being human, and pornographic images of some sort have been part of society since the dawn of our species. It's probably safe to assume that drawings of sexual activity were among the very first attempts at artistic expression.

As we've indicated, viewing porn together can function in more than one way. At a basic level, you can treat it as a kind of aphrodisiac, a way of getting turned on before or during a sexual encounter. This is perfectly fine, but porn can have more than just entertainment and titillation value. You can actually use it as a resource for discovering types of sexual

---

70 William Griffit, "Response to Erotica and the Projection of Response to Erotica in the Opposite Sex," *Journal of Experimental Research in Personality* 6, no. 4 (April 1973), 330–338, abstract available at http://psycnet.apa.org/psycinfo/1974-02447-001; Heather A. Rupp and Kim Wallen, "Sex Differences in Response to Visual Sexual Stimuli: A Review," *Archives of Sexual Behavior* 37, no. 2 (April 2008), 206–218, full text available at http://www.ncbi.nlm.nih.gov/pmc/articles/PMC2739403/.

activity that are exciting to you and then as the basis for scenarios that you can discuss or even act out.

Watching educational porn together can be very useful for learning techniques and for introducing new activities into your repertoire. For some people, the instructional content makes the explicitness a little easier to approach. There are those among us who learn best by observation. Sometimes there is no substitute for visual material. Some instructional films are a little too clinical, and it can be a challenge to balance erotic appeal with the need to convey information. Nevertheless, there are some great instructional DVDs and streaming videos available.

While some couples may find it easier to view porn together than to talk about their fantasies, others may find it more difficult. For those who have spent many years watching porn as a clandestine, solitary activity, suddenly doing it an open way, in the company of a loved one, can be jarring and uncomfortable at first.

Things have changed a great deal in recent years, and the erotica available today is considerably more diverse than it was a decade or two ago. Increasing numbers of women are making erotic films, often with an avowedly feminist slant. These filmmakers are working both inside and outside the conventional adult industry. They make a point of treating their performers with respect and casting people who are enthusiastic about their work. Contrary to the stereotype, many performers in adult films both freely choose their careers and enjoy what they do.

It is important to remember that the performers are actors

and that they are appearing in movies that are created to be sexually stimulating. Dr. Marty Klein describes the need for what he calls "pornography literacy." Regular people don't compare themselves with professional athletes when they're playing a friendly game of volleyball. Pornography is a production; you don't see the three hours a day the performers spend in the gym, the plastic surgeries, the behind-the-scenes preparation that happens for that perfect shot. People who are porn stars generally have unusual bodies and/or skills, and you should enjoy their performances and not compare yourself or your partner to them, any more than you would compare yourself to a professional athlete.[71]

To return to Maggie Mayhem's definition of porn, we think it is a very apt one. In the past, we've written about how using a vibrator can get you turned on before your mind has a chance to intervene. This makes it very useful if someone is feeling stressed or unfocused, since it goes directly to the body and produces a physical response, whether or not the mind is engaged. Visual erotica can have the same impact, since it is processed through the visual cortex, bypassing logical thought. The route to the body is not as direct as it is when you use a vibrator, but imagery can block out the mental chatter.

What people believe about themselves and the truths of their bodies are often two entirely different things. This can manifest itself in the way you respond to porn. You may start

---

71   Marty Klein, "How to Talk with Your Kids About Pornography: Example 3, the Search History," *New York Times*, May 12, 2012, http://www.nytimes.com/interactive/2012/05/10/garden/porn-searchhistory.html.

out thinking, *I don't want to watch that. That's gross,* and then discover that you haven't hit the pause button, or that during self-pleasuring you are mentally replaying the act you thought was so gross on screen. If this happens, you'll have to revise your self-definition and recognize that, at minimum, *I am not the kind of person who would do* that, *but watching it was really hot.*

MORE ABOUT FANTASY: PARTNERED AND SOLO

Fantasizing is an act of imagination and creativity, even if it continues to get a very bad name in certain quarters. ("Sex addiction" counselors consider it an obstacle to "recovery.") Most people think of imagination and creativity as highly individual. Despite the numerous examples of great artistic collaborations, the myth of the lone "artist as hero" is a powerful one. It is true, of course, that much great art has been produced by people toiling in solitude, but many great works are the result of a collaborative effort, whether the input was largely editorial or two or more people embarked on the project and worked together from start to finish. Similarly, when people talk about sexual fantasy, they think of it as essentially private, and fantasizing is usually deemed to be a solo rather than a partnered activity.

We'd like to add what may be a new dimension to your understanding of fantasy. Think of it as something you can do alone as well as together, and consider partnered fantasizing as another tool for expanding your erotic palette. If you start by talking about your personal fantasies, and perhaps enacting them, you are moving them out of the private realm and establishing the conditions for developing a creative sexual collaboration. Creating a fantasy together can feel more inclusive than one of you laying out a whole scenario. Of course, one of you will have to get things going, but that could be as simple as saying something like "I've always wondered what it would be like to have sex with a stranger." With this as a foundation, like Don and Eve, you can develop a whole scenario whereby you play out that fantasy in a way that works for both of you. In this context, we don't mean actually having sex with a stranger; we mean role-playing. Where you go from this basic idea is entirely up to you. It might involve just a blindfold and your mutual willingness to pretend that the blindfolded party doesn't know the person who is making love to him, or it could be considerably more elaborate.

There is a slight but important distinction to make here. Partnered fantasies are co-created, and this happens during conversations about sex and specifically about what turns you on. We're not talking about a fantasy in which you have cast your partner in a role to suit your own desires. That's still a solo fantasy. Partnered fantasies evolve in two primary ways: when you both share an interest that you discover while talking about your personal fantasies, or, if your inner sexual lives are different, by finding a common element to focus on so that you can play it out together. The first way is perhaps easier. Let's return to the sex-with-a-stranger scenario to illustrate how the second way can work: maybe one of you doesn't find the idea of sex with a stranger particularly appealing but finds exhibitionism exciting. In these circumstances, you may be able to include aspects of both fantasies in your scenario by dressing in provocative, revealing attire, and perhaps displaying affection a little more publicly than you otherwise would, and bringing in the blindfold once you're alone.

ACTING OUT FANTASIES

Make a mutual decision about how far to go when acting out your fantasies. Are you going to restrict yourselves to role play? Will you include other props or toys? Will you interact with other people? Will you do things that are somewhat bold? How much and what skin will you expose, and where? There are some whose fantasies are primarily about things that they would actually like to do, or have done in the past. Conversely, there are those who fantasize about things they would never want to do or experience in real life; rape fantasies are probably the most obvious and common example. Many people engage in both types of fantasizing. Some are really creative; skilled fantasy players may construct and enact elaborate scenarios that can have the complexity of a theatrical production.

Cara and Raphael both found the idea of sex with a stranger highly erotic, but they belonged to a very conservative religion. Their beliefs and the rules of their relationship meant that actually having sex with a stranger was unacceptable. Instead, they came up with a creative solution, one that allowed them to play out the fantasy without crossing the line into behavior that conflicted with their values but that was significantly bolder than Don and Eve's private role play.

Cara would dress in a way that was out of character for her, sometimes wearing a wig, and then go to a public place that was outside their community, where they would not encounter anyone they knew. Raphael would arrive at the appointed place, proceed to act out a pickup scene, and then take her to a seedy motel to have sex. They never needed to take the fantasy any further.

So, keep in mind that some fantasies work precisely because they exist in a realm outside of reality. Just because you fantasize about something doesn't mean you need to actually experience it. At the same time, if you want to live out a fantasy, there are many ways to achieve that end, including role play, incorporating elements of the fantasy into your interactions, and even engaging in the fantasized behavior. Having an appreciation for the range of available possibilities will make it much easier for you make a mutual decision about just how much reality you want to bring to your fantasy life.

TIP: Flirt with Each Other Outrageously Online

Set up anonymous email accounts or an account with a service like FetLife or Twitter. Send erotic messages to each other using your assumed names. You can use Twitter in a somewhat more public way, since the messages will be available to others; this can be a lot of fun if you're not overly concerned about online privacy.

SEX TOYS

Using sex toys can be a great way to start expanding your sexual horizons. In addition to the fact that they are designed to give you pleasure, they can also be used to enhance your fantasies. In recent years, the use of and access to toys has gone mainstream. You can find them easily on the Internet or even buy them at your local drugstore, so your options are virtually limitless. Humans have probably been using sex toys for almost as long as they have been using tools.[72] While there's no need to delve too deeply into the history of sex toys, it does merit noting that they went through a major evolution during the Victorian era, due in large part to the medical profession and what was, at the time, a standard treatment for "hysteria" and other purportedly "female" emotional problems. It may seem utterly bizarre today, but it was standard practice for doctors to bring their female patients to orgasm to relieve these ailments. The vibrator was invented to enable doctors to treat more patients in less time; in a matter of a few years, home units became available to the general public.[73]

In the following century, vibrators were sold by mail, often with euphemistic advertising copy promoting their health benefits. (Similarly, rectal dilators were sold for ostensibly medical purposes.) It wasn't until the early 1970s, when Betty

---

72 In 2005, a 28,000-year-old stone phallus that may have been used as a sex toy was found in a German cave. Jonathan Amos, "Ancient Phallus Unearthed in Cave," BBC News, July 25, 2005, http://news.bbc.co.uk/2/hi/science/nature/4713323.stm.

73 This history is explored in depth in Rachel P. Maines, *The Technology of Orgasm: "Hysteria," the Vibrator and Women's Sexual Satisfaction* (Baltimore: Johns Hopkins University Press, 2001). The play *In the Next Room* and the film *Hysteria* approach it from a less academic perspective.

Dodson started teaching women to masturbate with the Hitachi Magic Wand, that people started speaking openly about vibrators as sex toys. In addition, before the 1960s, any advertising that explained the vibrator's real use would probably have been considered obscene. Notwithstanding this increased openness, a mere three decades ago, toys that were explicitly for sexual use were almost universally very poorly made, often of potentially hazardous plastics, and were only available in sleazy adult bookstores or for order from dodgy-looking ads in the back pages of men's and pornographic magazines.

We've come a long way, thanks to people like Dodson and Dell Williams, founder of Eve's Garden. Today, there are many woman-owned, clean, bright, and friendly shops where people can purchase sex toys. If you have not visited one of these stores, they can be found in many North American cities, and shopping at one together can be a great sexual adventure. Go, talk to the staff, and learn how the various items work. Salespeople in these shops are knowledgeable about the products and very helpful. If there are no such shops in your area, or you live in one of the remaining states that restricts the sale of toys, there are plenty of online options.

So, what is a sex toy? Virtually anything that facilitates your pleasure and arousal. Some sex toys are popular simply because they can do what the human body cannot—even the most skilled and inventive lover can't replicate the sensations produced by the Hitachi Magic Wand, and no part of the human body is shaped like a string of Ben Wa balls. Of course, the human body is also capable of doing things that sex toys cannot, and this is good to remember, especially if you are feeling a little threatened by your partner's use and enjoyment of toys. As with pornography, think of them as enhancers not competitors.

TIP: Vibrators—Not Just for the Genitals

To increase your partner's enjoyment during oral sex, place a vibrator on your cheek while pleasuring him.

Try placing one in the center of the chest or using it to tease the nipples.

Use a vibrator to stroke up your partner's thighs during hand sex.

Hold the vibrator on your partner's perineum during oral or hand sex.

Apply between the shoulders while making love doggy style.

Spread the energy post-orgasm by running the vibrator up the abdomen.

Hold one to the back of your hand when giving a hand job.

Some people believe that sex should be "natural" and that artificial enhancements of any kind are somehow inferior to the "real thing." We've heard these attitudes expressed with regard to both the use of sex toys and the use of performance-enhancing drugs like Viagra. We have a more pragmatic view. Sexual pleasure is natural, so why not use whatever is available to enhance it? Toys can angle toward just the right spot, be more ergonomically suited to the contours of the anal canal than a finger or a penis, and provide hardness, different temperatures, a sense of heaviness and fullness. They can move back and forth, rotate, or vibrate at amazing speeds and never tire. As already mentioned, they can be used in fantasy as well. If you aren't interested in doing a double penetration with two real people but have a fantasy about it, one real penis and one dildo can approximate the fantasy without the complications or contortions that bringing a third person into bed would entail.

Now that sex toys have come out of the closet, we have entered an era in which art meets eroticism. Today you can find toys that are beautifully made of wood, carved crystal, hand-blown Pyrex, stainless steel, or a number of other materials. Some toys almost look like heirlooms, and in fact, we have a couple on display in our home. The design and craftsmanship are such that the uninitiated might not even recognize their purpose. This is quite a departure from the vibrator of the 1970s—the one that would break after the first use. Although the general quality has improved in recent years, you still need to be mindful about the materials, and remember that you get what you pay for. As sex educator Dr. Ruth Neustifter likes to say, "If it smells like a new shower curtain, the toy is toxic."

TIP: Pervertibles: DIY Sex Toys

Remember, anything can be a sex toy. All you have to do is apply a little creativity and erotic imagination when looking at the most mundane objects. This can be a lot of fun: a hand or wall mirror can help you see what you otherwise cannot; a shower massage makes a great vibrator; and while it's sometimes the subject of jokes, so can the spin cycle on the washing machine. You can use anything from ice cubes to toothpicks for sensation play. Kinky people call these repurposed household items "pervertibles." Here are some suggestions to get your creative juices flowing:

bamboo skewers
plastic wrap
ice cubes
snakebite kits (to provide suction)
mentholated rubs
feather duster
paint stirrers
clothespins
Ping-Pong paddle
small cutting board
spray bottle
Nerf bat
oars
sawhorse
toothpicks
scarves
belts
wet towel

FROM BEHIND CLOSED DOORS TO OUT IN THE OPEN

Perhaps the most advanced form of monogamous sexual adventuring involves bringing your erotic life out of the privacy of your home. This can be a very big step, especially at first, but once you get over the initial unease, it is likely to start feeling completely natural. The first stage of this kind of exploration often incorporates social nudism, a practice that remains taboo in the United States, even though it is common-place and widely accepted in much of Europe.

There are nudist resorts and nude beaches all over the country, and while a few of these places are very popular with people in alternative sexual lifestyles and may cater to them, the general emphasis is on social nudity; in many cases the resorts are family friendly. Open sexual activity is almost universally frowned upon in nudist resorts and on nude beaches (where it's also illegal). Contrary to what you might think if you've never experienced it, there is something about being with a group of naked people that lowers social barriers, makes conversation easier, and creates a feeling of camaraderie. Anecdotally, at least, the biggest hurdle for most people is that first moment of being naked around a group of strangers, but the discomfort tends to fade rapidly. While the environment at most nudist resorts is friendly rather than erotically charged, these are great places for shedding your clothes and some of your inhibitions and perhaps for opening new avenues of conversation.

If you're comfortable with social nudity, take a slightly more adventurous step: a couples sensual massage class or a

Tantra workshop. These workshops can range from mildly erotic, with most or all of the explicit, hands-on work done in private, to more advanced intensives in which you may be in a room full of people giving each other erotic massages. Choose carefully, based on your comfort level. Err on the side of milder when you're starting out, since pushing too far could produce emotional backlash and regret. Harbin Hot Springs in Northern California offers some great massage workshops for couples, in a sensual but not overly sexual, spiritually oriented environment. See the Resource Guide for additional suggestions.

We have very limited access to sexual education in our culture, and the overwhelming majority of people never have the opportunity to be in the presence of others who are having a sexual interaction. Nor do most people ever get to see explicit demonstrations of sexual techniques. To expose yourself to these things is to break some very powerful taboos. If you're on a joint quest to discover more, you are likely to find that these experiences generate a deeper erotic connection.

9

ADVANCED SEXUAL ADVENTURING: OPEN RELATING TO STRENGTHEN YOUR PARTNERSHIP

If unconscious monogamy can be stifling, consciously opening your relationship can enrich it. The words *monogamy* and *nonmonogamy* imply a binary opposition, but the reality is more complex. This is our personal perspective, but we hope it provides you with a useful conceptual framework.

Our definition of nonmonogamy is not limited to having sex with people outside your relationship. To us, nonmonogamy means acknowledging the erotic dimension that may exist in any human interaction. Anyone in a relationship who is exploring alternative forms of sexual expression or is comfortable sharing erotic space with other people is not fully monogamous and is in what might be called a "designer relationship." We got this term from Kenneth R. Haslam, MD, founder of the Kinsey Institute's Polyamory Archive Collection. We like the term because it avoids the binary opposition between monogamy and nonmonogamy, suggests that you can customize your partnership in a way that suits you, and points to the fact that every relationship is unique.

Strictly speaking, much of the behavior we described in the preceding chapter is not really monogamous by our definition. If you are exploring together, you have moved into the realm of nonmonogamy, even if only slightly; however, when we discuss nonmonogamy and various forms of nonmonogamous relating in this chapter, we are referring specifically to engaging in physical interactions with others. For many, making this choice can be a way to deepen intimacy.

Though we had already been exposed to many of the ideas about open relating that are current in the polyamorous community and elsewhere, we started thinking about this more deeply when some of our students wanted advice on how to open up their relationships. This was not something we offered as part of our teaching, but the issue kept arising, both in our private work and in some of our public talks. In one instance, we gave a lecture on Tantric philosophy and practice at a college. During the Q&A, questions about open relationships started coming our way, even though this was not a focus of our talk.

The discussion soon revealed that most of the students reflexively accepted the dominant relationship paradigm, as much as they seemed to be looking for an alternative. One of them asked, "Then it's okay for you to step out on your partner?" We did our best to explain that the "faithful/stepping out" dichotomy is a false one and that we were trying to articulate a more nuanced way of thinking in which no dichotomy exists. This idea—that you are either sexually exclusive or you are cheating—is prevalent. The concept that one can have multiple lovers while remaining faithful is baffling to many. Even when journalists try to present alternative relationship styles in relatively favorable terms, they frequently lapse into language that casts open and consensual nonmonogamy as a form of "cheating."

This confusion is perhaps not surprising. The public sees infidelity as a serious problem and a social evil. In recent years, polls have repeatedly shown that Americans view married men or women having affairs as immoral. Indeed, this view is a national consensus, with only 7 percent saying it is morally acceptable in the most recent Gallup poll on the subject.[74] In the same poll, 10 percent deemed human cloning to be morally acceptable, and 11 percent did not object to polygamy. While the definition of infidelity seems to be expanding to include viewing visually erotic material, 31 percent considered pornography morally acceptable. (The poll was silent as to how many people acknowledged either having had affairs or having watched pornography. There's undoubtedly a gap between expressed moral views and actual behavior.) This excessive, almost dogmatic, attitude toward infidelity is largely an American phenomenon.

We don't advocate having affairs, and betraying your

---

74 Frank Newport, "Americans, Including Catholics, Say Birth Control Is Morally OK: Birth Control has the Broadest Acceptance Among 18 Behaviors," *Gallup Politics,* May 22, 2012, http://www.gallup.com/poll/154799/Americans-Including-Catholics-Say-Birth-Control-Morally.aspx.

partner in this way is potentially damaging. Deception, dishonesty, or betrayal will harm a relationship, but the source of the problem may not be the sexual activity so much as the breach of trust. The way in which our society has constructed monogamy encourages clandestine and dishonest behavior; according to this model, desires have to be suppressed and denied, and if you are in a "committed" relationship, acting on those desires is at best dangerous and at worst pathological. This notion is common in the therapeutic community, and we've heard of therapists who've warned clients who express interest in opening their relationships that they are "playing with fire." The available research shows that this notion is false and there's little difference in marital stability between couples who have open relationships and those who do not. There's also considerable evidence that people practicing various forms of nonmonogamy have higher levels of relationship satisfaction than do people in monogamous ones.[75]

FORMS OF NONMONOGAMOUS EXPRESSION
Nonconsensual Nonmonogamy

Even though we do our best to be nonjudgmental when it comes to sex, we take a dim view of nonconsensual nonmonogamy, since it usually involves betrayal. The fact that one person has not agreed to it does indeed make this cheating,

---

75 See, for example, Edward M. Fernandes, "The Swinging Paradigm: An Evaluation of the Marital and Sexual Satisfaction of Swingers," *Electronic Journal of Human Sexuality* 12 (January 23, 2009), http://www.ejhs.org/Volume12/Swinging2.htm#t1.

or at the very least a violation of an implied agreement. There are many different ways in which people engage in nonconsensual nonmonogamous behavior. It's not the sex itself that is ethically problematic; it's the dishonesty and secretiveness that are unethical (except in rare instances) and potentially very damaging.

Ordinary people who claim to be monogamous engage in all sorts of behavior that is anything but. For starters, serial monogamy—a very common practice today—is not your great-grandmother's monogamy. Before the sexual revolution of the 1960s, it was assumed that one should be a virgin at the time of marriage and remain sexually exclusive. Needless to say, not everyone complied with these social expectations, but they were the norm. Today, the idea of having a single sexual partner for one's entire life is hardly mainstream, except in some conservative religious circles, so at the very baseline, monogamy as it is currently practiced isn't really monogamy at all. This form of nonmonogamy is not cheating, and consent is not an issue.

Nonconsensual nonmonogamy can take a wide variety of forms, including: clandestinely getting lap dances, employing sex workers, having affairs, and having same-sex liaisons "on the down low," to name a few. An additional variation is doubly nonconsensual—dating others while not disclosing one's marital status. We like to call these "deficient" forms of nonmonogamy because they are done in secret. The whole dynamic changes when the activity is consensual and agreed upon or shared by both partners.

Clandestine behavior is often very risky; there is generally no discussion about safer sex and no conscious, informed decision making regarding what precautions to take. This means that the risks are considerably higher in nonconsensual nonmonogamy than they are when everything is out in the open. In a recent study published in *The Journal of Sexual Medicine*, researchers found that those engaging in nonconsensual nonmonogamy are considerably more likely to have unprotected sex. Cheaters used condoms for oral and anal sex at a rate 27–35 percent lower than did those in open relationships and had a 64 percent higher rate of using drugs and alcohol during their extracurricular encounters.[76]

Semiconsensual Nonmonogamy

Semiconsensual nonmonogamy is somewhat more efficient than its nonconsensual counterpart because there is at least some measure of transparency, though it lacks the collaborative and mutual dimension that we think is optimal. This form of semiopen relating has much in common with some open relationship models, but the accompanying attitude is one of toleration not engagement. Under this model, a partner might say, "You can go get a lap dance when you are out of town, or have a fling with someone you meet on a business trip, and I'll tolerate it. Just don't tell me about it." The tolerance is often accompanied by a justification such as "That's just how men

76 Terri D. Conley, Amy C. Moors, Ali Ziegler, and Constantina Karathanasis, "Unfaithful Individuals Are Less Likely to Practice Safer Sex Than Openly Nonmonogamous Individuals," *Journal of Sexual Medicine* 9, no. 6 (June 2012), 1559–1565, abstract available at http://onlinelibrary.wiley.com/doi/10.1111/j.1743-6109.2012.02712.x/abstract;jsessionid=DA4B499B031 5176CAB55E38A11278B7B.d03t02.

are." Semiconsensual nonmonogamy is not an uncommon solution for couples dealing with illness or a major imbalance in sex drive, and it can work for some people.

Although it may work for some, merely tolerating a behavior is not embracing and supporting your partner's growth or using sexuality as a tool for evolving together. This is a very old-fashioned model, evoking certain European societies in which men of a certain class were expected to have mistresses, and the wife had no choice but to tolerate the infidelity. Some self-defined "open relationships" in which the policy is "don't ask, don't tell" also fall into this category. Of course, if this approach works for you, and you just prefer not to know about your partner's liaisons, that's fine, provided you are making informed safer sex decisions and have arrived at this style of relating in a way that is truly mutual.

Open Relationships

Now that we've given you an overview of what we consider to be less than optimal ways of being nonmonogamous, let's look at some more positive approaches. If you're interested in nonmonogamous sexual adventuring, you'll probably encounter a variety of terms for different ways of having open relationships, so we thought it would be valuable to provide a brief overview of some of the different styles and then share the model that is most in keeping with our philosophy. Bear in mind that there's often a great deal of overlap among the different forms of nonmonogamy, notwithstanding the terminology that people use to define themselves.

Many people use *open relationship* as a kind of shorthand,

so the intended meaning can vary a great deal. The origins of the term go back at least to 1972 and the publication of the bestselling *Open Marriage*, by Nena and George O'Neill. While the book did not focus on nonmonogamy, the topic was addressed, and in one chapter sexual nonexclusivity was presented as an option:

> We are not recommending outside sex, but we are not saying it should be avoided either. The choice is entirely up to you, and can be made only upon your own knowledge of the degree to which you have achieved, within your own marriage, the trust, identity, and open communication necessary to the eradication of jealousy.[77]

To a significant extent, the O'Neills' way of thinking about relationships helped lay the groundwork for the polyamory movement that emerged almost two decades later, but their vision of open marriage had little to do with sexual nonexclusivity. The brief section devoted to that topic probably accounts for the book's enduring fame, though Nena O'Neill later changed her stance. The O'Neills' book helped popularize alternative relationship models that had been percolating in various subcultures for nearly a decade. Many more books on the subject appeared in the wake of *Open Marriage*'s success.

The late 1960s and early '70s were an era of major cultural change and experimentation, but attitudes were in some

---

77 Nena O'Neill and George O'Neill, *Open Marriage: A New Lifestyle for Couples* (New York: Avon Books, 1972), 254.

respects considerably more conventional than they are today. Thus, *open marriage* has been replaced by *open relationship,* which is now one of the relationship status options on Facebook. ("It's complicated" is another.) In this sense, the O'Neills' legacy has endured, even if many of their ideas have fallen out of favor with the mainstream. Nena O'Neill died in 2006, and her obituary in the New York Times opined:

> Read today, "Open Marriage" is a period piece, a window onto a distant age of experimentation and abandon. Its ideas can appear shockingly ordinary, even quaint. In the shadow of AIDS, its bolder suggestions seem not so much daring as painfully naïve.[78]

At this writing, seven years after the publication of the obituary, and with a new explosion of interest in and books about nonmonogamous relating—Tristan Taormino's *Opening Up,* Jenny Block's *Open,* and Christopher Ryan and Cacilda Jethá's *Sex at Dawn,* among others—it seems the *New York Times* deserves the label naïve far more richly than do the O'Neills. While these books have not achieved *Open Marriage*'s notoriety, they reflect a significant public interest in alternative ways of relating and being sexual, an interest that is probably more thoughtful than it was during the tumultuous and experimental days of the sexual revolution.

The problem with the terms *open marriage* and *open*

---

78 Margalit Fox, "Nena O'Neill, 82, an Author of 'Open Marriage,' is Dead," *New York Times,* March 26, 2006, http://www.nytimes.com/2006/03/26/books/25oneill.html.

relationship is that they are very broad. If you choose "in an open relationship" as your status on Facebook, your closest friends are likely to know what you mean and what your arrangements are, but the other 1,000 may just assume that you sleep with random people. There are a numerous ways to have an open relationship. It can mean you're dating and have agreed it's too soon to be exclusive; it can mean you swing; it can mean you date multiple people; or any number of other things. Thus, it is a very generic statement about being nonmonogamous. It's useful as shorthand but no more than that. How you define it more deeply is up to you. As the O'Neills put it: "Open marriage is called open for that very reason: the options are there for you to take or leave according to your individual decision."[79] The great advantage to the term is that it is not limiting.

Friends with Benefits

This form of nonmonogamy seems to be increasingly common among young people. It usually refers to sexual relating without excessive emotional entanglement, though friendship, of course, can involve deep attachments. As others have observed and we've repeated, friendship is pretty much essential if you want to have an enduring, erotic relationship with a primary partner. "I don't like you, but I love you" may sound good in a song, but it's a terrible basis for a long-term relationship.[80] Thinking about your primary partner as a friend

---

79 O'Neill and O'Neill, *Open Marriage*, 254.
80 Smokey Robinson, "You've Really Got a Hold on Me," *The Fabulous Miracles*, Tamla Records, 1963.

with benefits (FWB) is a healthy attitude, and it can help keep things hot.

For the most part, FWB is applied to singles, so there has not been much examination of what it might mean to a couple. You can have a friend or friends with benefits even if you have a strong primary bond. You may have a friend with whom one or both of you is sexual, but with whom there is no romantic entanglement and no expectation that the relationship will turn into anything else.

It is not uncommon for a first nonmonogamous sexual experience to happen with friends. We've known people who were at a party where things got a little "crazy" and one thing led to another. Sometimes a conversation with friends about your sex life as a couple can lead to a discovery that there's a realm in which you wish to interact. For some, this is the preferred form of erotic adventuring, and if you are part of a community that supports sexual exploration, you have a much better chance of meeting potential FWBs. Deliberately setting out to seduce someone who may not be interested and who might even take offense can be very risky. In some cases, it's probably better to leave the seduction in the realm of fantasy.

This is a somewhat different arrangement from what is typical of either the swinger or polyamorous communities; the former tends to emphasize recreational sex, while the latter tends to focus on deeper attachments. These rough distinctions often have more to do with style and identity than with actual practice. Clearly, people in those communities can and do have FWB-type relationships.

In contrast to the nonconsensual nonmonogamy of an affair, an FWB relationship can nourish you as individuals and as a couple. An affair may provide an opportunity to grow and may even make your sex life with your primary partner hotter for a while, but in most cases, when an affair gets found out, either the affair or the primary relationship will have to end. In an FWB situation, there is transparency and, if you handle it well, no drama. You can feel affection and have an emotional connection with another person without putting the primary partnership at risk, and the friendship can take its natural course. You and your FWB may drift apart, or you may stop being sexual together while remaining close. Being open to this way of relating creates an array of possibilities for developing deep and enduring bonds with others while strengthening your partnership.

Swinging

Like *open marriage, swinging* is a term that has its origins in the 1960s and '70s, and swinging as practiced in the twenty-first century can sometimes partake of the cultural values of that era. Before the term became popular, "wife swapping" was a fairly common description of the practice. This reflects the dyadic, heterosexual model that is still prevalent in the swinging community and some of the now antiquated norms that were a factor when this subculture began to take shape. Wife swapping evokes even more antiquated ideas that date back to the era "when men were men and women were property." While wife swapping is not commonly used today, it still colors popular stereotypes about the scene. (There is a website called swappernet.com.) The term is not only quaint; it is inaccurate in its implication that women are unwilling participants who go along to please their husbands. We have the impression that the overwhelming majority of couples who swing do so based on a mutual interest, sometimes unexpressed for many years. And women in swinger culture usually determine both who participates in and the pace of each erotic encounter. Thus they are frequently more in touch with their own pleasure and sexual power than women in more conventional relationships.[81]

ONE COUPLE'S EROTIC AWAKENING

Don and Eve, in addition to having regular "stage nights," have been swinging on and off for over a decade. Their story is not unusual, and it illustrates how many women who explore swinging feel sexually empowered, even if they experience some initial unease.

Don and I got involved in the lifestyle over 10 years ago. Don brought it up, and I was kind of taken aback at first. I know a lot of women feel the same way: what's wrong, why am I not enough for him, what is he really looking for, what if he falls in love with someone else? etc. One summer, we were heading down to South Carolina for a NASCAR race. There's a chain of strip clubs along I-95, and Don suggested we visit one. I was nervous about it but agreed to go in. We nicknamed one

---

81   For a discussion of this subject, see Curtis R. Bergstrand and Jennifer Blevins Sinski, *Swinging in America: Love Sex and Marriage in the 21st Century* (Santa Barbara: Praeger, 2009), 62–63.

particular dancer "Shorts." (She was wearing the shortest shorts we had ever seen!) Very hot!

On the way home, we found a hotel with a Jacuzzi, and, oh yeah, a strip club right down the street! This was the turning point for me. That was the night I realized that women really turn me on. When we arrived we took a table. Don began asking questions about private dances. He wanted me to have a private dance performed by a woman. Strangely, they would not allow that in a booth; it had to be done at the table. Don paid, and Sunny (our choice) began to dance for me. At first I was fully aware of all the eyes on us, and I felt very uncomfortable. After a while everyone else went away for me, and it was just Sunny, Don, and me. I remember I was wearing white jeans and an orange halter. By the time Sunny was finished dancing for me, I swear my panties were so wet it would have been visible for all to see through my white jeans. We actually left the bar after that dance for that reason. I felt soaked.

We went back to the hotel and had amazing, hot, long-lasting sex.

When we got home, we started looking for swing clubs to go to. We found one nearby and frequented it for several years.

The terminology we're using is very broad. *Swinging* generally applies to couples who engage in sex with other people as a recreational activity. Swinging couples may play separately or together, and the idea of "swapping," as opposed to sharing, still exists among some members of this community. In any event, in swinging, the emphasis tends to be on sex, and in its deficient form this emphasis can be monolithic. We've heard of incidents in which one couple has not even wanted to speak to another after a sexual encounter. For some, sex with others may be fine, but only in the context of an anonymous or near-anonymous situation in which there is no chance that an emotional connection will develop.

SWINGING AND EMOTIONAL ATTACHMENTS

While some in the lifestyle seek to avoid forming emotional attachments with their partners, this is by no means always the case, and even hook-ups can have a strong emotional component. Several people in the lifestyle have described their experiences as being quite emotionally intense, even when they involve what might appear to be casual encounters. Swinging is not monolithic, and even when sex is recreational, people may feel strong emotional connections.

One person we spoke to even goes so far as to tell his partners that he expects to fall in love with each and every one of them, while at the same time making it clear that he will do his best to let go at the appropriate time. While not all of his partners have the same intensity of feeling, it's an important part of the experience for him, even though letting go can be a challenge.

Because many people who "swing" or identify themselves as being "in the lifestyle" are middle to upper-middle class, with families and mainstream careers, they may be closeted about their participation in alternative sexual activities. While we understand the need that many people feel to conceal this aspect of their lives, the clandestine element can sometimes contribute to behaviors and attitudes that are problematic. In its most deficient form, swinging can replicate sex-negative paradigms that are so prevalent in mainstream culture—conventional attitudes about gender roles, homophobia, and a less than fully integrated attitude toward sexuality and sexual adventuring. For example, same-sex interactions between women are almost expected in some segments of the community, but in much of mainstream swinger culture, similar interactions between men have yet to be accepted.

Many people in the lifestyle keep their lives compartmentalized, revealing their sexual interests only to fellow lifestylers. This compartmentalization can help to engender a "party" mentality as opposed to a more conscious approach to being sexual. It's no accident that one of the most popular lifestyle-oriented resorts is called Hedonism. We're not against hedonism at all and have argued that conscious hedonism can be a spiritual practice. We're also not against blowing off steam at times, but an excessive focus on partying means that some of the power and beauty of sex and the potential it carries will almost certainly be overlooked.

All of that said, the swinging world has changed a good deal over the last decade, and based on our experience at lifestyle events, there's considerably more openness to deeper and more varied explorations of sexuality than there was ten years ago. The interest in Tantra has increased significantly; kink of various kinds is more widely accepted; and male homophobia seems to have declined while the number of events that welcome bisexual men has increased. This is purely impressionistic, but attitudes seem to be evolving.

The North American Swing Club Association has listings for on- or off-premise clubs or groups in all but a handful of states.[82] *On-premise* means that sex is allowed on-site, and

---

82 NASCA International, www.nasca.com. The states without listings are Alaska, South Dakota, Utah, Arkansas, Vermont, and Nebraska.

off-premise refers to socials, which may get a little risqué but where genital contact is not allowed. There are also numerous resorts and conventions that cater to this community in the United States, Canada, and elsewhere. While swinging may not be for you, just visiting a swing club can be a very interesting sexual exploration, a much bigger step than going to a nudist resort or taking a couples' massage workshop. This can be a relatively unthreatening first step as you begin moving into more open adventuring, and there is no requirement that you do anything at all—you can just go to observe, flirt, dance, or make out. You can watch others or have sex without having to touch anyone. There is no obligation to have sex just because you visit one of these clubs.

If you go to a swing club, be prepared to stay out late; this is partly a function of the party atmosphere that we've already discussed. Lowering inhibitions can take a long time. That caveat aside, you are likely to find that people in the lifestyle are friendly and respectful. If you tell them you're new, you're unlikely to encounter much pressure, though you may get propositioned. People may be somewhat physical when they flirt, but it is well understood that no means no.

This understanding is central in alternative sexual communities. Most of us have a hard time taking rejection. Spurned sexual or romantic advances are a very unpleasant part of adolescent life, and the memory of these incidents can be painful. Most people in the lifestyle have gotten over this and take rejection in stride. Thus, in contrast to what's common in mainstream society, even in adult dating, a no is not a personal rejection and is not necessarily categorical.

Turning down an offer doesn't mean "I have no interest in talking to you." It just means "I'm not interested in engaging sexually with you." If you're attending a club with the intention of seeing and being seen, you may end up having sex in the same room with that person, and that can be fine. The lifestyle has its own unique set of social norms; this is true of every group that's outside the sexual mainstream. It's always good to learn something about a given community's prevailing etiquette before you attend an event.

Polyamory

Polyamory is a social movement that emerged in the early 1990s; the term, a neologism that combines the Greek for "many" and the Latin for "love," was coined in 1993. The deepest roots of this movement connect it to the utopian experiments of the nineteenth century and what was then referred to as "free love." More recent antecedents date to the 1960s and '70s, when the term *polyfidelity* was coined. They include the work of authors Robert A. Heinlein (*Stranger in a Strange Land*) and Robert Rimmer (*The Harrad Experiment*), the intentional communities and communal living experiments that flourished during that period, as well as the sexual adventuring of the early swingers and the human potential movement values expressed in *Open Marriage* and similar publications.

Polyamorous or "poly" relationships range from dating more than one person at the same time to group marriages and virtually anything in between. Many if not all of these experimental relationship models long predate the coining of the term. Some people simply lived, for example, in a ménage à trois. This term does not mean a onetime threesome, though it is sometimes used that way. Instead, it refers to a triadic domestic and sexual arrangement. The people in these arrangements did not identify themselves as polyamorous, and in many instances they were isolated and had no knowledge that there were others living in similar configurations. By the early 1970s, many more intentionally experimental arrangements were being attempted, from triads to group marriages. A study of these efforts published in 1973 included the "conservative" estimate that more than 1,000 group marriages were in existence at the time.[83] Even then, before polyamory had entered the lexicon, these ancestral polyamorists were laying the groundwork for the movement that would emerge a couple of decades later. Like contemporary poly people, many of those who participated in the research for *Group Marriage* emphasized communication and honesty and were "out" to others in their lives. Even in the midst of the sexual revolution, it took great courage to live as an openly nonmonogamous person. It still takes courage, but the poly movement has made it easier to do so and to find support from like-minded others.

In contrast to identifying your relationship as "open" or having recreational sex with others, calling yourself polyamorous carries with it at least the implication that you're emotionally involved (or willing to be emotionally involved) at a deep level with more than one person. Once you move beyond that very broad and general sense of the word, being polyamorous

---

83 Larry L. Constantine and Joan M. Constantine, *Group Marriage, "Marriages" of Three or More People, How and When They Work* (New York: MacMillan and Company, 1973). The estimate is from the jacket copy.

means different things to different people. For some, being poly involves focusing on the relationship as much as or more than sex; this can mean that love is a prerequisite for sex. At the same time, we know people who identify as poly and whose behavior is externally indistinguishable from that of self-identified swingers.

Some in the poly community seek to differentiate themselves from swingers, and as we've indicated, there are some significant differences between the communities. That said, it seems to us that the biggest differences are cultural and have much to do with the origins of the two groups, their politics, and to some degree their focus—sex for swingers and relationships for poly people. In contrast to swinging, polyamory has a theoretical basis and carries with it an implicit and sometimes explicit critique of conventional monogamy and even the dyadic relationship. We've always been attracted to this intellectual and theoretical aspect of polyamory. At the same time, some people who identify as poly are married couples who participate in casual, recreational sex, and some people who identify as swingers have long-term relationships with other couples or individuals. Thus, despite the many differences, the two communities have much in common.

If you are interested in exploring polyamory, we strongly encourage you to read some of the literature on the subject. It's sure to be thought provoking. We do have a big caveat: polyamory may involve bigger emotional risks than some other forms of open relating. If you're already in a pair-bonded relationship, poly may not be for you, and we'd like to highlight a few potential pitfalls. These problems are by no means universal, but we've seen them enough to think we should point them out.

- There can be a tendency to deemphasize the primary bond to a degree that leads people to move apart.

- There can be an overemphasis on the personal at the expense of the relational. "I am responsible for my feelings. You are responsible for yours, and if something is bothering you, you need to address it yourself."

- It can become overly focused on fulfilling personal needs and wants. "I want to have multiple lovers" or "I need to have this experience."

- Feelings of jealousy can be seen as a moral failure.

We are not suggesting that these problems are present in most poly relationships, but just as monogamous relationships can be dysfunctional, so can polyamorous ones. At their worst, poly discussions about relationships can have the quality of an interminable group therapy session, but at their best, poly gatherings can be love-fests that are both intellectually and erotically stimulating, and the poly community can be an incredible source of emotional support.

Designer Relationships

To reiterate, there is a great deal of overlap among these relationship models. What they all share is an approach that is radically different from the mainstream paradigm. Even though many members of the swinging community are externally quite mainstream, the lifestyle itself is anything but. The differences are more about style than substance, and people who live conventional lives probably view all forms of open relating with equal distaste. You don't have to identify yourself as belonging to any particular group. You may prefer to use sex advice columnist Dan Savage's term "monogamish," and as Savage asked in a hilarious appearance on the Stephen Colbert show, "Is it adultery if I'm committing it at one end of a guy, and he's committing it at the other end of that same guy?"[84] Ken Haslam, who has been one of the leading lights in the poly community since the mid-1990s, coined the term *swolly* to reflect his identification with both the poly and swing communities, though, as we've noted, his preferred descriptor is designer relationship.[85] So, feel free to choose a label that fits you

---

84 Dan Savage on *The Colbert Report*, July 12, 2011, http://www.colbertnation. com/the-colbert-report-videos/391692/july-12-2011/dan-savage.

85 Haslam wrote us in considerable detail about coining this term. We quote him at length because his perspective is so valuable: "Here is a letter I wrote in 2008 on the word 'swolly' to explain its origins. It has been used a couple of times in the literature and is actually in the Urban Dictionary. And you can now get a cup or tee shirt with 'swolly' on it along with a definition. So, it looks like the concept of that vast, ill-defined area between swinging and polyamory now has a descriptor. I always tell people that polyamory is all about choice and have now even started using the term 'designer relationships' to let people know that there are few, if any, rules for designing relationships these days—anything goes as long as everyone knows what is going on and agrees." In the original email Haslam explained that he used the word swolly "to indicate a person embracing both the swing and poly worlds. Although I 'coined' the word tongue-in-cheek during one of the Internet swing/poly wars, I find there is so much overlap that the word may actually have validity. It is well known that many polys come from the swing world when they tire of sport sex and begin to feel the need for more emotional closeness with their sex partners. And, being comfortable in the swing world, will occasionally go back for an evening of hot sex … This comfort of being able to choose what is right for us is what polyamory can teach the world." Kenneth R. Haslam, MD, pers. comm., September 20, 2012.

and take what you can from each community to develop your own paradigm. Our preferred term, which may resonate with you since this is a book for couples, is *pair-bonded nonmonogamy.* This term highlights the open aspect of the relationship, while also emphasizing the paramount importance of the primary bond. It works for us.

SAFER SEX

We are in no way supporters of abstinence-only sex education, but its advocates are right in one respect. The only kind of sex that is entirely risk-free is no sex at all. Next on the list is self-pleasuring, followed by total exclusivity between first-time sexual partners, and then total exclusivity between partners who have been thoroughly tested—though in the last two cases there remains a minuscule risk of sexually transmitting an infection that can be acquired nonsexually, hepatitis C for example.

For most people, these options are unrealistic. Thus, there is an element of risk in all sexual encounters (just as there is an element of risk in everything that you do, including sleeping). This is true even if you use barriers, since they sometimes fail. Certain infections can be transmitted even when barriers—male or female condoms, dental dams, plastic wrap, and gloves—are used. The term *safer sex, as* opposed to safe sex, which was current a couple of decades ago, is a way of acknowledging that using protection is not a guarantee.

There are definitely risks involved in having a nonexclusive relationship, and some of them are serious, most notably the risk of contracting HIV. Remember that research shows that people who cheat on their partners are more likely to behave irresponsibly when it comes to safer sex. If you're open sexually, it's your responsibility to educate yourself about the risks and to make informed decisions about how you will protect yourself and your partners.

The risks are real, so making conscious decisions about your safer sex practices is essential. At the same time, being excessively concerned about sexual risk can easily turn into sex-negativity, a mind-set in which infection is transformed into punishment and concern about risk becomes a receptacle for fears that are not proportionate to reality. We're not experts in public health or epidemiology, so we encourage you to inform yourself about the risks involved in given behaviors, which is crucial for making sound decisions about what chances you're willing to take. You'll find some links to sources of information in the Resource Guide.

Regular testing is essential for all sexual adventurers, and if you have multiple partners, it's wise to do it more than once a year. Testing should include a full panel of STIs (sexually transmitted infections): HIV, syphilis, gonorrhea, chlamydia, herpes 1 and 2 (type 1 is very common and is known as oral herpes; type 2 is known as genital herpes, but both can be contracted orally or genitally), human papilloma virus (there's currently no HPV test for men), and hepatitis B and C. An HIV test alone is not sufficient. At the time of writing, there is growing concern about drug-resistant gonorrhea, which can be transmitted to either partner during fellatio. While it may be emotionally easier to remain unaware, regular testing not only enables you to know your status, share it with prospective partners, and thereby avoid exposing them; it also ensures that if you do have an STI, you can get prompt treatment and minimize the negative impacts of that infection. We know people who test semiannually, others who do so quarterly, and people in the adult film industry who do so even more frequently. Your decision about how often to test may depend on how frequently you interact with others, but of course, there may be a time lag between exposure and a positive test, so clear test results are not a 100 percent guarantee of safety.

If you are in your fertile years, practicing safer sex includes avoiding unwanted pregnancies and making informed and intelligent decisions about birth control. While the pill is probably the most reliable method, it can have a negative impact on libido and pose other health risks. Other forms of contraception—intrauterine devices (IUDs), diaphragms, cervical caps, etc.—have their individual advantages and disadvantages. When used properly, condoms are very effective, and unlike other methods, provide protection against STIs. The decision about what method works for you as a couple is highly personal, and it may be appropriate to use two methods rather than one. For example, if you're fluid-bonded (use no protection with each other) and don't want to use condoms in your private interactions as a couple, the pill or an IUD may be an appropriate choice, even though you use condoms when you're playing in a group. In fact, many couples use condoms whenever they play together in a group setting, and condom use is required at some clubs and parties, regardless of whether the people interacting are fluid-bonded or not.

Different communities and cultures have different standards for what level of safer sex practices they use. Even within communities, the standards may vary, and they may not always be clearly articulated. Some insist on barriers for all penetrative and oral sex; others are willing to risk engaging in oral sex or digital penetration without barriers. (This seems to be a very common compromise; however, since fellatio is a high-risk activity when it comes to the transmission of gonorrhea, and drug resistant forms are now being identified, attitudes may very well change.) Some polyfidelitous groups (those who are exclusive within a closed circle) dispense with protection after everyone has been tested, and most people who are in long-term primary relationships are fluid-bonded with their primary partners.

If you are exploring interacting with other people, and you decide to use the most stringent possible safer sex protocols (barriers for all potentially risky contacts, including oral sex) your choice will generally be accepted. Deciding which specific trade-offs you want to make is a personal matter. Just make this decision with as complete an understanding as possible of the risks involved, both for yourself and for your partners. If you are uncomfortable with an activity, don't just do it either to please the person or because you're really turned on. This is why it's essential to have the safer sex conversations well before any sexual encounter begins and excitement impairs your judgment.

In recent years, studies have shown that the rate of STIs is increasing among those over forty-five.[86] People are living longer and are remaining sexual as they age. In addition to the increasing rate of infection among older people, there's evidence that the rate of condom use is lower than in the general population. This may be because people in this group came of age before the AIDS crisis of the 1980s, were in long-term relationships that have ended in recent years, and never got into the habit of using protection. It may also reflect a sense that there's no need to be concerned about STIs later in life. This is very unwise; reaching age forty-five doesn't mean you can forgo safer sex practices or be exempt from regular testing.

To return to the concept of fluid-bonding, in addition to health considerations, there is an important emotional and symbolic component to the decision to forgo barriers and become fluid-bonded. You may be having sex with multiple people, but if there are certain things you do only with your primary partner, it is likely that this will serve to deepen your emotional bond, creating a sense that unprotected sex is something different and special, something you don't do with other people. This can reinforce your feeling of connection and intimacy with each other.

---

86 Tiffany Sharples, "More Midlife (and Older) STDs," *Time*, July 2, 2008, http://www.time.com/time/health/article/0,8599,1819633,00.html. For a more recent study, see Rachel von Simson and Ranjababu Kulasegaram, "Sexual Health and the Older Adult: Trends Show That Doctors Must Be More Vigilant," *Student British Medical Journal* 20 (2012), e88, available at http://student.bmj.com/student/view-article.html?id=sbmj.e688.

Talking about Safer Sex

It's not easy to talk about safer sex practices and test results. Even people who are good communicators and experienced sexual adventurers can find it challenging. In some communities, these discussions do not take place at all; the underlying assumption is that people are basically healthy and that barriers will provide the necessary protection. This is not wise, but it is not unusual either, even among people and in environments where honest communication is highly valued. Almost everyone has bought into the idea that sex should be spontaneous (See Chapter 2: Good Relationships, Myth #8), and talking about protection and test status interferes with that spontaneity.

Of course, using protection does reduce your risk, but having the conversation is important nonetheless. Some people who host private sex parties hold opening circles in which everyone discloses their test status, sexual interests, and boundaries, so that everything is known and in the open before anyone consumes even a little alcohol or any sexual interactions have begun. This ice-breaking ritual ensures that people are making informed decisions, not acting on impulse.

TIP: Reid Mihalko's Safer Sex Elevator Speech

Sex educator Reid Mihalko has mastered the art of talking about safer sex decisions. This is his approach to getting the topic out of the way quickly and easily.

When were you last tested for STIs, what did you get tested for, and what was the status of those tests?

What is your current relationship status and sexual orientation, and what, if any, relationship agreements do you have that I should know about?

What are your safer sex protocols and needs?

What are one or two things that you know you like sexually (or might want to do with me)?

What is one thing you know you don't like sexually (or that you aren't up for today)?

Optional: Provide a quick rundown of any risky sexual things you've done since you were last tested.

Finally, ask the other person, "And how about you?" and listen to what they say and how they say it.[87]

Practice answering these questions with your partner until it becomes comfortable. This will not only make it easier to have this conversation with people you don't know quite as well, it will also help ensure that you both are on the same page before going on an adventure.

As is generally the case when it comes to sexual adventuring as a couple, you should reach agreements and understandings about your boundaries and stick to them. Accidents do

---

87 Reid's Safer Sex Elevator Speech, http://reidaboutsex.com/safersexelevator-speech/. Visit the site for additional details and more of Reid's perspective on this subject.

happen, and condoms may break or fall off. These mishaps can certainly be disturbing if they occur, and the risks of disease transmission or unintended pregnancy are real, but if you've built trust, they will be easier to navigate. In addition, if you've discussed your test status in full before having sexual contact, your knowledge should make such incidents less anxiety-provoking. Of course, all of this presupposes that people will be honest in their disclosures, which may not always be the case, but to reiterate, people in most alternative sexual communities are more likely to practice safer sex than those who are not.

SEXUAL RESPONSIBILITY

In many ways, having a discussion about safer sex is only the beginning when it comes to sexual safety, or perhaps *sexual responsibility* is a better term. It's undeniable that sexuality can be risky and unruly, and people often behave irresponsibly. In one form or another, the unruly nature of human sexuality is one of the great themes in literature. It is part of what makes sex interesting, and it would probably be impossible to completely control the chaotic aspect of human sexuality. No one is as rational or in control as he or she would like to think. Nevertheless, it is possible and desirable to do your best to be responsible, even as you embrace the wild, passionate, and unpredictable in your sexual adventures.

Sexual responsibility requires self-knowledge and self-awareness, clarity in your communication, and a determination to abide by your agreements. It means honoring each other's emotions, and those of the people with whom you interact, treating them with respect and consideration, even if it is a onetime encounter. It also means knowing and abiding by the standards of any community you choose to enter.

Sexual responsibility also entails doing your best to ensure that your actions are in harmony with your basic values. If they are not, it is irresponsible to expose others to them. If you consider transparency to be a basic value, to keep secrets from your partner is to violate your own integrity, and to make the person with whom you're engaging complicit in this is self-betrayal. There may not be immediate and obvious repercussions to such missteps, and if indeed they are missteps, there is room for correction or more self-awareness in the future. But if this happens repeatedly, your actions are likely to come back to haunt you. Bob Dylan famously sang, "To live outside the law you must be honest."[88] This is a typically cryptic Dylan line, but whatever Dylan may have intended, we think the saying is one to live by if you are going to live outside the sexual rules of mainstream society. Being honest begins with being honest with yourself. This is not easy.

---

88 Bob Dylan, "Absolutely Sweet Marie," *Blonde on Blonde,* Columbia Records, 1966.

SEXUAL RESPONSIBILITY IN ACTION

We've known Jennifer and David since before they got married. David is a foreign-born academic, and Jennifer is currently in graduate school. Their story is a very unusual and illuminating one, so much so that we quote them at length. What they have to say is relevant to many aspects of open relating but perhaps most directly to sexual responsibility.

First Contact/Escorting—David

When we were first married, Jennifer was working as an escort. Although she was beginning to slowly leave the escorting business and had only a handful of regular clients, she continued to escort for the first year of our marriage. I knew Jennifer was an escort when I first met her; in fact, we met because I was a client (my one and only time with an escort) on a trip to the USA.

On the days when she went to work as an escort, I would be lying if I said it was the same as the days she didn't. There was always a sense of uneasiness; the knowledge of what my wife was doing was always at the back of my mind all day. However, as soon as it was over, everything was all right and we were back to normal. There were never any lingering or lasting issues. Jennifer was always very good at reassuring me and reconfirming our love for each other. Jennifer also repeatedly promised that she would stop escorting immediately if I was not happy with what she was doing. I think knowing that this option was always there helped a lot in dealing with her escorting work on a day to day basis.

First Contact/Escorting—Jennifer

As a professional escort I tried to make it a hard and fast rule that I would not become romantically involved with my clients, but somehow David managed to work his way past my defenses. I think it helped that we lived on different continents and had to communicate through email. This amplified our ability to be ourselves without the awkwardness of traveling in the same social circles. At the time we met I was in my very first nonmonogamous relationship, one that was suffering from all the mistakes I could make and fading fast.

As a former "serial cheater" I had a lot to learn about honesty, trust, and self-restraint. I had fallen into a kind of "kid in a candy store" mentality about open-relationship sex and refused to comply with any rules that I felt hindered my powerful sexuality. The appeal of sex work for me was the simple fact that I could have the thrill of stranger sex over and over again. It was almost addictive. Meeting David proved to a blessing and a curse, as I was forced to accept that no relationship would ever be sustainable without my learning to compromise.

Separation—David

For the first eighteen months of our marriage we lived on different continents as I waited for my US visa to be processed. During this time we frequently flew back and forth to see each other, often spending months at a time on each continent. However, we also had long periods apart, which as newlyweds, desperately in love, was an incredibly difficult situation to deal with.

During these periods of separation, we had agreements about seeing other people. We talked extensively about what we were each comfortable with. Most of this activity involved attending BDSM/swinger events in our respective countries. The one thing that was always important to me about this was honesty; I always feel that something kept secret from your partner can take on a life of its own and has the ability to poison a relationship. Sometimes this was difficult and there were also some misunderstandings and some jealousy—this marriage thing was new to both of us. However, being open and honest was definitely the key aspect that allowed us to overcome many of these problems and cope with the extended separation.

Separation—Jennifer

Living apart and trying to navigate an open relationship can be like playing chess blindfolded. One of the biggest difficulties for me was keeping the lines of communication open at all times. I'll admit to being terrible at keeping time commitments, and with a 16-hour time difference to navigate it was hard to make sure our phone calls and Skype calls happened on a regular basis.

One of the most important things that David asked of me was to always share everything. That sounds so simple and it really should have been but I was accustomed to lying about my desires, following that old adage "What he doesn't know won't hurt him." The first time I had to "confess" to rule breaking it was overwhelmingly painful for me, but I pressed on and promised to show respect to this person who meant so much to me.

Monogamy—David

Once I moved over to the USA to live with Jennifer, we made a mutual decision to concentrate on each other for a while and not see other people. This was made easier by a move to a different state for work, an area where we did not know anyone. It felt like a fresh start for us and our marriage. Being able to finally live together as a married couple was such a relief after being apart so long. I had been in a reasonably long term monogamous relationship before, but Jennifer never had, so this transition was harder for her than me. However, I think we both managed to ease into this new way of life very well and were very happy with each other—in fact I can honestly say I have never been happier than I am in my marriage. I have often said to Jennifer that if we decided never to play with other people again, I would still be content—and I mean it, I have never met anyone like her. We have a great sex life and five years into our marriage I still find her sexy and attractive—all the time.

However, this period of monogamy was also not perfect. We both travel extensively with work/family commitments and so there are periods where we are apart. There were temptations, flirtations, and drunken missteps—but at the end of the day, we both love and trust each other. Again, for me the important thing is honesty. If a mistake was made, we owned up to it—this may have created unhappiness at the time but that dissipates and goes away. Finding out about a secret that has been kept from you by someone you trust so intimately and implicitly would be a much bigger problem.

Monogamy—Jennifer

It was my favorite joke to tell my friends that I always thought "monogamy" was a type of wood. All joking aside, it took me a long time, with quite a few broken hearts along the way, to realize that I was a nonmonogamous person. My commitment to David was going to be the first time I tried to fight the urge to sneak in just one little "no one will ever know" one-night stand, and it was harder than I thought.

When sex was my profession it was never a problem for us, as it was always out in the open. Seeking out the "forbidden fruit" was what I had to avoid, and in doing so I learned a lot about my self-destructive tendencies and issues with low self-esteem. It took all of David's love and patience for me to understand that I was pushing his boundaries on purpose to see if he would stick with me. I had to realize this was toxic behavior and it took some outside counseling and a great deal of personal reflection and meditation to get past what I call the "needy demon."

Opening Up—David

We have now been married for five years. Over the past year or so we have started opening up and playing with other people a little. Initially we tried reaching out to local BDSM and swingers groups and found little connection/attraction and had a few not so successful experiences. Eventually we decided to go back to larger BDSM events in remote cities that were run by friends of ours. We had great experiences at these events, but it also felt like we were gently dipping our toes back in the water, so we took things slowly and mainly played together with others.

Last year we again tried to connect with others in our area through the swinger community with more success. So far, we have done all of these things together, as a couple. An interesting aspect of playing together with others is that, for me, the jealousy aspect vanishes alto-gether. I feel none of the uneasiness I felt when Jennifer was escorting or playing with others when we lived apart.

Recently, Jennifer was in India and rang me to ask if she could play with someone she had met there and was sexually attracted to. This is a big step; I said yes but once again immediately felt that uneasiness. However, I know that my wife will come home to me enlivened by this experience; she will be honest with me and always consult me. As Jennifer and I continue to explore each other and our sexualities, even when we play with others, this is a journey we are making together. All these experi-ences make our amazing marriage even stronger. I feel so blessed to have a partner like J with whom I can be so honest about sex and with whom I can explore so many exciting opportunities.

Opening Up—Jennifer

One of the greatest aspects of an open relationship is the ability to find fulfillment in your partner's pleasure with others. After a turbulent start and some bumps along the way, I am happy to say that David and I are enjoying the fruits of our labor. I still notice that I have a lump in my throat whenever I ask for what I want, but it is something I know I can push through for the sake of my treasured partnership.

This happened fairly recently on an overseas trip when I approached the subject of having sex apart from each other. David was hesitant at first but let the idea settle in his mind before telling me how he felt. I was ready to let the answer be whatever it was going to be and know that I would have earned trust and respect from the person I love, the greatest gift I could ask for in our fantastic marriage. My husband gives me the space to explore others within a solid relationship, and in return this has given me more joy and pleasure with him, along with everyone else with whom I have the honor of spending quality time.

Mindfulness and Respect

Another aspect of sexual responsibility is respect for others—their boundaries, their health, and their emotional well-being. This means not only treating them with respect during your interactions; it also means honoring their wishes, starting with the assumption that what you do is private and confidential, in the absence of a specific statement to the contrary. Some people can face serious consequences in their everyday lives should their private actions be made public, so don't kiss and tell. All of these rules apply regardless of the person with whom you're interacting. This includes, perhaps above all, sex workers, a group of people who are scorned by mainstream society. If any of your adventures involve paying for erotic interactions or entertainment, remember that you are a participant, and treat the person you are paying as an equal and a professional.

Sexual adventuring calls for a high level of mindfulness. If you care passionately about sex, why not pay attention and strive to live in accordance with your highest ideals? In mainstream society, sex and money are probably the two most common motivators that cause people to violate their own ethical standards. Most people who are motivated primarily by greed are probably not all that ethical to begin with, but countless others—even those with generally high levels of integrity—have betrayed and even destroyed themselves for sexual reasons. Part of the problem is that society's standards are contrary to human nature, and even those who would like to live in accordance with them are very hard pressed to do so. In addition, self-deception and impulsivity make it easy to lose one's way. Behaving more honorably when it comes to sex can serve as a template for behaving honorably in all aspects of life.

FIRST STEPS TOWARD OPENING YOUR RELATIONSHIP

By now you should have an understanding of some approaches to open relating, and some of the theoretical, relational, and ethical elements that are implicated if you decide you want to explore having sexual interactions with others in a way that not only maintains but nurtures your connection with each other. Conventional wisdom says this is impossible, but in reality it works very well for many people; most of the evidence indicates that relationship satisfaction and divorce rates are roughly the same, at least when swingers are compared to conventionally monogamous couples. One study suggests that swingers report greater relationship satisfaction and overall happiness in life. [89] We would go on to contend that when approached with consciousness, awareness, and a sense of mutuality, nonmonogamy can often produce a deeper and more satisfying relationship with your partner.

It's our general feeling that the best way to keep focused on your primary bond and your connection, especially in the early stages, is to explore together. For this reason, the approach we propose will slant slightly toward the model that exists within the swinging community, and going to a swing club

---

89 Bergstrand and Sinski, *Swinging in America*, 57–59.

can be a very good way to start moving into more advanced forms of sexual adventuring. This is not for everyone, and you should only take our suggestions to the extent that they resonate for you; you may feel that attending a polyamory or kink event is a better fit, or you may feel that being in an environment where people are openly having sex would make you too uncomfortable. If this is the case, follow your instincts, and ignore our specific ideas. The following general principles should still apply.

The most important general principle is DON'T RUSH! It is far better to attend an event or a party and to go home thinking, *Wow, there's so much more I could have done,* than it is to wake up the next morning feeling some emotional backlash, tension between you, or the sense that you've gone too far. Almost equally important is agreeing that you will explore at a rate that is comfortable for whichever one of you is the more hesitant, and that the partner who's eager for more will not pressure the other or insist on anything. It's OK to say, "Even though I would have liked to play with other people, I'm really glad you were so eager to go to the party with me, and I'm comfortable with where you are." It's not OK to say something along the lines of "Why wouldn't you let me try to join that scene?" or even worse, something like "I wish you weren't so inhibited." Remember that you're collaborators, partners in crime. No one wins, no one loses; and there's always next time.

If you decide to go to a swing club together, you should research the clubs in your vicinity, and find one that seems congenial—that is, if you live in an area where you can choose from more than one. Of course, you can't really know what any club is like until you've been there, so there's no guarantee that it will be the kind of environment you imagined. There's a good deal of variety, both in the clubs and in individual esthetics, so it's best to go in with no expectations.

You may decide that you want to start with an off-premise event. Attending this kind of event will enable you to flirt, get a little risqué, and make out with others, if that's what you've agreed upon. You will also be able to watch others flirting, exposing some skin, and generally behaving in a more openly erotic way than what you'd expect to see in a regular bar or nightclub. Some couples go to off-premise clubs and parties, enjoy them immensely, and bring the erotic energy home to unleash on each other. Others find this type of event to be tedious and a little strange. You probably won't know until you've tried it.

GETTING TURNED ON AND BRINGING THE ENERGY BACK HOME

Jack and Diane are a professional couple in their fifties. They identify themselves as being "in the lifestyle" and have for years. They limit their interactions with others to public displays of affection on the dance floor. They have been to resorts like Hedonism and attend on-premise events. They have experimented with more intimate forms of play but did not enjoy them and have no current interest in more overtly sexual activities.

Diane: We don't switch partners. On the dance floor, yes, we'll fool around, but we won't go to someone's place or play in the backroom. It's an openness to enjoying sex for what it is. It's not like I'm jealous if Jack notices someone else. I think it's great he is sexual. I know he doesn't want to have sex with her. It's like foreplay for us. For people who are solid, it opens you up to being freer and open to all the fun stuff there is to do out there.

Jack: It's a turn-on. Everyone's dressed up and feeling sexy; we're on the dance floor, and people are noticing other people. It raises our sexual feeling and awareness and brings us closer to each other.

Diane: It is nice to not feel jealous. We don't feel it. There's not a lot of jealousy in the lifestyle. I think most regular people feel it because of their own insecurity. If you feel solid in your relationship, it shouldn't be an issue. If he didn't notice other people, I would be concerned—what, he doesn't want to feel sexual? I like it when he notices others because I know he's turned on.

We asked: "Do you have explicit agreements? Or is it situational?"

Jack: We have agreements. There's always the possibility that we'll modify them, but we know we will check in with each other first. We're happy with where things are, but we also realize that things can change.

Diane: We have gone back to a room maybe 5 times over the years, but I haven't usually liked it. We will always check in with each other if we want to do something different. But that hardly ever happens.

Whether or not you enjoy the off-premise experience, there's much to be gained from being in an environment where people are actually having sex in a more open and public way than is familiar to most of us. This is true whether you opt to be sexual together in the presence of others or not. It's probably safe to say that only a small minority of modern Westerners have been present when others are actually having sex. It can be an incredibly profound and liberating experience to share erotic space with more than one other person.

INTERACTING WITH OTHERS

There is a significant physical and psychological difference between sharing erotic space with others, including having sex in the same room, and making the decision to interact physically. Similarly, notwithstanding what we've said about how limiting it is to think of genital intercourse as sex and anything else as something less, there's a significant physical and psychological difference between caressing and other lighter forms of erotic play and having genital contact. Beyond that, some in the swinging community make a distinction between people who draw the line at oral sex and those who have genital intercourse with others. The terms *soft swap* and *full swap* are commonly used. Although there may be some regional variations, soft swap usually refers to all sexual activity excluding anal and vaginal sex, and full swap usually pertains to PVI, but may also include anal sex. As much as we don't like the way these terms rely on the outmoded and misleading "wife swapping" paradigm, they do reflect the reality that having genital intercourse with someone other than a primary partner, perhaps in the presence of that partner, is a very big step for many people.

EXAMPLES OF AGREEMENTS FOR INTERACTING WITH OTHERS

Making out and touching are OK.

Oral sex is OK, but not PVI.

Genital contact is OK, but no open-mouth kissing.

No ejaculation, male or female, inside the mouth.

We will only interact with others if we are in the same room.

We will not interact with others in the same room.

Same-sex interactions are OK but opposite-sex interactions are not.

Barriers are required for all forms of potentially risky sex.

In fact, every step on this path is a pretty big one. By opening up just a little, you're moving into unknown territory and relating to each other in ways that are not commonly accepted in our society. There's no obligation to push yourselves to the limit, and if you find yourself approaching an edge, be careful to push very gently, if you push at all. And, of course, if you discover that something is not for you, there's no obligation to go forward. If you decide to interact with others, remember to take it slow, and do your utmost to nurture your connection with each other. Keep your statement of purpose in mind, and if one of you has any misgivings, or your activities don't seem to be enriching your relationship, then it's probably wise to pause and reassess. While we have met at least one couple who decided to open their relationship at a time of crisis and rediscovered their love and desire for each other in the process, this is the exception not the rule. If you're having significant problems in your relationship, it's probably not the time to interact with others. It's generally best to start when things are going well.

When you are playing with others—whether it's an individual, another couple, or a group of people—make a plan; decide on your limits in advance, and stick to them. Keep your agreements in mind, and do everything possible to stay on the same page emotionally. Make frequent eye contact and find additional ways to stay connected. Check in with each other verbally during any activity at the first hint of discomfort. Sometimes this is all the reassurance that's needed. If one of you is feeling overwhelmed or distressed, extricate yourselves politely, and if something has triggered anger or jealousy, try to postpone discussing the issue if possible. Our rule is that you should avoid intense conversations while you're in the heat of erotic excitement or immediately thereafter. This is even more important when multiple people are involved, since everyone present is in a very open and vulnerable state. We've found that next-day conversations usually provide valuable insights and generate deeper feelings of solidarity, even when they're about something that didn't work well or that was uncomfortable.

WHERE AND HOW TO MEET SIMILAR PEOPLE

Meeting others is often one of the biggest challenges facing those who wish to open up and explore. The issues are similar to those faced by singles, but they can be more complex because your activities are unconventional. Some rely on the Internet, where there are numerous sites, some catering to the swing community and others that are more polyamorous in focus. OK Cupid is mostly a dating site for singles, but it provides the option of identifying yourself as "seeing someone" or "married and available." It is fairly mainstream, but it is one of the few such sites that welcome people in alternative relationships and it has become popular in the polyamorous community. Adultfriendfinder.com caters to the worldwide swinger contingent. It offers personals and resources for same-sex as well as heterosexual couples and is the largest adult website in the world, with more than 40 million members. (See Chapter 13: Resource Guide, for additional sites.)

We are somewhat uneasy about relying on the Internet, despite its ever-increasing popularity and its utility. It is possible to meet some interesting people, but it can also lead to greater isolation. This may seem paradoxical, but if you're on the sexual fringe, it's important to find community with people who share your sensibilities and with whom you have common ground. This is true even if Internet dating works for you. If you build face-to-face social networks, you'll be more likely to find not only playmates but also friends and fellow travelers. If you're merely searching for hookups online, you're likely to find some, but you may miss out on making more meaningful connections. Despite our misgivings about the Internet, we've listed some of the more popular sites in the Resource Guide, since some people prefer this way of meeting.

Because we value community, we co-founded the Pleasure Salon in 2007. This monthly gathering in New York City brings people from different alternative sexual communities together for the purpose of creating solidarity and building networks. There have been various spinoffs, and at the time of writing, there are Pleasure Salons in Portland, Oregon; Vermont; Singapore; and Melbourne and Adelaide, Australia. In New York, the polyamory group Open Love NY has similar monthly gatherings. There are various meet-and-greets and "munches" (casual gatherings centered around sharing a meal) held regularly around the country, in cities large and small. In this context, the Internet is your friend. You can search for local, regional, and national gatherings of all kinds. We have listed some of the more established events in the Resource Guide.

DEALING WITH JEALOUSY

Some people open their relationships naturally and feel little or no jealousy. For others, jealousy can be an enormous issue. To some degree, the extent to which you experience turmoil may be a function of your personal makeup and history, but your feelings may reflect how skillfully you are exploring openness and how well you are adhering to your statement of purpose. Whatever the case, jealousy is a real, legitimate, and understandable emotion. Thus, it is necessary to develop the skills to manage these feelings.

If you experience feelings of jealousy, you don't need to justify them. Nor are such feelings a personal problem. They are something that exists within the relationship, so they need to be addressed. We've noticed a widespread tendency to say or imply that if you are jealous, it is because you have personal issues and your buttons are being pushed. This is a kind of willful blindness to the fact that feelings of jealousy are relational. If you're basically in good mental health and you feel that your partner is being inconsiderate or acting in ways that may be hurting you, there is usually a dynamic that you need to look at as a couple. To think otherwise is naïve and potentially harmful.

While statements such as "You create your own reality" or "I can't make you feel anything—you're responsible for your own feelings" may have some validity, to take them as literal and absolute truths is to embrace a solipsistic worldview. It may sell books—*The Law of Attraction* and *The Secret* come to mind—but it's a pernicious way of thinking. At its worst, it can lead to a "blame the victim" mentality. At best, it amounts to an extreme form of individualism that is more akin to Calvinist Christianity than anything else.

There are countless subtle emotional factors and inter-personal dynamics that can provoke feelings of jealousy, so sometimes an activity that always seemed problem-free may suddenly feel uncomfortable. You should always have the right to express your feelings of discomfort and jealousy if they emerge, and it's best to pay attention to these feelings and address them as a couple. This can be a powerful way to build intimacy. Examining when and why something may have gone awry for you can be a way to connect and under-stand each other more deeply.

If one of you expresses feelings of jealousy, and the other is thinking or saying, "That's not true," you have gone off track.

Drop the need to be right or the desire to avoid causing your partner pain, and listen until you fully understand the feelings. For example, if your partner says, "I was upset by the way you caressed Karen's hand," replying, "I wasn't caressing her hand; she was showing me her bracelet" is not going to bring you closer or give you any insight into what has gone awry. An answer along the lines of "I'm sorry it upset you. Your feelings are important to me, so let's look at what was going on and why," may actually lead to greater closeness and reduce the chance that jealousy will be an issue in the future.

Polyamory activist Anita Wagner Illig has wisely observed that jealousy often stems from buying into the conventional relationship model that we've examined so critically here. According to Wagner Illig, commitment without trust is one of the most common sources, if not the primary source, of jealousy. Building trust may not eliminate jealousy altogether, but it can certainly transform what some experience as a "green-eyed monster" into a mild, transient twinge.

It may also be helpful to be a little more specific about jealousy and think about it as a group of different emotions, or as a single emotion that takes somewhat different forms. The mildest form of jealousy is akin to, or perhaps synonymous with, envy: "She's having more fun than I am, and I don't like it." This can be inconsequential and fleeting, but if one of you experiences it on a regular basis, it can be a warning sign that things are a little out of balance. If one partner is consistently left behind while the other is having a blast, you probably need to step back, think about it, and discuss the dynamic or dynamics that are at work.

Possessive jealousy is the form of jealousy that is probably most common in the monogamous world. It's also perhaps the most adolescent. It has been the trigger for many a barroom brawl, or worse. This form of jealousy is often disconnected from the reality of a relationship, and may have nothing to do with trust (although such is by no means always the case). This is jealousy of the "you better not look at my girlfriend, or I'll beat you up" variety. It is rooted in a proprietary model of relationship (although it is not limited to men) and in deep-seated personal insecurities. If you're prone to feeling this type of jealousy, now probably isn't the time to explore open relating.

Jealousy that is triggered by fear of abandonment is also common. This feeling can emerge in response to an array of stimuli and need not have to do with sex or intimacy with another person. In its mild form, abandonment jealousy can stem from a concern that something—a job, a hobby, or another person—is taking more of your partner's time and attention than you would like. This can feel like abandonment and therefore seem threatening and distressing. Your partner is not actually leaving, but is instead allocating emotional energy in a certain way that results in your getting less attention.

In its more severe form, abandonment jealousy is triggered by the reality that the person is actually leaving. In this situation, the one feeling jealous is intuiting that a connection with another person or a passion for something else signals that the relationship is severely eroded and at risk of breaking entirely. There is, of course, a vast middle ground, but whether the cause is circumstantial and minor (increased responsibilities at work, the demands of child rearing, etc.) or it is more significant (dissatisfaction with the relationship or infatuation with a new lover), abandonment jealousy needs to be addressed with kindness, honesty, and awareness. Sometimes just expressing the feelings and knowing they've been heard and understood is all it takes to alleviate them. Thus, if your partner is feeling abandonment jealousy, it can be very helpful to listen carefully and acknowledge how your behavior may have contributed.

Being in a relationship requires dedication. This is not to say that you cannot love your other partners, but as sex and couples therapist Tammy Nelson, PhD, has pointed out, everyone wants to feel special to a beloved. Even if someone is deeply polyamorous, there's still a strong human drive to form pair-bonds. Some poly people can form deep bonds with several partners, but since most of our readers are in dyadic relationships, we'll focus on maintaining that special sense in the context of being a couple.

In mainstream society, the need to feel special is often related to sex and the desire that many people have to believe that they are "the one" for someone else. This usually means foreswearing having sex with anyone but that "one." It's fine to break out of the box of conventional monogamy, but it's also important to recognize that there are sound psychological reasons both for the convention and for the role that jealousy has played in literature since long before modern ideas about love and marriage became the cultural norm.

In order to keep your primary bond strong, you have to find a way to reassure your partner about the value of your connection and do so on a regular basis. You can be fucking twenty people, and that can be fine as long as you maintain this sense of specialness. The same is true for polyamorous people in triads or group relationships. If the bonds are to remain strong, there has to be something that the members do among themselves that reinforces the specialness of each connection. If you can constantly assure your partner that the connection has special value, it will make it much easier to manage any feelings of jealousy that may emerge.

COMPERSION AND JEALOUSY

While compersion is not exactly the opposite of jealousy, it can function as an antidote. Taking pleasure in the pleasurable experiences of others can be a kind of kink. There's an element of compersion in some cuckold fantasies, in which men get turned on by their wives' extracurricular sexual activities. The cuckold fantasy typically involves humiliation, so compersion is usually secondary and may only be relevant to the extent that it demonstrates how inadequate the cuckolded husband has shown himself to be.

Cuckoldry aside, we suspect that compersion is an important element in many open relationships, especially for those in the swinging community who engage in same-room sex with other people. For many, the experience of seeing a partner having sex with another person, giving and receiving pleasure from that other person, is an enormous turn-on and a source of pride and satisfaction. People can also experience feelings of compersion when hearing about a partner's sexual experiences with another (without the quality of fetish that undergirds the cuckold fantasy).

COMPERSION IN ACTION

Kendra and Robert are in a designer relationship that most would probably define as polyamorous, though like many other poly people, they have also explored swinging. Kendra is highly skilled at feeling compersion, and her experience with the emotion illustrates how it can enrich a relationship.

For Robert and me, I think it started when we joined the swinger scene. When we're out together, if only one of us is having a good time, then there's a good chance the other won't want to go out as much, so we started looking for the other to be enjoying the party, meaning finding somebody to be sexual with.

So it became a habit to think, I hope he has a good time tonight. We also just enjoy seeing each other happy. We have different ways of trying to keep each other happy, and as long as we feel such a strong connection with each other, comprising many dimensions, another relationship is nothing to be afraid of. Basically, he's my Robert and I love to see him happy.

Currently Robert has a steady girlfriend, but I don't have a steady boyfriend. All the same, he is happy for me when I do connect with somebody, and I am happy for his relationship and other connections. Although I do miss him when he's out, it's an enhancement to his life and gives me a bit of freedom to be myself alone for a couple of hours … It's a good freedom.

We can't guarantee that you'll feel compersion just because you've decided to explore a more open way of relating. It may not be a feeling that is available to everyone, but if you continually build trust and reinforce your connection with each other, even as you explore being sexual with other people, you'll create the conditions in which compersion is possible. If you experience it, you are likely to feel a very deep connection. This kind of bonding can be more profound than what is available to most people in conventional relationships.

BONDING THROUGH KINK

Like *open relationship,* kink is a term that covers a variety of activities and forms of sexual expression. It is a catchall word for sexual practices and interests that are outside the mainstream—from role play to dominance and submission, a vast array of fetishes, and sadism and masochism. We'll explore some of the terminology of the kink world in more depth a little later, but at the outset, it's important to take note of this diversity because outsiders often think of kink in limited and perhaps somewhat sensational terms.

For a long time, kink was considered extreme. The world of kink has been shrouded in secrecy, even if it was sometimes treated as glamorously gritty, as in the Velvet Underground's 1967 song "Venus in Furs," a demimonde anthem inspired by Leopold von Sacher-Masoch's novel of the same title. In the late 1970s and early '80s, there was overlap between the kink and swinging communities, at least in New York and San Francisco, but kink generally remained outré. In recent years, kink has become more mainstream both as fashion (the Velvet Underground and Andy Warhol's Factory crowd were four and a half decades ahead of their time) and as an acceptable form of sexual expression. Even so, the world of kink can seem strange and a little scary to those who are unfamiliar with it. That was certainly true for us, but if you can get past any misgivings and explore kink with an open mind, you're likely to learn more about yourselves as sexual beings, and you may be lucky enough to find previously untapped sources of pleasure. While we hardly qualify as serious kinksters, our experience exploring this scene should be illustrative.

Even before we met, we both had a deep curiosity about sex and had visited clubs that cater to the kink community. We were outsiders with very little knowledge, and what we observed ranged from mildly erotic to unsettling. Sometimes, the enthusiasm displayed by people in the scene came across as a kind of zeal, an effort to convert. This probably had more to do with our anxieties than with the reality of what was taking place.

Shortly after we met, when we were just starting out as Tantra teachers, we went to a presentation on Tantra and BDSM given by someone who called himself Dr. Chakra. BDSM stands for bondage, discipline, sadism, masochism; the acronym also contains dominance and submission as well as slave and master or mistress, so it encompasses a substantial segment of the interests that fall under the kink rubric. We were very impressed by his talk. Nevertheless, we remained somewhat skeptical about whether there could be any real connection between Tantra and BDSM. We had a lot to learn.

A few months later, we gave a presentation to a BDSM group and remained at the venue for a party that took place after our talk. People were friendly and very interested in the material we presented. At this event, we began to understand that some of what we had previously perceived to be aggressive come-ons stemmed more from an enthusiastic desire to share interests than from a hidden agenda around converting newbies. In spite of having had this generally positive exposure to the world of kink, we still had a lot of judgments about it and remained uneasy.

This was due in part to our background in Tantra, which is predicated on maintaining balance and parity between partners. After all, in traditional sexual Tantra, the partners go so far as to worship each other as manifestations of the divine. At the time, we struggled to fathom how dominating or inflicting pain on someone you love could be congruent with something as spiritual as Tantra. This was so even though we knew that at least one Tantric text explicitly mentions pain as a path to experiencing the mystical states of consciousness that are central to Tantric practice.

In spite of our preconceptions, we were sufficiently interested in understanding as much as we could about the myriad forms of human sexual expression that we decided to go to Dark Odyssey. At the time, the event was very BDSM focused, and this one was a five-day gathering at a private campground.

In the days leading up to our attendance, we were extremely nervous. In order to be sure that we would be comfortable, we reserved a hotel room, so we could retreat if things got too intense or if either one of us started to feel overwhelmed. This is an important principle to keep in mind whenever you are pushing your boundaries sexually. Make sure that you have taken measures to protect yourselves in case you start to feel uncomfortable. Arranging for a refuge, either physical or emotional, is likely to make you feel freer and less pressured.

While we slept at our hotel for the entire weekend, this had far more to do with our physical comfort than with any of the goings-on at the campground. To our surprise and delight, the event opened us to new and much deeper understandings about the world of kink and the community of people who define themselves as "kinky." We discovered that serious BDSM practitioners are often far more Tantric in their interactions than many who identify themselves as "Tantric" and certainly more than most "vanilla" people.

We also discovered that there is a self-policing aspect to the scene. In the past, this included a strong emphasis on ensuring that everything was "safe, sane, and consensual." Although this phrase is still commonly used, there is now a movement within the kink community to replace it with the acronym RACK (risk-aware consensual kink), since a lot of play does involve risk. There is also an ongoing discussion about the nature of consent and the importance of keeping agreements. Dungeon rules and protocols are usually posted; the use of alcohol (not to mention drugs) is generally forbidden in play spaces; and all but a few players make use of safewords. A safeword is a clearly defined and previously agreed upon expression that empowers a person who is bottoming (being the submissive or the person receiving) to have control over whether a scene is to slow down or stop altogether. The safeword *yellow* is often used for "ease up/I'm near the limit" and *red* for "stop."[90]

All of these elements serve as checks against reckless and harmful behavior. Those who step out of line will develop bad reputations and are likely to be shunned. This is not to say there are no irresponsible people in the scene or that bad behavior never happens, and even if an event is described as taking place in a "safe space," you should always be mindful of your own security and self-protection, just as you would in any other context. If you maintain your boundaries, there's little reason to worry and lots of fun to be had.

WHAT IS KINK?

If the words pertaining to open relationships are vague and indefinite, the definition of kink is even more slippery. To some people, activities described in earlier chapters—talking openly about fantasies, watching porn, going to strip clubs, being in the same room when other people are having sex— would all qualify as kinky. There are no doubt some people who consider oral sex or the use of toys to be extreme forms

---

90 The Lesbian Sex Mafia has a checklist identifying what constitutes abuse specifically within the context of an S/M scene, though the principles have a far broader application: "The Difference Between SM and Abuse," http://lesbiansexmafia.org/lsmnyc/bdsm-is-not-abuse/.

of sexual behavior that they wouldn't dare try, and for whom virtually anything outside of PVI sex in the bedroom, with the lights out, is adventurous. If you've read this far, it's not likely that you're one of those people. To some degree, what's kinky is in the eye of the beholder and is a matter of self-definition. Many people who don't identify themselves as kinky play with sensation (whether it's using ice cubes, feathers, or spanking), sensory deprivation (blindfolds), or light bondage, so you may already be kinkier than you think.

Although the meaning of kink is somewhat elusive, there are some good working definitions available, and we think Tristan Taormino's is one of the best:

> I use the word *kink* as an all-encompassing term to describe the people, practices, and communities that move beyond traditional ideas about sex to explore the edges of eroticism. Kink is meant to include BDSM, sadomasochism, kinky sex, dominance and submission, role play, sex games, fantasy, fetish, and other alternative erotic expressions.[91]

We admire Tristan for, among other things, her inclusive vision and tireless efforts to build bridges among sexual communities that might never have interacted a decade or two ago. Her definition is an invitation; it's up to you to discover your own kinks and to find ways to use them to enrich your relationship

---

91 Tristan Taormino, ed., *The Ultimate Guide to Kink: BDSM Role Play and The Erotic Edge* (Berkeley: Cleis Press, 2012), ix-x. If you're interested in delving into the theory and practice of kink, Taormino's book is an outstanding resource.

and your erotic life together. You may use what you learn to provide a little added spice to your sex life, or you may find that you want to participate more fully in the lifestyle and become a committed kinkster.

Communities often define themselves in part by creating a vocabulary that is well understood by insiders but confusing to outsiders, and the kink community is no different. An outsider might see the acronym BDSM and recognize that it stands for bondage, discipline, sadism, masochism, or bondage, dominance, slave, master/mistress, or some combination thereof, but the actual meanings of the words may not be entirely clear on the surface. This hypothetical outsider might well find these words a little frightening. The same outsider might see some of the attire and trappings of the BDSM world—leather, dungeons, manacles, floggers, scary-looking wooden structures—as fraught with menace. It's certainly true some people play hard, and we've observed scenes that made us uncomfortable, but for the most part, the menace is in the language and the trappings.

SADISM AND MASOCHISM

Let's start with sadism and masochism (S/M). Sadism is derived from the name of the Marquis de Sade, the infamous French revolutionary figure known for his prodigious literary output and scandalous personal life. Sadism became a psychiatric term for a person who gets pleasure from inflicting pain on others. It applies to sexual sadism or emotional sadism. Masochism has similar roots, derived as it is from the name of the aforementioned Leopold von Sacher-Masoch. Like sadism, masochism is a term that is often used in a clinical context, to apply to a person who seeks either physical or emotional pain.

There can be no denying that some people enjoy inflicting emotional or physical pain on others, and some get a sexual charge out of doing so. This can become problematic or worse in extreme cases, if it's compulsive or the erotic element is tied to victimizing others. Such behavior is unrelated to consensual S/M. Similarly, there are also those who seek emotional or physical pain in self-destructive ways. People who intentionally include an S/M element in their sexual play should not be confused with those for whom sadism or masochism is pathological.

S/M play usually involves a number of different components. Giving and receiving stimulation of various kinds, energetic exchange, and bringing about an altered state of consciousness are often foremost among them. On the level of sensation, pleasure and pain are very closely connected in everyone, more in some than in others. A great deal of S/M play involves exploring this interconnection between pleasure and pain and a process of moving back and forth between the two.

For people who enjoy this process and find it erotic, the slow build can be indescribably delightful, and by giving up control and placing oneself in the hands of a skilled *top* (the person who is providing the stimulation or sensation), the bottom is free to surrender completely. In many cases, the receiver enters what is called subspace, an altered state of consciousness. This state is essentially identical to the one that practitioners of Tantric sex seek to achieve through prolonged lovemaking.

The skilled top will stay connected and acutely aware of the bottom's physical and mental state. The exchange we're describing here is fundamentally an energetic one, and as in Tantric giving and receiving sessions, the top is providing a kind of energetic gift to the bottom, who is striving to receive that gift as fully as possible. The energy is returned to the top as the bottom gets aroused and goes into subspace. This process of building and exchanging energy can be an enormous turn-on.

Luc Wylder, who has had a long career as an adult performer and director and is well known for his topping skills, once told us that the reason he enjoys that role is because it gives so much pleasure to the bottom and he finds this a huge turn-on. There is no single reason why people enjoy playing the role of top (or bottom), but to assume that being the top is all about taking pleasure in inflicting pain or a desire to have power and control over others is to miss nuances that are present in most BDSM interactions. There is a vast difference between being of service and being servile, and as Luc's description of why he enjoys topping makes clear, there are multiple elements involved. There is, of course, a certain ego gratification in knowing you are skilled enough to turn your partner on and perhaps even induce an ecstatic state. At the same time, as a top you are also serving the bottom or receiver, regardless of external appearances.

BDSM relationships are often very complex. While the same can be said about any relationship, one of the most interesting things about the BDSM/kink world is that these complexities are in the forefront and are not being denied as they so often are among "vanilla" people. Many highly skilled players in the scene are in fact experimenting with these complexities, often by deliberately making them central to their interactions.

These are the elements that led us to recognize that when kink is done well, it can be very Tantric. The truly conscious and intelligent people in the kink world are very cognizant of these elements. Their involvement in kink is often based in the desire to delve deeply into how power and control, pleasure and pain, and giving and receiving factor into the human experience. If you can approach BDSM with this in mind, what may seem exotic and perhaps a little frightening from the outside can become a vehicle for a deeper understanding of human psychology in general, and your own psyche in particular.

Some people identify as switches, meaning they enjoy both topping and bottoming. In life, all of us are both givers and receivers, but few of us are equally comfortable in both roles. If you are willing and able to switch, you may find that it brings to the surface aspects of your relationship and personal behavior patterns that existed at a level below your conscious awareness. Exploring the dynamics involved, and the roles you are comfortable playing, can be extremely revealing in addition to being very erotic.

DOMINANCE AND SUBMISSION

Dominance and submission (D/S) involves an exchange of

power: the bottom surrenders control to the top, something that many experience as liberating. This can happen in the context of a scene, or it can be a full-time relationship structure. Just as S/M is about far more than the artificial, binary opposition between pleasure and pain, D/S is about far more than a power dynamic in which one person exercises total control over another. While such relationships exist, they are by no means typical of what is defined as dominance and submission in the BDSM/kink scene. D/S relationships are also complex. D/S players who are conscious of the power dynamics within a relationship often engage with these issues far more deeply than conventional couples. Even very conscious and politically aware people may be uncomfortable looking so closely at power dynamics and relationship roles that are, like monogamy, often embraced simply because they are the societal default.

S/M scenes include a psychological component, but it is often in the background. Consensual D/S brings this psychological element to the fore; it's often more about the mind than the body. S/M is more transactional, with one person giving sensation and the other receiving. While there are many nuances, D/S differs from S/M in significant part because it is relational.

Thus, the S/M top may not have a particularly dominant personality, and once a scene is over, the relationship can and often does revert to its idiosyncratic structure. The same can be true in a D/S setting if you're role-playing, but for some, the relationship is something that's agreed upon and lived. If you're living a D/S relationship full time, you are still relating in a way that requires you to look at things that most people in "vanilla" relationships spend their lifetimes trying to avoid.

To return to switching, it seems to be more common among people who engage in sensation play, since it's not unusual to enjoy both giving and receiving. It can also be found among those who are exploring D/S, especially those who identify as polyamorous; sometimes people will be dominant in a relationship with one partner and submissive with another. It is also true that not all BDSM relationships involve sexual activity (many dungeons or clubs have strict limits on sexual contact); and D/S relationships can be egalitarian in the bedroom, even if the interpersonal dynamic is primarily dominant/submissive, with one partner dictating, for example, when the other eats, sleeps, or exercises.

At the extreme end of the D/S spectrum is the 24/7 master or mistress/slave relationship. In some respects, the master or mistress/slave dynamic, with its terminology and trappings, was the most off-putting aspect of kink for us. The term *slavery* was inextricably linked in our minds with abuse, oppression, racism, and the denial of basic human dignity. The idea that people would willingly be called slaves was very troubling, and the fact that various BDSM clubs hold "slave auctions" was horrifying. This element, as well as some of the quasi-Nazi attire that can pass for fetish wear, can still be troubling for us, but after talking to seasoned players and people who have lived these relationships, we also understand that some of our discomfort was the discomfort of the outsider. There is no doubt a kind of glamour and allure in embracing these darker sides of the human experience, at least for some, but the master or mistress/slave dynamic, as practiced by many in the BDSM community, is more interesting and complex than we imagined it to be.

As outsiders, we assumed that the master or mistress/slave relationship would be one of total domination and exploitation, because in real human slavery, that is essentially the truth. The real slave has not consented to being enslaved, and one synonym for slavery is involuntary servitude. In the BDSM world, the servitude is not only voluntary; it is agreed upon and contractual. It is founded on egalitarian premises, and it is an agreement that can be dissolved. Thus, even if it may have some of the external trappings of chattel slavery, it is an intentional and consensual arrangement.

More importantly, the responsibilities that it involves for the master or mistress are very significant. As Raven Kaldera told us, his role as a master is to guide his slave in ways that will facilitate the slave's personal development—not just to benefit from being served. The level of engagement Kaldera described is far deeper than what exists in many more conventional relationships, and it requires profound interest on his part. We're not suggesting that master or mistress/slave relationships are for everyone. The model would certainly not work for us, but as with less extreme forms of D/S, suspending judgment and seeing past the trappings enabled us to recognize that these relationships can be healthy and nurturing for all concerned.

KINK AND STEREOTYPES

Our judgments about the scene in general, and master or mistress/slave relationships in particular, reflected many of the stereotypes about kink that exist in the mainstream, and we were on the open-minded end of the "vanilla" spectrum. Even as kink becomes more widely understood and accepted, and a book like *Fifty Shades of Grey* is at the top of the best seller list, these stereotypes persist.

One of the stereotypes is that anyone who engages in kinky activities of any kind must have been abused as a child. As Barbara Carrellas has pointed out, some people may get interested in kink in response to having been abused, and for many, this can be a form of homeopathic healing, a framework for repeating the traumatic experience in a way that is reparative.[92] Carrellas has also observed that the reparative element often involves reclaiming control, since the consent of the bottom/ submissive is required, and this can be empowering.[93] Even if there is a history of abuse that's connected with a person's interest in BDSM, the question remains, So what? Beyond that, it is by no means a given that everyone interested in kink is working out a childhood trauma. People are drawn to kink for a multitude of reasons, sometimes simply because they're responsive to certain sensations or because they enjoy the altered state of consciousness that a flood of endorphins can produce. It's the height of arrogance to assume that those reasons are necessarily pathological. Fortunately, the therapeutic community is somewhat more enlightened on this subject than the public at

---

92 Carrellas, *Urban Tantra*, 249–251. While Carrellas mentions BDSM in passing in her discussion of homeopathic sexuality, she has made it clear in lectures that she had BDSM in mind as one form of sexual homeopathy. She also makes it clear that not all those who are interested in BDSM have been abused and that not all those who have been abused will be attracted to kink.

93 Barbara Carrellas, pers. comm., October 27, 2012.

large, and kinky sexual practices are no longer deemed to be evidence of pathology in the absence of other indicators.

TIP: Kink Is Not Abuse

There is a very clear difference between abuse and kinky practices, and it bears remembering this whether you're interested in exploring kink or not. Abuse is abuse; what's abusive in a kinky relationship is what's abusive in a vanilla relationship. It's probably abuse if one or more of the following is taking place without your explicit request and agreement:

Someone is controlling you financially or taking advantage of your dependence.

You do not have the right to say no or stop a scene.

The confines of your agreements are not being honored (for example, you are being humiliated in ways that are not part of your role play).

Your self-esteem is being damaged.

You want to leave but can't.

You're being isolated from family and friends.

While individual therapists may still reflexively treat kink as mental illness, the general trend is positive. Upward of 10 percent of adults have engaged in some form of kinky behavior (and this may well be a low estimate if you choose to define kink as expansively as we do).[94] Thus, while it may not be normal in the strictest sense of the word, it is certainly

---

94 https://ncsfreedom.org/key-programs/education-outreach/education-out-reach-program-page/item/364-what-is-sm-how-many-people-engage-in-sm?. html.

common, and depathologizing it reflects a more evolved understanding that is taking hold in much of the therapeutic community. The human brain is highly malleable, and we are uniquely capable of eroticizing virtually anything. The really skillful players in the kink scene are conscious, creative, and imaginative sexual explorers. Most of them get up in the morning, go to work, and lead perfectly normal lives.

Intimacy in Kink

As with nonmonogamy, the idea that participating in BDSM or other forms of kinky behavior can create more intimacy may seem counterintuitive. We certainly approached kink with this prejudice. The fact that many activities involve physical risk actually contributes to the level of intimacy that BDSM can engender. If someone is going to bind your wrists or tie you to a Saint Andrew's cross and flog you, there has to be a high level of trust at work. This is also why you should seek instruction before trying anything but the mildest forms of kinky play.

Doing BDSM well requires presence, awareness, communication, and attunement—all of which are building blocks for intimacy. Many players have in-depth discussions in which a scene is mutually developed and ground rules for an interaction or even a relationship are established through a process of negotiation, something that can lead to a sense of shared purpose and mutuality. Much BDSM play is prolonged, lasting far longer than conventional sexual encounters, so presence, awareness, and attunement have to be sustained. Many scenes conclude with a period of aftercare in which the bottom is pampered and attended to for as long as is necessary to return to a more normal state of consciousness. This too can lead to a very deep sense of connection and bonding, and it takes basking in the afterglow to an entirely different level.

Of course, greater intimacy is not an inevitable outcome, and sometimes highly skilled BDSM practitioners can hide behind their technical proficiency while remaining somewhat disconnected from their partners. Midori (a brilliant sexuality educator, artist, and BDSM expert) has written about this disconnect with the suggestion that keeping it simple is often the solution.[95] Her perspective is worth bearing in mind. If you have any lingering doubts about BDSM and intimacy, we refer you to a peer-reviewed study in which researchers found that even when scenes went badly some couples reported feeling greater intimacy, and when scenes went well couples reported feeling greater intimacy and had reduced levels of cortisol, a major stress hormone.[96]

FETISH, ROLE PLAY, AND DRESSING UP

Kink is by no means limited to BDSM. There are also the overlapping realms of fetish and role play. Role-playing can include aspects of BDSM—the naughty schoolgirl sent to the principal's office for a punishment that might include both

95 Midori, "BDSM's Dirty Secret—The Real Risk of Kinky Sex," http://www.edenfantasys.com/sexis/sex/midori-real-risk-kinky-sex-0815111/.

96 Brad J. Sagarin, Bert Cutler, Nadine Cutler, Kimberly A. Lawler-Sagarin, and Leslie Matuszewich, "Hormonal Changes and Couple Bonding in Consensual Sadomasochistic Activity," *Archives of Sexual Behavior* 38 (2009), 186–200, full text available at http://www.niu.edu/user/tj0bjs1/papers/scclm09.pdf.

spanking and sex, for example—but it need not. Role-playing scenarios are limited only by your creative imagination, and if you start attending kink events, you are sure to see all sorts of inventive role play—people dressed in animal costumes, age play, staged kidnappings, and possibly even kinky clowns. Role play can run the gamut from playful and silly scenarios to elaborately staged and highly erotic ones.

For some, dressing up, in leather, latex, or drag, may be the extent of their kinky activity. They may just go out to a club dressed in fetish wear, check out the various scenes, and use this as an appetizer for erotic encounters they have in private. This is more than mere posturing. It is a kind of kink in itself, with the clothes and the energy of the environment providing erotic fuel.

We'd like to use an example from our own lives to illustrate the learning potential that exists in fetish, role play, and BDSM. We were teaching at Hedonism in Jamaica, where we happened to encounter some friends who were experienced BDSM players; one of them is skilled at rope bondage. One night, a costume party was planned, and we decided that we would play the roles of pirate and "a wench captured in the South Seas." Phantom bound Patricia's body, leaving her forearms free. The harness had a rope handle at the back that made it possible to lead her around. (There was thus a modest D/S component in the role-playing.) We just allowed ourselves to be goofy, which took away some of the unease that we might have felt. We have a very egalitarian relationship, and while each of us may have certain dominant and submissive traits, D/S has never been a significant interest or component of our erotic repertoire. For added amusement, the toy parrot that came with the costume was also in bondage.

The experience was not much of a turn-on, though playing around with control in this way was enjoyable for us both. Patricia was surprised to find that being bound felt good, akin to being in a constant hug. Because her forearms were free, the restraint was not overwhelming, and she was able to surrender to being led around. It was very interesting to observe how people (many of whom were swingers) reacted; some couldn't look at us, while others seemed riveted. Mark enjoyed the power and control, and the reactions. There was nothing extreme about what we were doing, but even something as playful and mild as this little game gave us some new perspectives on our relationship dynamic.

If our mild D/S role play was provocative to some in this crowd, we can only guess how they would have reacted if we had added gender ambiguity to the mix. Playing with gender roles and cross-dressing is a radical and very interesting aspect of the kink world. For some, dressing up as another gender itself is a fetish and can be a turn-on independent of other factors. When it comes to gender, gender roles, and gender ambiguity, there are many different ways that people explore and play around with identity and appearance. If you start exploring the kink scene, you will probably get a crash course in these topics. For present purposes, we will limit the discussion to heterosexual people who are cis-gendered (who identify with the bodies in which they were born).

If your physical body and biological gender feel congruent and you don't find dressing up as the "opposite" sex to be a turn-on in itself, it can still be immensely valuable and inter-esting to play around with your identity and the role in which your chromosomes have cast you. In our Tantric training, we were taught that everyone has both masculine and feminine aspects, and many practices are intended to unite the inner male and female and familiarize us with the full spectrum of gender, not just the polarities. There are a variety of ways to do this. We have often encouraged people to imagine themselves as the other sex, using visualization to create the feeling of having male or female genitalia instead of whatever was there at birth. Clothing can make this imaginative process far more visceral.

If you put on clothing and makeup (if you were born male, a woman's makeup, and if you were born female, a penciled-in mustache and five o'clock shadow), you may discover some-thing interesting. If you're doing it at home as a couple, the way each of you reacts to the other embodying the "oppo-site" sex can reveal a lot about how gender stereotypes impact you. This isn't about dressing up for a thrill or about sexual orientation; it's about exploring the nuances of gender and freeing oneself from convention. In the era of glam rock, many heterosexual men discovered that by dressing in drag they suddenly became objects of female (and sometimes male) desire. Throughout history, there has been something incred-ibly alluring about gender ambiguity—the *castrati,* figures such as George Sand, and the gender-bending characters in Shakespeare's plays all partook of this allure. You may find that playing with gender and embracing fluidity and ambi-guity not only function as erotic enhancers but also provide you with a way of understanding yourself more deeply.

TANTRA, KINK, AND A CAVEAT

In the Tantric tradition, there is a significant emphasis on boundary crossing and taboo breaking, and for many modern people, kink is perhaps the most fertile realm for exploring the violation of cultural taboos. This exploration of boundaries, the often highly ritualized nature of BDSM play, the pursuit of altered states of consciousness, and the emphasis on energetic exchange combine to make us think that traditional Tantra and kink have a great deal in common.

Notwithstanding these similarities, it is very important to bear in mind the distinction between breaking taboos and becoming increasingly narrow in your erotic life. If you're exploring kink and you feel compelled to pursue ever more extreme erotic pleasures, you may be missing the point. At their best, both kink and Tantra are about expanding your sexuality and adding to your existing repertoire.

TIP: Kinky Practices: A Panorama

Seasoned kinksters have a great appreciation for the human mind's capacity to eroticize anything. Here is a list of some interesting kinks from FetLife. Search for their definitions on the Internet, and discuss your reactions. Were you curious, turned on, grossed out, indifferent, amused, baffled?

auralism
behavior modification
blushing
edging play
erotic hypnosis
forniphilia
graphoerotica
impact play
kilts
kitten petplay
nyotaimori
psycholagny
retifism
sleepy sex
socks
superheroes
Victorian lifestyles
Wartenberg pinwheels

This list is only a small sampler. If you do your own research, you're sure to find many others. This can be a very interesting way of discovering what other people are doing, opening up some interesting conversations, and gaining a greater appreciation for the endless variety of erotic options that human beings have available.

GETTING STARTED

We don't qualify as experienced, expert BDSM players. At best, we are dabblers and fellow travelers who have learned a lot from our friends in the community. Given our somewhat limited experience and skill sets, we thought it wise to provide you with a general and broad overview of the scene and how we, as predominantly "vanilla" people, have incorporated kink into our own lives. The appeal of any given item from the sometimes overwhelmingly stocked kink smorgasbord is going to be highly personal.

You may already have certain fantasies that you want to explore. If that's the case, you can do research online or consult one of the ever-growing number of BDSM/kink-centric books that are available. You can also take classes online at kinkacademy.com. And don't forget that many communities have public meet-ups and munches and that workshops can be found in many major cities.

Regardless of whether you have specific fantasies, it's often the case that you don't know whether you will like something until you actually experience it. Your rational mind may tell you, for example, that you're not the kind of person who enjoys being spanked, but your body (and your genitals) may tell a different story. For this reason, the best way to explore is to attend events or workshops and try things out.

Many kink events offer samplers, and these can be a great way to experiment and learn. Just a couple of minutes of an activity may be enough to tell you whether you like it or might acquire a taste for it. Even if the experience is not a turn-on for you, it may be an opportunity to develop new insights. We've always found these samplers to be very valuable, a great way to break personal taboos without investing a lot of time or risking too much discomfort. The kink community is filled with people who have developed their skills to such an extent that they display real artistry. They're often passionate about what they do and are willing to share their knowledge if they're approached sincerely and respectfully.

The sincere and respectful component is important for any interaction, but it has particular relevance if you're exploring BDSM/kink, a world in which protocol is often highly important. There are many different protocols within the community, and some are determined by relationships. Thus, in the broad sense, you should be quiet and keep a safe and respectful distance when watching a scene in a dungeon. In the narrow sense, you should be aware that some submissives cannot speak or act without permission from their master or mistress, and some dominants may expect a certain kind of treatment, even from strangers. If you play it somewhat cool and take time to observe unobtrusively, you should be able to get a sense of what the rules are, both in a particular environment and in a particular relationship.

We would be remiss to ignore the fact that some people on the scene are lacking in social skills. This is true of humanity in general, but BDSM/kink does attract people who are into pushing boundaries and/or posturing. Thus, it's wise to be a little wary of those who too aggressively offer to share their knowledge with you. Like swingers, BDSM/kink players are accustomed to being politely rejected. Most offers come with no expectations or strings attached, and a polite no is usually sufficient. In rare instances, the no may have to be repeated, and in the worst-case scenario, the host or dungeon monitor may have to be notified. This is a last resort, but you should have no hesitation about speaking up if someone is behaving inappropriately.

TIP: Saying No Politely

When someone approaches you at an event and you are interested in the person but not the proposed activity, a polite no can take the following form: "I'm not really interested in being caned, but maybe you could tie me up instead. (Just be sure the person knows something about ropes.) If your no is really a no, you can simply say, "No, thank you," but it's a little more gracious to say, "Thanks for the offer, but I'm not interested in trying that," or "I've tried that, and it's not really my thing." Whatever you do, do not say, "Not now, but maybe later," unless that's exactly what you mean. If that's the case, say something like "I don't play with strangers, but if there's a chance to get to know you socially, I might be interested at another time," or "I'm not sure whether I'm interested in trying that and need some time to think about it. I'll let you know."

One final observation: for most beginners, attending a kink event or visiting a dungeon is likely to be a big stretch, and that first excursion may be accompanied by some anxiety. To reiterate, as with any sexual adventure, it's best to have clear understandings and ground rules established before you start, and if it's totally new for you, it may be best to plan on watching the first time. At events where sex does not take place on the premises, your agreements about sexual activity will not be in play, but it's still wise to have talked things through and to be sure that if one of you is feeling uncomfortable, that feeling will be addressed. Leaving early should always be an option, but chances are you'll find something that is fascinating, at least to watch. While some draw a distinction between kinky and nonkinky people, we suspect that virtually everyone is at least a little kinky. It's just a matter of identifying those kinks and figuring out how they can sweeten your sex life.

DEALING WITH DISCREPANCIES, DISTRACTIONS, AND DISRUPTIONS

No matter how good your relationship may be, no matter how deeply connected you may feel and how sexually compatible you are, long-term relationships will inevitably change, go through ebbs and flows and ups and downs. You won't always be in harmony physically or emotionally. You will certainly experience distractions and disruptions and are likely to go through periods when you are sexually out of sync.

Sometimes these rough patches are due to external circumstances—medical or financial issues, for example. Even if you've made a conscious and sustained effort to build goodwill and trust, you may still betray or feel betrayed; even if the betrayal is of the careless or inadvertent variety, it can still sting. Your relationship and your erotic life together may be subjected to challenges that develop due to responsibilities to others, especially children. Medical issues can emerge at any time, so the longer you're together, the more likely it is that you'll have to contend with health problems. Differences in your sexual styles or levels of desire can be either deep rooted or transient. We hope to have provided you with a skill set that will make it easier to manage these more difficult periods and build enough goodwill to maintain your solidarity.

Given that no relationship is problem free, the nature of the discrepancies themselves is relatively unimportant; what really matters is how you handle them—optimally with grace, empathy, and love for each other. If things get overly difficult, there is absolutely nothing wrong with seeking couples therapy or sex therapy. Just be sure to shop around and choose professionals who are well qualified and with whom you resonate personally. Bad therapy or counseling or a poor therapist-client match can easily do as much harm as good, and, as we've mentioned, many couples therapists are not very knowledgeable about or comfortable with sexual matters.

TIP: How to Select a Sex Therapist

Check credentials, degrees, certifications (including AASECT), and state licensure. In some states, people calling themselves "counselors" or "psychotherapists" may not be licensed because the term is outside existing regulatory structures.

Avoid "reparative therapy" and 12-step style programs for "sex addiction." The former approach has been widely debunked. The latter is scientifically questionable, and the American Psychiatric Association's Diagnostic and Statistical Manual (DSM) does not recognize sex addiction as a valid diagnostic category.

Verify that the therapist is in fact sex-positive, kink-friendly, and poly-friendly and will refrain from judging the ways in which you are exploring your sexuality as a couple.

Be sure that you both feel personally comfortable with the therapist. The success of any form of psychotherapy depends in part on the relationship between client(s) and practitioner.

Sometimes couples therapy's primary function seems to be helping people part in the most amicable way possible. That should never be the starting point, but realistically, if the rough patch is more like a bridge collapse, the discrepancies are too great, and your relationship is fundamentally unhappy, the healthier thing to do is to move on and stop trying to fix something that is irreparable. A book like this one cannot be a cure-all, but if you apply some skills and are cognizant that things are likely to change in the future, if you can be flexible and refrain from insisting that things should remain as they always have been, you are much more likely to retain your composure and your connection during challenging times.

When difficulties arise, dealing with them can be emotionally demanding. There's an old saying that every wall is a door, and while the claim that the Chinese word for crisis is composed of two characters, one meaning danger and the other meaning opportunity, has been debunked, there is some truth in these simplistic formulations. Satya, Mark's first Tantra teacher, has a more humorous and apt acronym—AFGO (another fucking growth opportunity)—that accurately reflects the emotional reality of crisis and opportunity. Perhaps the greatest opportunity at the heart of many rough patches, and indeed of many crises, lies in the possibility that instead of pushing you apart, the problem and the process of resolving it can create more solidarity and bring you together.

While most conventional wisdom says otherwise, this can often be true in the aftermath of a major betrayal, including a clandestine affair. It is well known that some people's married sex lives experience a resurgence during an affair. Nevertheless, cultural judgments about cheating lead many to assume that affairs are either the product of deep and probably irreconcilable problems in the relationship, or that the breach of trust is at worst irreparable and at best can only be healed slowly and gradually but with lingering scars. This is by no means always so. As therapist and author Tammy Nelson has observed, in many instances, the aftermath of an affair is an opportunity for partners to reconnect and perhaps deepen their love for each other.[97] Seen from this perspective, the betrayal is a prelude to an awakening, and without it, some relationships would almost certainly deteriorate gradually, with the partners taking each other for granted, continuing to disengage, and moving further and further apart emotionally.

When you encounter difficulties, you need to be able to draw on both your verbal and nonverbal communication skills. Always do your best to reestablish your connection before having difficult conversations and to keep your conflicts as separate from your romantic and sexual life as possible. This is a matter of dealing wisely with both physical and emotional space.

Remember to avoid discussing any dissatisfaction you may be feeling before, during, or immediately after you have sex. It can be challenging to keep silent in these contexts, especially if something deep-seated and long-term is involved. Also remember that repeated criticism of your partner's lovemaking skills, especially in such a naked and vulnerable moment, is likely to be counterproductive, leading to a kind of paralysis based on feelings of incompetence, or even to withdrawal and depression.

More broadly, we suggest scheduling a specific time to have any kind of difficult discussion. In some instances, this may mean putting it off for several days, but it prevents blindsiding, creates more mutuality, and can help you avoid falling into a pattern in which one partner pushes for a conversation

---

97 Tammy Nelson, PhD, *The New Monogamy: Redefining Your Relationship After Infidelity* (Oakland: New Harbinger Publications, 2013).

while the other repeatedly says, "Not now," with the result that the topic is never addressed. Scheduling is not always an option, but it is helpful to make it a practice whenever possible. Just be sure to keep your appointments.

Of course, you should avoid having intense, emotionally loaded conversations if you've consumed any alcohol or recreational drugs. The same applies when you're sleep-deprived or have lowered defenses for any other reason. All of this can be tricky, and it demands a high level of self-discipline.

One of our favorite books on relationships is a brief text titled *The Relationship Handbook,* by George S. Pransky. The primary and very profound point at the heart of the book pertains to mood. The key concept is that when one or the other of you is in a low mood, which is not to be confused with clinical depression, you should probably refrain from having difficult conversations. This concept was a revelation for us. It requires enormous self-awareness and a good deal of effort to apply the understanding that combining low mood and discussions of serious issues is a prescription for trouble.

Mood is just one factor in making the decision about when to have difficult discussions. It's always best to find ways to connect and establish a sense that you are allies before starting these conversations. This requires presence of mind and an ability to control your impulses. If at all possible, avoid surprising your partner. Don't raise issues at inopportune times or in inappropriate places—for example, when you aren't likely to have time to reach a resolution, in public, or in the car (when one of you should be focused on driving).

TIP: Beyond the Six Questions: Examine Yourself

Recall the six questions to ask yourself before speaking (see Tip 11, "Is Honesty Appropriate," in Chapter 4): Is it true; is this an appropriate time; is it necessary; is it kind; is it helpful; does it improve upon the silence? In addition to the six questions, ask yourself:

Is it just a personal preference, or is it something that's really important to me?

Is talking about it likely improve our relationship?

Can I express it in terms that my partner will hear and understand?

Is what I am requesting something I am confident my partner can do?

If not, is there an alternative request I can make or compromise I can propose that will produce some positive change and that may open a pathway to my desired outcome?

Is there a clear objective and a way for us to recognize when that objective has been achieved?

Will I be able to express my appreciation for both my partner's efforts and the results?

These questions will help you focus and be specific, and will make it easier to avoid griping or blanket criticisms. It's good to engage in this kind of self-examination whether the issue is significant or comparatively minor.

There may be times when you answer most of these questions in the negative and still conclude that it's necessary to have the conversation. We are not suggesting that you silence yourself or stifle your feelings. Conflicts exist in even the happiest relationships, and tough conversations are sometimes necessary. The key element is finding ways to make those tough conversations somewhat less loaded. It's counterproductive to allow resentments to build. This can lead to dogpiling and case building. It often ends in what is sometimes called "venting." Although the word implies a gradual release of pressure to prevent an explosion, in common usage venting really means exploding, and explosive venting is likely to be destructive. Words can injure, and once spoken, they cannot be unsaid. Instead of venting, do whatever you can to ensure that your interactions, even those with difficult or unpleasant elements, remain positive and continue to reflect your determination to hold each other in high esteem and treat each other with as much kindness as you can muster.

DESIRE DISCREPANCY

A major discrepancy in sexual desire is one of the most widely cited factors that lead couples to seek sex therapy.[98] This problem is frequently characterized as being due to the woman's "low libido," an idea that is deeply rooted in cultural beliefs about gender and sex. While aspects of cultural stereotypes may sometimes be true, desire is a complicated subject, and gender stereotypes tend to reduce it to a very simplistic formulation: men are dogs, and women are passive vessels

---

98 In 1986, it was the leading factor. Peter R. Kilmann, Joseph P. Boland, Shelley P. Norton, Edward Davidson, and Charlene Caid, "Perspectives of Sex Therapy Outcome: A Survey of AASECT Providers," *Journal of Sex & Marital Therapy* 12, no. 2 (1986), 116–138, abstract available at http://www.tandfonline.com/doi/abs/10.1080/00926238608415400.

who acquiesce sexually to keep men happy. Ever since the late eighteenth century, the idea that women could seek and enjoy sex has been something of a taboo. Thus, for some women, acknowledging and embracing the capacity to feel desire and to be a truly sexual being is incompatible with received ideas about what it means to be feminine. We'd suggest that this goes very deep and often operates on an unconscious level.

It's important to distinguish between discrepancies in desire and sexual incompatibility, which is a much broader category. Couples can be sexually incompatible in many ways and for many reasons. Major long-standing disjunctions in sex drive or sexual interest are best addressed by a professional not by reading a book. Some people may be able to live with discrepancies in desire and find other aspects of the relationship sufficiently rewarding to stay; some may choose the "don't ask, don't tell" form of open relationship; and others may separate when things become intolerable. It is probably easier to overcome desire discrepancies if there's a reasonable degree of general sexual compatibility, and if sex was at least good and mutually satisfying in the early stages of the relationship.

If you encounter a sudden discrepancy, begin by ruling out any physical causes. Any number of conditions (some of them serious), from hormonal imbalance to depression, can affect desire. The same is true for medications. The birth control pill, because it overrides natural hormonal cycles, can often diminish libido. Antidepressants are notorious for their impact on sexual function—broadly on libido and more narrowly on response. Even some over-the-counter medications can affect sexual interest and function. Doctors often do not disclose potential sexual side effects when recommending drugs to their patients. This may be due to ignorance in many cases, but even very knowledgeable and skilled physicians may hesitate to do so, perhaps out of fear that the warning will become a self-fulfilling prophecy.

If there's no evidence of a physical or medication-induced cause for the discrepancy, then it does behoove you to examine both your general relationship dynamic and the way you interact sexually. You may have fallen into a pattern in which you are just not meeting each other as fully as you might, or you may have said and done things that wounded one, the other, or both of you. You may be responding to each other based on deeply held, even unconscious, understandings about gender roles.

One common negative dynamic relates to sexual competence. Comments that are all-encompassing, such as "You're a clumsy lover," are obviously toxic. They provide no guidance about what is desired, but even more specific instructions, like "Slow down," are often not specific enough to be helpful and can leave your lover feeling baffled and incompetent. It is more helpful to be specific, to express what it is that you do like, and to ask for it kindly. Even more importantly, acknowledge your partner either for doing what you requested or for making the effort. Accentuating the positive can also be a big help: "I really love the way you were licking my clit, and I'd love more of that kind of attention, but when you entered me, I wasn't quite ready" is likely to get a much better reception than "You really need to learn how to give a good blow job."

We are not suggesting that desire imbalances arise due solely to one partner's making impossible or incomprehensible demands. The dynamic we've described is just as co-created as the best sexual relationships. In many instances, the complaints are rooted in deep, unspoken dissatisfactions that have a long history. As a result, when this dynamic is in play, there has often been years of perceived neglect. When we've encountered it, the anger has been palpable, and it's hard for the person to express it with consideration or restraint when it has been building for years.

Feeling incompetent or that your wishes are being neglected is likely to diminish your general level of sexual desire and your specific interest in interacting with your partner. Many imbalances in desire can more accurately be described as a form of giving up or learned helplessness, in which one partner either feels unable to satisfy the other or one partner feels that the other is uncaring, unwilling, or unable to be an attentive lover. In order to break this logjam, the person who is frustrated must learn to make suggestions in a way that is not blaming. The person who is being less than fully attentive must become more skillful—by developing a greater ability to focus and the capacity to be less defensive and more understanding. It's perhaps most important to communicate a determination to provide at least some of what the other person feels is missing, whether it's quality of touch, attentiveness outside the bedroom, or specific forms of stimulation.

This can be a real test of your ability to turn toward each other. It takes flexibility, humility, and humor on both sides. In some ways, it's easier if the cause is physiological. If the problems are interpersonal, the more you can be kind and empathic with each other, and the more you can express things in clear, nonblaming terms, the more likely you are to resolve them. Labeling a problem a "discrepancy in desire" is not specific enough. If you can figure out exactly what's going on, you will have the tools to get back into sync.

Sometimes discrepancies in desire are really a reflection of a much deeper set of issues that is better described as sexual polarization. This polarization is an extreme form of what we've been discussing. In couples for whom this is an issue,

BAD SEX HABITS THAT CAN LEAD TO DIMINISHED DESIRE

- Checking out or disassociating

- Engaging in activities you don't enjoy to appease your partner

- Having sex in exchange for gifts or good treatment

- Keeping silent about physical or emotional discomfort

- Coercing or cajoling your partner for your own gratification

- Not paying attention to the quality of touch and the way touch is received

- Making disparaging remarks about performance, appearance, or any other deeply personal aspect of your partner's sexuality

the more libidinous partner may not only be unskilled as a lover but may demand sex or be oblivious, unempathic, and pushy when advances are rebuffed. If even a hint of this dynamic is present, seek professional help without delay, and do everything possible to forestall any further erosion in your relationship.

In the absence of deep and complicated issues, regular or maintenance sex (see Chapter 12: Going the Distance) can be very helpful for keeping your level of desire elevated and at least approximately congruent. According to a 2012 paper published in *Social Psychological and Personality Science,* low desire is the most common reason couples seek sex therapy.[99] Low desire and low mood are interconnected, and each can exacerbate the other. Recent research suggests that "bibliotherapy," reading a self-help book on sex as the primary component in treatment, boosts both desire and responsiveness.[100] We suspect that one reason this type of therapeutic approach may be effective has nothing to do with the treatment itself or with the specific content. Instead, the mere fact

---

99 Amy Muise, Emily A. Impett, Aleksandr Kogan, and Serge Desmarais, "Keeping the Spark Alive: Being Motivated to Meet a Partner's Sexual Needs Sustains Sexual Desire in Long-Term Romantic Relationships," *Social Psychological and Personality Science,* abstract online at http://spp.sagepub.com/content/early/2012/08/26/1948550612457185. This may reflect a change since 1986, although there is obviously a significant area of overlap between "low desire" in an individual and a discrepancy in desire between partners.

100 Laurie Mintz, Andrea Balzer, and Hannah Bush, "Bibliotherapy for Low Sexual Desire among Women: Evidence for Effectiveness," presented at the 118th Convention of the American Psychological Association, San Diego, August 2010, full text available online at http://www.psychologytoday.com/files/attachments/44385/study-showing-tired-womans-guide-increases-sexual-desire-and-satisfaction.pdf. Mintz wrote the book that was used in the study.

that people are devoting time and attention to their sexuality may contribute to the increased desire and responsiveness. If you make sex a priority and take steps to make sure it remains that way—from exercising your PC muscles to having regular sex, whether or not you're "in the mood"—you're likely to avoid or minimize this common modern problem.

OTHER DISCREPANCIES

Uneven desire is just one form of discrepancy. Some couples have different sexual tastes: one may be kinky and the other not; one partner may be polyamorous and the other monogamous; one may be bisexual and want to act on it and the other straight. There are many ways to resolve these kinds of differences, and the process is highly individual. A common form of discrepancy that sometimes overlaps with an imbalance in desire is an imbalance in sexual response.

While it would be a wonderful world if every couple were always well matched sexually, the truth is that we're all wired differently and may function differently in different circumstances and in different life stages. It's generally assumed that women are slower to respond than men and that they need an extended period of foreplay to get turned on. This is often the case, but it is by no means universal. Some women are quick to arousal and quick to orgasm, and some need a lot more buildup. If anything, the variability increases as people age; many (though by no means all) women grow more responsive through their thirties, forties, and fifties, whereas men tend to slow down in these years and often find that it takes longer to get an erection and have an ejaculatory orgasm. Of course, the refractory period also gets longer as men age.

The key to dealing with these differences in response is to remain attentive to each other and to recognize and address them head on, to pace yourselves and collaborate so that even if you are not in exactly the same state at the same time, you can still keep your trajectories more or less in sync. There are a number of specific steps you can take to do this effectively.

If you know your general arousal patterns are divergent, it's somewhat unreasonable to assume that you will follow similar arcs if you both start out in a cold state. If one of you tends to be fast and the other slow, it's likely one of you will be left behind. Don't be disappointed or resentful when this happens. While it may seem inconsiderate, it's just biology. What you can do is take measures to get around this imbalance.

The most obvious first step is for the person who's faster to begin by pleasuring the slower one. This will not only build arousal in the partner who needs more time; it is also likely to help you feel more emotionally connected. Beyond that, giving pleasure can be an enormous turn-on, so use your compersion skills, and focus on getting your partner going before you get started.

Another strategy is for the person who is slower to take steps to get turned on prior to the encounter. (Of course, the encounter has to be planned or at least anticipated for this strategy to work.) These measures can include pumping the PC muscles, thinking about sex, fantasizing, and masturbating, with or without orgasm. By preparing yourself and getting turned on before the encounter begins, you will have given yourself a head start, and even though your arc is longer, you can meet your partner on the way up, and you can track each other through the apex.

If you're prone to coming quickly, you can use the old trick of masturbating to orgasm prior to a sexual encounter. Exactly how long before is highly individual and probably can only be learned by trial and error. This may mean that you're actually in the refractory period when the encounter begins or simply that the recent ejaculation will slow your response for the next round.

If you're very well attuned to each other, the faster partner may want to build up to a high level of arousal at first and back off repeatedly before having an orgasm. This will allow the slower responder to catch up. One way to do this during penetrative sex is to stop and switch to oral pleasuring for a while, then resume having genital intercourse, and repeat as needed. This can be a particularly gratifying approach because it helps the person who comes easily to build a lot of arousal as the encounter progresses.

While simultaneous orgasms are delightful, we're not suggesting that you make it a goal to have them. The important thing is to collaborate on making your general track as compatible and congruent as you possibly can. With practice, you'll be much more likely to have simultaneous orgasms as a by-product of becoming more aware of how your arousal patterns are similar and how they differ. This should be an organic process, not one that's aimed at achieving anything except an enhanced ability to be attuned to each other.

Psychological issues can also lead to discrepancies. The

issue may be something as ordinary and familiar as anxiety. According to sex therapist Dr. Marty Klein, many people are continually anxious or can never fully relax during sexual encounters.[101] In some instances, frequent or seemingly compulsive masturbation and viewing of erotica may be a way of managing not only generalized anxiety, but also anxiety about sex itself.[102] While we are not in a position to make diagnoses or discuss the array of clinical forms of sexual problems, we have already expressed our doubts about the validity of "sex addiction" as a diagnostic category. But we do recognize that compulsive behavior of any kind, including sexual behavior, can become a serious problem.

Thus, if you're compulsively watching porn and are unable to regulate your viewing, if you're compulsively engaging in sexual behaviors that put you or others at risk, or if you are finding it difficult to resist urges that conflict with your basic values or involve any form of nonconsensual activity, you should seek professional help. We also think it's best to look at the issue from as many perspectives as possible and try to work through it as a couple; in our experience, there's often an interpersonal dynamic that's fueling the problem.

Frequently, the interpersonal dynamic involves guilt and shame, and these feelings can fuel the compulsivity. We're reminded of a story Daniel Odier (an outstanding Tantra teacher with a deep knowledge of the tradition) told in a

---

101 For example, Klein criticized "National Orgasm Day" and proposed replacing it with "National Relax and Enjoy Sex Day," http://www.sexualintelligence.org/newsletters/issue102.html#one.

102 Klein addresses this issue as well in "Male Sexuality: Selfishness or Insecurity?," http://www.sexualintelligence.org/newsletters/issue111.html#two.

workshop that Mark attended. It's very useful for what it can reveal about guilt and shame and how they operate. Years ago, a man visited Odier with a problem. He was about to be ordained as a Catholic priest, but he was compulsively going to peep shows and sometimes paying for sexual contact. He asked Odier what he should do and specifically whether he should give up on the priesthood.

Odier's response was that he should neither change his plans nor stop engaging in the activities but rather that he should approach these excursions differently by bringing as much awareness as he could muster to them and cultivating an attitude of respect for the women with whom he was interacting. The seminarian was outraged and left in a huff. A few weeks later, he returned and apologized for his bad behavior. He had taken Odier's advice, and something significant had shifted. He had not stopped going to the peep shows, but the power that the fantasy had over him was not as strong. As we see it, this story illustrates how guilt and shame can fuel sexual compulsion, and also how the choice to stop hiding coupled with a slight shift in attitude can be transformational.

Although people often use them interchangeably or as a pair, there are some important distinctions between guilt and shame. Guilt is a more specific term that generally applies to a particular act or incident. It can be a valuable tool for self-monitoring. In mentally healthy people, feelings of guilt are often a sign that one has betrayed one's own values. We like to call this efficient guilt.

By contrast, deficient guilt is the feeling of having done something wrong in the eyes of others, or of God. Your own inner compass may not tell you there's anything wrong with it, but you worry that you might be judged or punished. This is the kind of guilt that is sometimes labeled "Catholic" or "Jewish"; it's about failing to live up to the standards of others or failing to do what others might expect of you—for example, by masturbating or not calling your mother every day.

Shame is a broader category and generally a deeper and more vexing one as well. Although it often has its origins in a person's being repeatedly made to feel guilty about certain behaviors, it is not as attached to a specific action. It generally relates to a pattern of behavior or a core pain about the essential self. Daniel Odier's seminarian was struggling with both shame and guilt—guilt over his actions and shame about his sexuality, and we'd speculate that it was the feelings of shame, far more than the feelings of guilt, that were fueling the compulsion. The would-be priest felt unworthy at some deep level, and the activity fed his feelings of unworthiness. He also expected that if anyone found out, he'd be condemned not only for what he was doing (guilt) but for his very nature (shame). Odier's response was brilliant because it forced the young man to face these feelings head-on and deprived him of the harsh judgment he was expecting and perhaps even seeking.

If you encounter feelings of guilt and especially shame about yourself as a sexual being, it's best not to conceal them. When you feel efficient guilt, you are likely to acknowledge whatever you've done and try to make amends. When guilt is deficient, the temptation to hide it gets stronger. Deficient guilt can easily turn into shame, and shame demands secrecy and thrives on clandestine behavior. The more honest you can be with yourself and your beloved, the less likely you are to get caught up in compulsive behaviors and the less likely you are to feel ashamed about your sexuality. To reiterate a point that we raised earlier, maintaining a certain realm of personal and private thoughts and behaviors is entirely appropriate. We are not advocating total disclosure, but excessive secrecy, especially when it is driven by shame, is almost sure to erode your connection.

SEXUAL FUNCTION

A multitude of factors affecting sexual relating can arise over the years, and the ones we've discussed thus far are the ones we feel most capable of addressing based on our own experience, our training, and our work with students. Some of the others are more remote from our personal knowledge base, but they are important to mention nonetheless.

The first category of issues includes problems that are physical in nature. They may also have psychological components in terms of origin, but even if they don't, their psychological ramifications are significant. These include premature ejaculation, delayed ejaculation, erectile dysfunction, anorgasmia, vaginismus, and vulvar pain.

Premature Ejaculation

While many men experience an occasional incident that they perceive as involving premature ejaculation (PE), the clinical standard for a diagnosis is specific: the problem must have persisted consistently for a minimum of three months, and ejaculation must occur within two minutes of intromission. This rapid response should be accompanied by a consistent inability to delay or control it, and by feelings of distress. [103]

There are many reasons why people experience premature ejaculation; stress and anxiety are frequent contributing factors. If the sympathetic nervous system (which is responsible for the fight-or-flight response) is overly active, premature ejaculation is more likely to take place. Some men are so consumed by the sexual experience that they may lose self-awareness and fail to recognize their level of arousal, or they may not have learned to slow down, breathe deeply, or do something different. Becoming skilled at working the PC muscles, and especially learning to relax them, can often be very helpful. In many instances, dealing with PE involves little more than developing new skill sets and becoming more attentive.

Delayed Ejaculation

Delayed ejaculation (DE) is more common than many people think. When it is sufficiently serious, it is sometimes called male orgasmic disorder or *anorgasmia* (a term we'll discuss in more detail in the context of female sexual dysfunction). This is an issue that doesn't get nearly as much publicity as premature ejaculation, because the common stereotype is that men have a hair trigger and have to learn to delay. Much of the hype around Tantra involves sexual marathons, and it's

---

103 Komisaruk et al, *The Science of Orgasm*, 56–57.

not uncommon for us to receive inquiries from men who want to last for hours. While it is true that many men need to learn to regulate the ejaculatory response, this need is by no means universal. Some men are fully capable of getting an erection but find it difficult to ejaculate. The problem can be limited to genital intercourse, or it may be more general.

Sometimes this has its origins in masturbatory habits that cannot be replicated during partnered sex. Developing a more flexible sexuality by gradually conditioning yourself to respond to different types of stimulation may be helpful. Antidepressants and other medications may also cause DE. Some people are just wired to come less easily than others, but even so, it is often possible to develop skills that make it easier. As with other problems of sexual function, it's important to be open and flexible, and to find a qualified professional with whom you can be fully honest.

Erectile Dysfunction

The National Institutes of Health coined the term *erectile dysfunction (ED)* in 1992 to replace the old, somewhat disparaging term for the condition—impotence. While the neologism is overly clinical and transforms what was more like a status into a pathology, as does the newly coined DSM-5 term, Erectile Disorder, it is helpful insofar as it decouples the capacity to have an erection from any issues of power. Nevertheless, ED is not really a single condition or disease. More often than not, it is a symptom of something else (whether physical or psychological), and thinking about it this way may ultimately be a more helpful approach. As with PE, virtually all men will be unable to have an erection at some point in their lives, especially as they age, but the occasional experience of not being able to get it up does not mean you have a serious problem.

Sometimes, ED is a response to stress, depression, anxiety, relationship dissatisfaction, or any number of other psychological issues. In these instances, drugs like Viagra, Cialis, and Levitra are not likely to be of much help, since they tend to work only if you're in the right mental state. While they're readily available on the Internet, it has been widely reported that counterfeits are common. Aside from the question of quality, it is a bad idea to take these medications without seeing your doctor in person. There is often an association between erectile dysfunction and high blood pressure, and ED can also be an early warning sign of vascular disease.

There's a significant distinction to be made between erectile dysfunction and erectile dissatisfaction.[104] Erectile dysfunction is the inability to achieve an erection; it's not the isolated incident of not being able to get it up for circumstantial reasons, nor is it a feeling of unhappiness with the firmness of your erection. As men age, erections are often less firm, and the refractory period gets longer. That's not ED; that's a normal part of life. While we have no objection to using medications that are designed to treat ED for producing stronger erections (which are often accompanied by increased pleasure) or shortening the refractory period, that's not really

---

104 Michael Castleman quoted in Joan Price, *Naked at Our Age: Talking Out Loud About Senior Sex* (Berkeley: Seal Press, 2011), 224–225.

the purpose for which they are intended. If you are capable of getting an erection that's firm enough for penetration, you may have erectile dissatisfaction, but you don't have erectile dysfunction. And remember, you can have a lot of fun with a flaccid or semierect penis. To return to impotence: although the word has been superseded, men tend to associate firm erections not only with sexual prowess but also with personal power. This is probably partly natural and partly cultural, but there is more to being a man than being able to produce a hard dick on demand.

GENERAL FEMALE SEXUAL ISSUES

There are a number of female sexual issues that are in some ways comparable to premature ejaculation, delayed ejaculation, and erectile dysfunction. Like these male conditions, they should be taken seriously, as they can be indicators of medical problems. Some may require surgical intervention, while others may be much easier to treat. As with male problems, it is especially important to seek immediate medical attention if there is an abrupt and noticeable change in sexual function or response.

Naomi Wolf, who describes her own experience with nerve compression and changes in sexual response in her book *Vagina: A New Biography,* points out that this is very important for women to bear in mind, given the nature of female anatomy. While men are vulnerable insofar as their genitalia are external, the nerves that govern male sexual response are more protected by the body cavity. Women's sexual nerves are more exposed; this means that women are more vulnerable to injury, up to and including permanent nerve damage. There are reports of impaired sexual function in women due to bicycle riding, injuries suffered while practicing Yoga, and childbirth.

The conditions that are frequently painful and that impair sexual functioning in women have even more clinical sounding names than their male counterparts. Vaginismus refers to an involuntary tightening of the vaginal muscles that makes PVI sex uncomfortable or impossible. Vestibulitis and vulvo-dynia are terms for chronic vulvar pain affecting any part of the urogenital tract that has no detectable infection or other pathology as the cause. The DSM-5 includes these conditions under the general rubric Genito-Pelvic Pain/Penetration Disorder. These conditions obviously interfere with sexual functioning and desire. They are also not very well understood, and treatment success is variable. If you encounter these issues, you need to get the best available medical help to address both the physical and emotional challenges you are facing; even if there's no psychological component to the condition itself, you will have to find effective coping mechanisms, both individually and as a couple.

Anorgasmia

Just as the word *impotent* has been officially discarded from the diagnostic lexicon, the general term for female sexual dysfunction, frigidity, has been out of favor for many years. Needless to say, the word frigid carries very negative overtones and reflects a stereotypical understanding of gender. The old diagnostic categories described male sexuality in terms of power and female sexuality in terms of warmth, with the implication that men who have sexual dysfunctions are weak and women who have them are cold and cold-hearted. In addition to being sexist, the term frigid is very broad, and several diagnoses have supplanted it. In the DSM-5, female disorders of desire and arousal have been combined under a single rubric: Female Sexual Interest/Arousal Disorder. (The male counterpart is called Male Hypoactive Desire Disorder.) Desire disorders are believed to be more common in women than in men—35 percent of women as opposed to 15 percent of men are said to suffer from what was formerly called "hypoactive sexual desire disorder"—and thus problems with desire have been more thoroughly studied in women.[105]

Anorgasmia simply means the absence of orgasm. In DSM-5, anorgasmia is called Female Orgasmic Disorder. There are basically two categories: (1) secondary anorgasmia, which applies to people who were formerly orgasmic and have lost the ability, and (2) primary anorgasmia, a state that some prefer to call preorgasmic to identify it as a state rather than a condition, in which the person has never experienced orgasm. If you have been orgasmic and you experience a change in or a loss of your orgasmic response, a medical condition may well be the cause. Secondary anorgasmia may be caused by anti-depressants, certain other prescribed and over-the-counter medications, menopause, and stress, to name a few.

While physiological problems, such as injury, may be

---

105 Stephen B. Levine, "Hypoactive Sexual Desire Disorder in Men: Basic Types, Causes, and Treatment," *Psychiatric Times,* June 2010.

responsible for primary anorgasmia in some instances, this is usually not the case. There may be psychological factors—anxiety, trauma, problems with attention, extreme inhibition—that need to be addressed professionally. As Betty Dodson has shown, the problem is often due to a lack of education. Female sexuality still tends to be treated as secret and shameful; in many segments of American society, it is still acceptable for women who acknowledge their sexuality and speak out about using contraception to be branded as "sluts." Estimates of the prevalence of primary anorgasmia in women range from 5 to 37 percent.[106]

There is research suggesting that religious and cultural factors play some role in sexual response, at least in the context of masturbation. In one study, 87 percent of women with advanced degrees reported that they usually or always experienced orgasm when masturbating, while only 42 percent of high school–educated women could say the same. (This difference was not found in partnered sex.) Similarly, 79 percent of women who had no religious affiliation were orgasmic when they masturbated, as opposed to 53–67 percent who professed a religious affiliation.[107]

If there is no physiological impediment or severe psycho-

---

106 Bruce J. Cohen, *Theory and Practice of Psychiatry* (New York: Oxford University Press, 2003), 417, gives the figure 5–10 percent; Beverly Whipple and Alessandra Graziottin, "Orgasmic Disorders in Women," in H. Porst and J. Buvat, eds., *ISSM (International Society of Sexual Medicine) Standard Committee Book, Standard practice in Sexual Medicine* (Blackwell, Oxford, UK, 2006), 334–341, full text available at http://www.alessandragraziottin.it/ew/ew_voceall/36/1532%20porst%20-%20orgasmic%20disorders.pdf. Whipple and Graziottin state the prevalence has been estimated at 24–37 percent for anorgasmia generally.

107 Ibid.

logical issue, primary anorgasmia may be the result of insufficient self-knowledge. There is so much variety in female sexual response that becoming orgasmic is often a matter of discovering which neural pathways work for you. Some women respond best to direct clitoral stimulation; others are more responsive anally; still others may need penetration; and some will require two or more of the foregoing. If you're anorgasmic, it may just take time and experimentation. If you have tried on your own to become orgasmic and have not succeeded, we suggest that you find a skilled sex therapist to help you. The prognosis is generally good.

The ability to experience orgasm is not a prerequisite for having a satisfying sex life, and notwithstanding archaic but persistent ideas about frigidity, it's not a prerequisite for having a warm and loving relationship either. If you're preorgasmic but enjoy sex, being overly focused on the goal of becoming orgasmic will not serve you or your relationship and will deprive you of pleasure and intimacy; it can also set you up for feelings of failure if the goal is not achieved. This is not to say you shouldn't try at all; orgasms are both healthy and deeply satisfying, so making an effort to develop the capacity to have them is a good idea, provided you don't lose perspective and get consumed by the idea that you must "achieve" your goal.

Pregnancy and Childbirth

In most if not all societies, it's expected that people will have children. The pressures to do so are more significant than you might imagine, and while the desire to reproduce is biologically driven, the message that you should have children (and that if you don't, there's something not quite right about you) is pervasive. The fact is that you can live happily without children. (We do.) From an environmental standpoint, not reproducing is probably the greenest thing you can do. As with monogamy, the decision to have children is something you should make consciously, not just because it's expected.

If you decide to have children, it will affect your sex life and your relationship. This is something that few people seem to recognize or consider. Similarly, people often tend to treat sex and childbearing as if they were somehow independent of each other. While the advent of reproductive technologies has to some degree separated sex from pregnancy and childbirth, they remain entwined.

Many people have the misguided notion that having a child will solve their relationship problems. This is unlikely at best, and if your problems are sexual in nature, pregnancy and childbirth are likely to exacerbate them. If you're relatively happy together and sex is good, having children will present some challenges and is likely to stress your relationship. Knowing this at the outset will make it easier for you to manage the changes and face the challenges.

Since we don't have children and don't have firsthand experience with what happens during pregnancy and parenthood, we won't presume to give you specific advice on how to deal with these potentially major distractions. Most of the general principles we've discussed throughout this book still apply in the context of pregnancy and parenthood. In fact, the physical and emotional demands of these periods mean that you should be even more diligent about putting them into practice.

The process of having a child produces significant hormonal changes that often have an impact on libido. Lou Paget, a leading expert on sex, pregnancy, and parenting, writes that 58 percent of women "feel sexually encumbered by the challenges of pregnancy."[108] According to the Centers for Disease Control and Prevention (CDC), postpartum depression, which can be a very serious condition, affects 10–15 percent of women during the first year after giving birth.[109] While hormonal changes are a significant factor in a woman's response to pregnancy and childbirth, there are also psychological elements that will affect both partners. The bonding process between infant and mother alters the parents' relationship dynamic, and it is not uncommon for men to feel excluded when the dyad becomes a triad. Cultural factors also come into play. Many men have consciously or unconsciously accepted the Madonna/whore dichotomy and may find it difficult to sexualize their partners both during pregnancy and after delivery. Even those who do not may find initiating sex to be more challenging—out of respect for and concern about the new mother's level of fatigue, due to feelings of being overwhelmed by the responsibilities of parenthood, or in response to other shifts in interpersonal dynamics that new parenthood can engender.

This is not always the case. Some men get turned on by

108 Lou Paget, "Your Orgasmic Pregnancy: Little Sex Secrets Every Hot Mama Should Know," in *Hot Mamas—The Ultimate Guide to Staying Sexy Throughout Your Pregnancy and the Months Beyond* (New York: Gotham Books, 2005), 5.
109 K. Brett, W. Barfield, and C. Williams, "Prevalence of Self-Reported Postpartum Depressive Symptoms—17 States, 2004–2005," *Morbidity and Mortality Weekly Report* 57, no. 14 (April 11, 2008), 361–366, full text available at http://www.cdc.gov/mmwr/preview/mmwrhtml/mm5714a1.htm.

their partners' pregnancy, maternity, or both; some women feel more erotically engaged while pregnant; and others may experience a renewed interest in sex after they've recovered from giving birth. As with so many aspects of human sexuality, there's no single way in which people are affected and no universal set of answers, but you can use techniques such as eye-gazing, karezza, and scheduling sex to stay connected. If the disruptions are significant, or if serious issues such as postpartum depression arise, the suggestions we've provided are likely to be of little help. In some instances, immediate psychological or pharmacological interventions may be crucial, but whatever the case, be an informed consumer; choose your doctors wisely and research any prescribed drugs for side effects.

MAINTAINING AN EROTIC CONNECTION DURING AND AFTER PREGNANCY

Kathleen and Jason had known each other in high school but got together as a couple many years later. Three months after they started seeing each other, Kathleen got pregnant, and they got married shortly after the birth of their first child, so in her words, they "built the relationship and built the family" simultaneously. They now have two children and have been diligent about maintaining their erotic connection during and after pregnancy. Kathleen's story illustrates the importance of making sex a priority and resisting the urge to become fully immersed in the parental role.

One of the things I really loved about being pregnant was that feeling of being full and shiny; if you always wanted bigger breasts, you've got them. I felt very healthy. Jason was really good about celebrating my belly as the new baby grew, so I didn't feel fat. I especially enjoyed sex from behind. My orgasms were very different, and they lasted much longer. There was so much blood flow to the vagina that I felt like I was "fluffed" all of the time. Being turned on was my default way of being, and we had a lot of fun of with the new sensations.

The second time, I didn't feel so beautiful. It was really a struggle. Once I got pregnant I was too emotional for the athletic, wrestly, aggressive sex we'd been enjoying. Lovemaking had to be more about sensuality and taking time. Jason took a lot of pictures and kept on showing and telling me how sexy I was, and that was really important to me.

Jason was determined to keep our sex life going. With our first, he had heard all the stories and was worried that the sex would end once the baby came. Two weeks after I gave birth, we started asking about what kind of sexual play we could do. Still, it was really hard sometimes. Our first didn't nurse well, so I was always pumping, and with the second, it felt like I was always breast-feeding.

Still, we determined from the start that we would do date nights.

We would go out to dinner. We started having sitters; even if the baby screamed for two hours, she wasn't going to die. I got to walk away from her, have a coherent thought, and look into my partner's eyes.

After you give birth, it is easy to feel some sort of shame around your body. Jason kept on making me feel good about my body. When you have a baby, don't get hung up on "I want to be skinny." Forget the magazine model and tap into earth momma. Think I am beautiful for all the ages. Then it gets really fun.

When the kids were a little older the most erotic thing we did was put locks on our bedroom doors. We did not want to lose each other. Our parents have been divorced multiple times. We felt staying connected was of utmost importance—so, date nights and locked doors!

Jason said: I don't want you to cling to the children instead of me; I want you to cling to me too. I agree. You can't wait until your kids go to college to discover each other.

The impact of having children often persists beyond the early stages of infancy. Breast-feeding affects libido and fertility and has been widely used as a form of birth control in nonindustrial and tribal cultures. This suggests that there is more to the deeroticizing effect of maternity than just the Madonna/whore dichotomy of Western culture. Motherhood, at least as long as the child is dependent, tends to desexualize women, not necessarily in terms of male attitudes but sometimes in terms of their own sense of themselves as sexual beings. If you are one of the lucky women who is not affected by this change, these ideas may seem strange, but if you are more typical, you can still choose to resist the influence of your hormones. This may not be easy, but it is possible.

So, take active steps to keep your relationship and sex life healthy after you have children. For the reasons we've just outlined, among others, marital satisfaction tends to decrease with children in the picture.[110] Even if you're unaffected by any of these physiological and emotional issues, you're likely to be tired and even sleep-deprived, especially during the first year of your child's life. It's very hard to feel sexy if you're exhausted, so there will be times when you need to overcome your fatigue. The rewards of doing so can be substantial and may even help you feel more energized.

When you have young children, it may take some effort to turn toward each other. It can be difficult to make time for yourselves and leave your baby in someone else's care. We've known couples for whom that first night away from home was wrenching, but it's essential that you do this for yourselves. In most societies, child rearing was not the exclusive province of the parents. Extended family and other community members were typically available to provide cost-free support and assistance. The nuclear family is largely an invention of twentieth-century American culture. It's unnatural and highly stress inducing. Nevertheless, it remains the dominant paradigm, and chances are it's the one you're living. Even so, finding

---

110 John Gottman and Nan Silver, *The Seven Principles for Making Marriage Work: A Practical Guide from the Country's Foremost Relationship Expert* (New York: Three Rivers Press, 1999), 211–213. According to Gottman and Silver, upward of two-thirds of women experience a dramatic decline in marital satisfaction in the first year after childbirth. They suggest that the men experience a similar decline in satisfaction but that the process is somewhat slower. According to Gottman, the minority of couples who manage to avoid these negative consequences are able to do so because "the husband experiences the transformation to parenthood along with his wife" instead of being 'left behind.'"

MANAGING THE DEMANDS OF PARENTING

Ted is a freelance artist and web designer. He is a stay-at-home father with multiple children and stepchildren. He had this to say about managing the demands of parenting.

The physical and emotional demands of raising kids/babies mean that you should be even more diligent about your sex life. What I often find is it is really easy to be tired (whether from kids or work), and it's easy to not engage with my partner—but with just a little effort, I can overcome this and actually get more energy.

help and taking some time away to reconnect with each other will make you more effective parents.

This does not have to be an extended vacation. If money's tight, try to leave the baby with a friend or relative and go camping, or find some other inexpensive overnight or weekend getaway. As a woman we met at Hedonism in Jamaica told us, "One of the best things my husband ever did was make me go for a long weekend away when my son was just two months old. We have never neglected this part of our relationship ever since." Thus, even a brief respite can relieve some of the pressure of parenting and renew your relationship.

Older children sometimes seem to have a kind of sex radar and are able to intuit from your interactions that something is different. While young children are unlikely to have a conscious awareness that you're planning to have sex, they can be keenly attuned to nuances, and your erotic interest in each other may pique their curiosity. This can have disturbing consequences for some parents. In one instance, a woman named Gina wrote in to dick-n-jane.com and described how their children frequently interrupted her lovemaking sessions by knocking on the locked bedroom door. One night, they neglected to lock the door, and their youngest, a seven-year-old, walked in and caught her giving her husband, Ben, a blow job.

The child was quite upset by the experience, and their reaction may have increased the distress. Your child will probably not be severely traumatized by catching you *in flagrante delicto*, especially if you don't freak out and behave as if you've been caught doing something bad. If your child asks questions about what was going on, explain it honestly, succinctly, and in an age-appropriate manner. To do otherwise is to send a sex-negative message, something that is more likely to be traumatic than merely witnessing the "primal scene."

This also points to something that is more significant than the issue of being caught. In the incident we've just described, the child who walked in on the parents was seven years old and the youngest of three. The couple in question had apparently neglected to establish clear boundaries and to educate their children about the need for privacy. Here is the advice we gave to Gina:

By the age of seven a child should be starting to develop an understanding of boundaries and personal privacy, obviously in terms that a seven-year-old can understand—that Mommy and Daddy sometimes need alone time and should only be disturbed if there is an emergency, and that closed doors are a sign you want to be left alone. This should go both ways, and your daughter should have a right to choose, within reason, to close her door and invite you in—after you knock or ask—except in truly urgent situations. We think establishing this kind of boundary and making it clear to your daughter that she has a right to establish boundaries of her own is a great way to start educating her about what she is entitled to as a person and is likely to help her grow up stronger and with a well-developed sense of autonomy. You might also convey to her that your bedroom is your personal space (just as her bedroom is hers), and this is true whether or not you are having sex. You should probably teach her to ask permission to enter your bedroom, even when the door is open. This is not just about good manners; it is a way of teaching how to treat others with respect and consideration.[111]

Although our comments also addressed a specific set of circumstances, the general point is valid for anyone with children. It's important to be vigilant in maintaining boundaries. Your children don't own you, and you don't own them. We're not advocating neglect or irresponsible behavior. We're suggesting that allowing your children to consume your lives to the point

111 "What To Do About Kids Walking In," http://dick-n-jane.com/2012/03/what-to-do-about-kids-walking-in.html.

where you're not able to have sex without interruption doesn't serve you or them. Happy, sexually satisfied parents are likely to be better parents, and children who understand the importance of respecting others' privacy and who have their privacy respected in turn are likely to be better-adjusted human beings with a healthier sense of personal boundaries.

If you already have children and they have left home or are getting ready to do so, "empty nest" syndrome will present you with an opportunity to be much freer sexually. For some couples, this new freedom can lead to a kind of second honeymoon. We've also met quite a few people who opened their relationships at this point in their lives. Those whose sexual habits have been overly shaped by their years of parenthood may not recognize this freedom and may continue to make love silently, with lights off, behind closed bedroom doors. Breaking out of these patterns can be somewhat awkward at first, but you're adults, and you can make your entire home your playground.

There are undoubtedly many other issues and challenges related to maintaining an erotic connection in the context of being parents, but the foregoing observations are the ones that seemed most important. If you are planning on having children, or have children and are finding it difficult to keep your sex life vibrant, even if you're doing everything we suggested, consult the Resource Guide for more information.

SEPARATION

Spending a little time apart is often very good for a relationship. It gives you a break from each other and can afford you the opportunity to focus on yourself. In addition, there is some truth to the cliché that absence makes the heart grow fonder. In our own lives, we've often found that when one us goes out of town, the other enjoys the solitude for the first few days and the one who's away is usually so focused on whatever the trip involves that neither one misses the other. As time goes on, however, the separation starts to wear, usually more on the one at home than the one who's traveling.

During our first ten years together, when Patricia was performing regularly, work often required her to be away for periods of a month or more. This was difficult, and to manage it we made it a point to talk at least once a day and usually more often. We also agreed not to be apart for more than two weeks at a time. This worked pretty well for us, but we realize that many do not have that option, for financial or other reasons.

Whether or not you can manage to see each other during periods of separation, you can maintain your erotic connection with phone sex, masturbating for each other via Skype, and sending erotic texts and instant messages. If you're not concerned about security and are using private computers and phones, you can share sexy photographs and erotic emails. Of course, you can also use snail mail, which is more secure even if it's no longer fashionable. Activities like these can generate feelings of yearning and desire for each other and can keep you excited about opening your mail. You will undoubtedly miss the physical contact, but at least you can titillate each other and build anticipation for when you are together again in the flesh.

People often ask us if there is a "Tantric" way of staying connected during separation and whether they can exchange erotic or loving energy with each other while they're apart. The answer is obviously yes, but perhaps not in the way that the questioners intend. Having phone sex or sharing erotic photographs is a form of energetic exchange, though of course this is not the same as having physical contact. Similarly, even if you're a dedicated practitioner of Reiki or any other form of distance energy transmission, your attempts to connect astrally are not going to affect you in the same way as actually having sex. Nevertheless, you can play around with some kind of energetic, nonphysical connection whether you believe in this kind of thing or not. One approach is to agree on a time when you'll both masturbate and fantasize about each other. At the moment of orgasm, you can either imagine coming together or that you are sending that orgasmic experience to each other, no matter how far apart you may be physically. We can't guarantee that you'll actually feel each other come, but it's still a great way to maintain and share your erotic focus.

FINANCIAL DIFFICULTIES

Disagreements about money and how it is spent are extremely common, if not universal. These disagreements may be the primary cause of relationship dissolution, especially among younger couples. A 2008 study published in *Financial Counseling and Planning* suggests that negative perceptions about spending are among the most significant contributing factors to relationship dissatisfaction.[112] In our own experience, financial discussions have been among the most difficult and emotionally charged conversations we've had, even though our basic values and attitudes are not all that far apart. In addition, our experience reflects what some of the research suggests: this issue has become less loaded as we've gotten older. This has been a gradual process, influenced in part by the fact that we've built great reserves of trust over the years, but also because we've compromised and grown together, and our way of thinking about financial matters has become more congruent.

The study focused on discrepancies in spending habits, including what we call nonconsensual spending—one partner making purchases or accruing debt without consulting the other. This unilateral activity and the concealment that often accompanies it undoubtedly contribute to the relationship dissatisfaction that the authors described. It's even possible to argue that the researchers mistook symptom for cause and that a divergence in spending habits was not the core issue. These behaviors suggest something deeper, a fundamental lack of respect and the absence of mutuality and transparency.

If disagreements about finances can be challenging when times are good, they can be devastating when money is tight. The authors of the study suggested that collaboration among marriage and family therapists, financial consultants, and

---

112 Sonya Britt, John E. Grable, Briana S. Nelson Goff, and Mark White, "The Influence of Perceived Spending Behaviors on Relationship Satisfaction," *Financial Counseling and Planning* 19, no. 1 (2008), 31–43, full text available at http://www.afcpe.org/assets/pdf/6-2877-volume-19-issue-1.pdf.

financial planners could lead to improvements in the way money matters are handled in a therapeutic context, but if you're in severe financial straits, the cost of therapy may be more than you can manage. If that's the case, you may find a clinic that operates on a sliding scale basis, but even then, the expense may be a significant burden. It's far better to establish a good foundation well before you're facing a financial challenge. If money and spending habits are big issues for you, it is wise to see a financially astute couples therapist and find ways to alter your habitual patterns.

If you are going through a difficult period financially, you should do your best to apply the skills that you have already developed: to treat each other kindly, to remember that the problem is external and not organic to the relationship, and finally to be sure to have regular sex. Sex is therapeutic. It will reduce your stress levels, and it is free. By contrast, many of the things we have been conditioned to believe will make us feel better are expensive and will only add to our economic woes. Retail therapy is contraindicated when you are in financial straits.

OTHER STRESSES

Any prolonged physical or mental illness is likely to create stress in a relationship. While we've mentioned a number of physical and mental health issues in various contexts, the subject of sexuality and chronic illness or disability is not something we're qualified to address. We can only suggest that you do everything you can to stay physically engaged with each other, even if explicit sexual activity is not an option, and be forthright with your doctors about your desire to remain sexual. You may have to be assertive and determined in order to get the information and care you need.

Whatever the source of the stress, meditation and exercise can be very helpful. The same is true of getting out into nature. A walk in the woods can inspire feelings of relaxation and well-being. Our meditation CD set *Ananda Nidra: Blissful Sleep i*s specifically designed to combine relaxation with pleasurable and erotically charged imagery. It requires no effort or prior experience with meditation; you just sit or lie back and listen. We use it ourselves—probably not as much as we should because, ironically, it is during times of stress when you are least likely to make use of these natural (and often cost-free) countermeasures.

It's easy to fall into habitual and unhealthy patterns of behaving and interacting when you're stressed. In addition to meditation and exercise, one way to combat this is to create new habits. If, for example, you notice that stress is making you feel less sexy and you're spending your evenings together in front of the television, sharing a pint of ice cream, you can replace this ritual with a nightly walk. Holding hands will keep you connected physically. It's also a great context for having positive conversations that can build solidarity and bring you closer emotionally. Eliminating the dessert and getting some exercise are not only healthier options; they're also likely to give you more energy and sexier bodies. You can even treat the walk as a kind of foreplay and have a date when you get back home.

A final note regarding television: we encourage you to either get rid of it or, at a minimum, only have it on when necessary. And keep it out of the bedroom. In our increasingly distracted society, television remains one of the biggest distractions of all. Television has its uses, as do computers, tablets, and smartphones, but when they start taking your attention away from each other, they're ruling your life instead of serving as tools for enriching it.

12

GOING THE DISTANCE

Our deadline for completing this manuscript came a few days after our twelfth wedding anniversary and almost fourteen years after we first met. By some standards, ours is a very long term relationship, but by others, it's little more than a fling. Both our sets of parents have been married for more than sixty years, Mark's for nearly seventy, and started dating as teenagers. By comparison, we're still in a new relationship. Nevertheless, we became lovers when we were both in our thirties, so we have experienced some of the changes that take place as people age.

There's no single way of defining a long-term relationship. For some it's a year; for others it may be forty. Generally speaking, the longer a relationship has lasted, the longer it is likely to last. This is true because people continually invest in their partnerships as time passes, and have more to lose if they end. Needless to say, in some cases, the investment can be an unsound one, and staying is throwing good emotional currency after bad. For the most part, we don't think that staying together for a long time is something to value for its own sake. This attitude can be a prescription for strife and unhappiness. Even if the relationship is not dramatically contentious, some couples seem to be united by mutual contempt and hostility, and that's not optimal; however, if there's a reasonable amount of goodwill and the balance of positive to negative interactions is favorable overall, the benefits of staying together may outweigh the negative impacts of frequent low-level bickering.[113]

We hope and expect to stay together for the rest of our lives, but we also recognize that nothing is certain and we may come to a point where it's necessary for us to part. It's important to be mindful that things change and that relationships are dynamic. Active engagement, turning toward, and an ongoing determination to cultivate profound interest in each other are far more important than "commitment" or marriage contracts.

In some respects, our parents—who lived through the liberalization of divorce laws that took place in the 1960s and '70s—were on the cusp of a dramatic change. Regardless of their personal relationship dynamics, they were part of the

---

113 John Gottman, *What Predicts Divorce: The Relationship Between Marital Processes and Marital Outcomes* (Hillsdale, NJ: Lawrence Earlbaum Associates, 1994), 36.

first generation that had a meaningful choice about remaining together. Nevertheless, their choices were still considerably more constrained by social conditioning than ours have been and certainly than those of people younger than we are. Social conservatives bemoan the erosion of the family and of marriage, but as with Nietzsche's death of God, the change in cultural norms around marriage and relationship can be viewed as being filled with liberating potential.[114] We stay together because we choose to do so, not because society and the law say we must.

Thus, there is no easy way to define long-term relationship. It's probably more productive to think about this subject in terms of turning points. As we discussed in Chapter 1, the first big change occurs after approximately six months to two years at the most. It is nearly universal and is probably the most important. Other changes, from the birth of a child to the "seven-year itch" to the midlife crisis, are more varied and individual.

We opened this book with an exploration of NRE and some of the popular myths about relationships. We'll end where we began by examining another prevailing cultural myth—the one that celebrates doomed or "star-crossed" young lovers. *Romeo and Juliet* is one of the most memorable, enduring, and influential works in the Western literary canon. It has shaped cultural beliefs about love, even though it is over 400

---

114 Nietzsche's statement is often described as nihilistic, but it is probably more accurate to understand it as meaning "Unshackled by the chains of God and Christianity, humans are now fully able to create their own destiny." Kevin Kole, "The Meaning of Nietzsche's Death of God," http://www.kevers.net/nietzsche.html.

years old and belongs to a genre that is far older. Romeo and Juliet love passionately, against odds, and die young due to a misunderstanding. One thing that makes the story so poignant is that it expresses a central truth about life and love: the kind of romance that Romeo and Juliet share must die. Had they survived, their relationship would have ended or evolved into something different. Virtually everyone can identify with Romeo and Juliet and their experience of that first bloom of love. Almost everyone has been through it and knows that it must come to an end, and that the neurochemical flood that accompanies it will subside.

The tragedy of *Romeo and Juliet* is not so much the death of the star-crossed lovers as it is the death of that new love, and therein lies the negative and harmful message of the play. On some levels, the play trains all of us to celebrate this ephemeral, overheated emotional state and experience its inevitable end as tragic, as something irreplaceable, the loss of which leaves us with nothing to do but mourn.

Romeo and Juliet is just a play, and we are not arguing that Shakespeare intended to influence people living hundreds of years later when he wrote it. The play wouldn't have endured and wouldn't continue to move people if it didn't speak to something very deep in the human psyche, and of course, it wouldn't have been very dramatic for the lovers to have survived and escaped. The problem is that there are not enough positive models for what to do when the initial intensity starts to dissipate. *Romeo and Juliet* celebrates that intensity and the drama that surrounds it as if they were the essence of love.

Drama is not a prerequisite for love. You can experience

strong emotions and infatuation without having to overcome obstacles or suffer unrequited longing. Some teachers of Western forms of Tantra object to the phrase "falling in love" and encourage students to "rise in love" instead. While this formulation is a little simplistic, it has an element of truth to it. Our personal experience of falling in love was one of coming home, of falling gently into each other's arms. We had passion and intensity but little of what passes for romance as it is popularly depicted. We always felt safe with each other, and because we got together to explore sexually and were open about our interests from the start, there was no need for longing. The love grew organically and has remained passionate all these years later. Perhaps things have worked so well for us because it was so uncomplicated in the beginning. There was intensity in those early days but there was also a sense of ease, and we suspect that the ease is what kept the fire from burning itself out.

We are not fans of manipulative courting. If you're following *The Rules* or think you're playing *The Game*, you're not engaging in behavior that will help you have an enduring, sustainable relationship that is founded on trust. The appeal of these books lies in the widely held belief that gaining the upper hand over another person is the key to succeeding in love (and by extension, in life). While we reject this kind of thinking, we also recognize that these authors are on to something, though their insights and intentions may not be congruent.

What we think these authors have understood is that the early stages of a relationship are potentially perilous. It is easy to be overwhelmed during this stage, but if one can exercise self-restraint, maintain a degree of cool-headedness, and even some measure of detachment, it is possible to enjoy the delights of infatuation without being consumed.

Meditation teachers talk about noticing the gap between a thought or emotion and the action that follows from it. This is a very useful skill to develop because noticing the gap enables you to choose more freely and decide whether to take the action. What we're describing is similar. If you can stay aware of what's happening as you fall in love and make a conscious effort to slow down and take a somewhat longer view, you will be actively creating the conditions in which a deeper and longer-term bond can emerge. Doing so will mean that your initial period of infatuation can be a time for mutual discovery and the building of trust, instead of being filled with *Sturm und Drang* (storm and stress), waiting by the phone, and suffering for the sake of love.

Similarly, staying aware that people are biologically programmed so that this initial fervor will die puts you in a better position to deal with the change. By being conscious and taking action, it is possible to sustain some of the intensity that is typically associated with the early stages of love. In the case of Romeo and Juliet, the end of their infatuated love is presented as tragic. Change doesn't have to be a tragedy; it can be an opening, and you can make of it what you will.

KARL AND CHRISTOPHER: FROM LOVE AT FIRST SIGHT TO TWENTY-SIX YEARS OF PARTNERSHIP

Karl and Christopher reside in the outer suburbs of New York City. One day in the late 1980s, Karl was thumbing through a fashion magazine and a picture of Christopher caught his eye. Later that evening, the man in the magazine—Christopher—stood in the flesh before him in a famous NYC club. They exchanged a dance and a few words, but nothing more. Over the course of the next three years they met only by coincidence on a few separate occasions. On the third encounter, they finally talked and initiated what is now a twenty-six-year relationship. Over that time they moved to other states, earned their graduate degrees, and adopted two children. They grew to know each other deeply and remained committed to keeping the passion alive by allowing time for each other as a couple. Special nights, long weekends, and intimate conversations never waned. They had this to say about long-term love:

Think back and remember what brought you and your partner together. For most, it was a strong desire for intimacy, love, and sex. When love is young, we long for daily doses of touching, kissing, caressing, and sex. However, the daily doses begin to subside with the passing of time and the responsibilities that come with it. A loving relationship that stands the test of time is one in which a deep and spiritual connectedness has evolved. This connectedness is much more powerful than early passion. When love is no longer new, it is palpable and its physical expressions— whether making love or just having sex—require no pretext, negotiating, or apologies. When you and your partner have arrived at this place in your relationship, you have mentally tuned in to each other's core and the essence of your sexuality.

Sexuality is a continuum and you must stay in touch with your own sexiness in order to fully embrace your partner's. Ask yourself: if you had the opportunity, would you want to make love or have sex with your-

self? Would you find your own body sexy enough to fantasize about? Not only do you want to desire your partner, but you want the desire to be returned.

In the course of our twenty-six years together, the allure and attraction have grown in this familiarity. As a relationship grows, partners more fully understand each other's wants and needs. Nonverbal communication becomes natural and is practiced with little or no thought. Familiarity with your partner becomes the real aphrodisiac. Knowing the touches that hit the spot, the words—soft or harsh—that arouse the senses, and the scents that recall images and deliver pleasure is the secret to maintaining a full, erotic relationship.

To return to a related but distinct point about *Romeo and Juliet,* the play is also a kind of blueprint for the way modern culture glorifies youth. It is a prototype for "Live fast, die young, and leave a beautiful corpse."[115] The line from *Romeo and Juliet* to *West Side Story* is direct, and the teenage love and death songs of the late 1950s and early '60s partake of similar mythology. All of this material celebrates the youthful experience of madly passionate love that is even more hormonally driven than the mostly adult forms of falling in love we've been discussing. Just as infatuation must end or evolve, we all must transition from youth to young adulthood to middle age and then to old age. While much has been made of the aging baby boomer generation and there's an increasing awareness

---

115 This phrase is often associated with James Dean, but John Derek delivered it in *Knock on Any Door,* a 1949 film with Humphrey Bogart. Derek's character, Johnny Romano, said, "I wanna live fast, die young and leave a beautiful corpse."

that growing older doesn't mean the end of sexuality, the prevailing model is still that youth is hot and sexy, while more mature passion is vaguely ridiculous.

TECHNIQUES FOR FALLING IN LOVE AGAIN AND AGAIN

From a sexual standpoint, during the first six months to two years, most people find that it's easy to have sex; they have it often and they enjoy it a great deal. As the hormonal flood of that first few months begins to ebb, sexual encounters become less frequent and less intense. If you are cohabiting and are basically always available to each other, it's easy to start taking sex for granted; it may become more difficult to initiate encounters, and one partner may become the sole initiator. This can be a heavy burden.

All these elements factor into the celebration of hormonal love and the view that its end is tragic. It's also why many people think that it's "never as good as the first time," as the Sadé song goes.[116] The truth is more complex, and comparing the first time with the thousandth time is probably inapt. Novelty can be exciting, intense, and thrilling. It may lead us to behave boldly or even recklessly. The familiar is, well, familiar, and it doesn't have the same fervid quality. Nevertheless, if you have taken the time to know each other deeply and have developed the skills to focus on each other's pleasure, you are likely to continue to have a high-quality sex life,

---

116 Sadé, "Never as Good as the First Time," *Promise,* Portrait Records, 1985.

even if the quantity is somewhat diminished.

There's often an enormous amount of psychic noise when you're interacting with a new partner or someone with whom you're falling in love. That noise, the intensity of the emotional and physical attraction, can drown out the finer tones. Much of our Tantric training involved developing the capacity to become facile with our awareness, and in a sexual context that means tuning in to the more subtle aspects of sex, to notice the tastes, smells, sounds, and sensations that are often missed during more frenzied lovemaking. There's nothing wrong with novelty and intensity. Even in the context of long-term sex, the capacity to make love with abandon, to surrender fully, is an important component, but comparing the satisfactions of having sex with a new partner to the satisfactions of having sex with someone you've known and loved for years doesn't do justice to either experience. Of course, if you're in an open relationship that works well, you can have your cake and eat it too, and we're not being facetious. Having the option to be with new partners can give you access to some of that intensity even as you continue to deepen your primary bond. Some people set up a false dichotomy by suggesting that those who are in open relationships are not going deep with their primary partners. As should be clear by now, we think this is a badly misguided belief.

Before we get into specific sexual suggestions, we'd like to touch on something that often gets overlooked when it comes to talking about sex, and especially sex in long-term relationships. This is a major problem in twenty-first-century America: poor physical fitness. Staying as fit as you can is crucial for maintaining a healthy and happy sex life, and as people settle into partnerships, they frequently pay less attention not only to their appearance but also to their overall condition. We've experienced this tendency to become neglectful at a number of points in our own relationship. It's very easy for this to happen, and the longer you let things go, the harder it becomes to get back into a healthy pattern. Nevertheless, the effort is always worthwhile. (Of course, if you have any significant health concerns, you should get a doctor's advice before starting an exercise program.)

Taking steps to remain physically fit will likely increase your level of desire, not to mention help you with issues of body image and feeling sexy. Recent research has suggested that Yoga may be particularly beneficial for building libido.[117] Although the contemporary practice of Yoga tends to be focused on health and fitness, Yoga and Tantra are closely related traditions, and both place a heavy emphasis on refining awareness, including paying attention to one's own physical processes. While there are some potential pitfalls related to Yoga and other forms of exercise (see the section "General Female Sexual Issues" in Chapter 11), generally speaking the advantages far outweigh the risks. Just be careful to select your teachers and trainers wisely. It is best to start very, very slowly, especially if you are not particularly fit. If you are middle-aged, you may find that Tai Chi or another gentler form of exercise is a better choice.

---

117 William J. Broad, "Yoga and Sex Scandals: No Surprise Here," *New York Times*, February 27, 2012, http://www.nytimes.com/2012/02/28/health/nutrition/yoga-fans-sexual-flames-and-predictably-plenty-of-scandal.html?_r=1&pagewanted=all percent3Fsrc percent3Dtp&smid=fb-share&fb_source=message.

Certain Yoga practices and postures are effective for bringing attention and increasing blood flow to the pelvic region, since they are specific to the pelvic floor and hence the sex organs. Nonetheless, other forms of exercise, especially any that engage the core muscles, are likely to have the same impact. If you work out, you can make a point of working your core and PC muscles whenever you exercise. If working out seems like a chore to you, this enhancement can make it more fun. If you're doing weight training, try adding PC pulses between sets to pass the time.

We have also found that working out as a couple can be a way of making the whole process both more tolerable and more collaborative (even when one of us jokingly blames the other for sore muscles). Not everyone has the luxury of being able to schedule workout times together, and it may not make you feel sexy in and of itself. But we have found that sharing exercise time and following a similar workout routine helps keep us motivated.

Sex itself involves using your muscles, and like muscles, your sexual life can start to atrophy if it isn't exercised regularly. In the words of Gabriel García Márquez, "While a person does not give up on sex, sex does not give up on the person. What you cannot do is to stop for a long time because then it is very hard to start up again. So, you always have to keep the engine running."[118]

---

118 Gabriel García Márquez quoted in Marlise Simons, "Love and Age: A Talk with Garcia Marquez," *New York Times*, April 7, 1985, http://www.nytimes.com/1985/04/07/books/love-and-age-a-talk-with-garcia-marquez.html?scp=1293&sq=By percent20MARLISE percent20SIMONS&st=nyt.

MAINTENANCE SEX

We've discussed the value of choosing to engage erotically, the importance of making dates, and the misguided idea that spontaneous sex is better sex. We'd like to dig into this subject a little more deeply and explore how choosing to be sexual can function as a lifetime program for sustaining your relationship and keeping it happy and harmonious. You can almost always choose to be sexual; just as you can choose to work out and maintain some level of physical fitness. As with physical exercise, you may not always be able to stick to the program, whether due to illness, injury, or emotional disruption. If there's an emotional disruption, it may not be wise to be sexual together until you've gotten back into a more harmonious state, and if there's an illness or an injury, it may be necessary to wait until you're both well. Nevertheless, as with physical exercise, if you've devoted yourselves to staying sexually fit, it will be a lot easier to return to your routine when you're ready to do so.

While a relationship is more like a living entity than a machine, it can be helpful to think about this in mechanical and specifically automotive terms. For the sake of this analogy, let's think about dating as taking various models of cars for test drives. If you fall in love with a particular model and bring it home, you will not only have to put fuel in the tank, you'll have to change the oil, get the tires rotated, flush the radiator, and do whatever else is necessary to maintain the vehicle and keep it running well.

When we see a well-maintained antique car, we often say,

"Look, there's somebody's baby." Auto enthusiasts spend hours caring for their prized possessions, attending to every detail. Most people value their sexuality and their relationships, but in many cases, they don't treat them with anything approaching the same level of care and attention. In our stressed-out society, the issue is often how much time we have to devote to sex, or how much time we believe we have. Whatever the reasons, make sure that you nurture your connection by having maintenance sex on a regular basis. It is a way of ensuring that your relationship will continue to run on all cylinders.

This may or may not involve genital intercourse. What's important is staying connected, keeping the erotic charge going. You may think this is too time-consuming, but make it a priority and make the time. It doesn't have to be a two-hour Tantric marathon. Sometimes a quickie is a great form of maintenance sex. A satisfying sexual encounter may not take as long as you think. The benefits of dedicating twenty minutes to sex can outweigh the time lost and can even outweigh the benefits of using that time to sleep.

MAINTENANCE SEX IN ACTION

Carole and Michael reside in a Rust Belt city and have been married for twenty-nine years. They have been swinging for six. They're low-key and playful with each other and probably fall well outside the popular stereotype of the swinger. When Carole says she enjoys having time to herself when Michael goes away for a few days on hunting trips, she does so in a matter-of-fact, playful tone of voice that is devoid of rancor; he takes the remark in stride. Their affection for each other and their connection are evident, but otherwise, they could be any other middle-aged American couple. For the last twenty-nine years, they have set their alarms to awaken them twenty minutes early so they can make love. They had the following to say about their experience and about maintenance sex in general:

Morning sex for the two of us started right from the time we said, "I do." This has been something that has flourished in our relationship—being able to wake up every morning and start the day sharing each other and making each other feel the love and affection between us. The simple thought of skin-to-skin contact and knowing that your partner is enjoying the start of the day just as much as you are. We enjoy starting in the morning with light finger touches under the covers or a soft dragging of the fingertips down Carole's back and down her leg. We love to begin in the spooning position. Her breathing and movements show her enjoyment. What better way to wake up every morning than to be touching, feeling, and caressing each other to the point of ecstasy? Sharing the love we have for each other and starting our day with the wonderful thought of how we woke up is beautiful. The shower after is always nice when we can share it together as well.

Morning sex isn't to everyone's liking, and making love every day may be more than you feel is necessary. Find a time frame and a level of frequency that works for you. If you're like many long-term couples, you probably could be having sex more frequently. If you choose to do this, you'll probably enjoy it more and also nurture the nonsexual aspects of your relationship. If you make it to an advanced age, you probably won't look back on your life together and think, *Gee, I wish we hadn't had so much sex.*

CONSCIOUSLY CONTINUE YOUR COURTSHIP

Having regular maintenance sex is valuable in itself, but there's more you can do to keep things vibrant and build up your erotic reserves for difficult times. We always encourage couples to find ways to continue their courtship for the long term. For most people, after infatuation subsides, some measure of complacency takes hold. When people are dating, they're not only flooded with hormones, they're eager to impress the other person and to gain or secure their love. This is true even if the courtship and early stages of the relationship are not particularly tumultuous.

Because of the way courtship is structured in our society, much of this effort to "win" the other person's heart and affections is undertaken by men. Even now, the expectation is generally that men will take the lead and do the courting, while women wait by the phone. When courtship is over and hearts have been won, women often complain that their partners no longer do things to make them feel special.

The reality is usually somewhat more complex. Even if men are more often than not the active courters, women too have to convey not only attraction but also a sense that the potential partner is special. Their ways of doing this may tend to be subtler, but they're no less important for being so. As the flood of hormones that accompanies NRE subsides, and after the pair-bond has been established, the need to court and impress tends to vanish as well. This can influence a wide range of behaviors from gift giving to personal hygiene.

Of course, people change; as your relationship grows and evolves, the things that mattered early on may not have the same appeal. In our own lives, for example, we did a lot of gift giving during our courtship. Over the years, we have become increasingly aware of how much stuff we have accumulated, so buying gifts for each other has become far less important. We have found other ways to court each other instead. Sometimes small acts of consideration can be the most meaningful.

TIP: How to Keep Courting Each Other

List the things you did to make each other feel special during courtship. Would the same things make you feel special today, or have your desires and interests changed? Think of what you're doing now to court each other, and come up with five simple ideas each to add to that list. Make sure your proposals are feasible. Plan to do one item each per week, and be sure to trade off as you romance each other.

It's safe to say that many women feel that being romanced is an important prelude to sex. In reality, there must be constant romancing on both sides. Men need to feel wanted and desired as well. This is not quite the same thing as courtship, which is a broader category. *Romancing,* as we use the term, involves creating an ambience that's conducive to being sexual, establishing a place, time, and mood that give your lovemaking a sense of specialness, and making it clear that you have each other's undivided attention. This does not have to be elaborate—although some people may prefer grand gestures—and it can be lighthearted. Our basic ritual is a simple one. When one of us says, "Do you want to join me for a bath?" the stock response is "Are you flirting with me?"

There's often a significant difference between what's romantic and what's a turn-on, though some people experience being romanced as intrinsically erotic. Romance can create the conditions for getting turned on, laying the groundwork for the erotic to take hold. The candlelit dinner, the walk on the beach, the ride in the horse-drawn carriage can help engender a special feeling. In Tantra, we talk about the *bhava*, which means a kind of elevated mood, a state produced through the enactment of a ritual in which the partners worship each other. Romancing each other is similar, even if it doesn't have the spiritual implications.

The Tantric ritual can involve the creation of a sensual and protected environment, and at the very least, it entails a deliberate awakening of all the senses by various means—flowers, music, incense, food, wine. Naomi Wolf has suggested that women, in particular, need to feel safe and relaxed in order to be sexual.[119] While we find Wolf's perspective to be somewhat extreme in its embrace of gender binaries, we also recognize that she makes some excellent points. Women may generally want more romance, as well as more attention to detail and physical environment. They may also tend to require a greater degree of relaxation to be open to sex. It does seem that many of the complaints we've heard from women about men and sex are related to a lack of attentiveness and insufficient buildup.

TIP: Keep Your Bedroom Sexy

Since a majority of couples have most of their sexual encounters in bed, it is important to do whatever you can in terms of lighting and décor to ensure that your bedroom functions as an erotic space. Make sure your bed is as comfortable as possible. Keep wedges and bolsters on hand to make experimenting with different angles and positions easier. Keep toys and supplies within reach; something as simple as a Rubbermaid bin under the bed is all you need. Consider investing in a massage table. If you want to get really creative, you can purchase several hand soap dispensers and keep a different kind of lube in each one. To ensure privacy, make sure you can lock the door. While keeping your bedroom sexy is always a good idea, don't forget that you can make love in other places too. Wherever you choose to have sex, be sure you turn off your phone before you start.

---

119 Naomi Wolf, *Vagina: A Biography* (New York: HarperCollins, 2012), 188–198.

SEX AND AGING

There are a number of books dealing with sex and aging, but the subject merits far more serious attention than it has received to date. We prefer to think of aging as a process that begins in adolescence and continues through the rest of life. This strikes us as a healthy and holistic way of understanding the changes that take place. As with so much of human sexuality, and life in general, there is a lot of variation in how the process of aging affects a given individual, but there are also quite a few broader, more general facts and emotional components that apply to virtually everyone.

We've already touched on the relationship between physical fitness and sexual responsiveness. If this is important when you're young, it is even more so as you grow older. This is partly because the health of your circulatory system is closely related to sexual functioning. Beyond that, diseases that are related to age and poor health, such as Type 2 diabetes, can cause impairment. In addition, if you can remain mobile and flexible, you'll have more sexual options as years go by.[120] Even if you have led a largely sedentary life, or simply are not very athletic, it's never too late to start. Our mothers, like many women of their generation, did not exercise. They took up the practice very late in life and have benefitted from it greatly. Our fathers were somewhat more physically active, but they too started doing more formal workout routines later in life and have reaped the rewards. Of course, the older

---

120 W. M. Bortz and D. H. Wallace, "Physical Fitness, Aging, and Sexuality," *Western Journal of Medicine* 170, no. 3 (March 1999), 167–169, abstract available at http://www.ncbi.nlm.nih.gov/pmc/articles/PMC1305535/.

you are, the more mindful you have to be of the downsides. Getting medical advice and finding instruction that is geared toward your particular circumstances are crucial after about age forty, or even younger if you have any significant health issues or weight problems.

Because they happen so gradually, the changes that occur in the twenties, thirties, and even into the early forties may not be terribly dramatic. There are many variables, but as you reach your mid-forties, there's a good chance you will realize that sex is not quite the same as it used to be, and of course, you will observe that your body is different too.

For men, erectile firmness is likely to decrease (in the absence of pharmaceutical or mechanical assistance), and as time goes on it may become difficult to get an erection without direct stimulation. As women go through perimenopause and menopause, there are changes in the vaginal tissue and in the lubrication process. These physiological changes are common to all of us, though there's enormous variability in terms of when and how much they affect us. If you took a random group of fifty-year-olds and tried to judge each person's age based on appearance alone, you'd probably guess that some were forty, some were fifty, and others were closer to sixty. The same is true of sexual functioning. Some retain a much more youthful sexuality for many years, while some start aging before their time. A multitude of factors, some genetic, some psychological, and some related to your conscious choices, come into play. While the totality of these factors is far beyond your ability to control, you can take steps that will make your sexual life more satisfying as you grow older. Staying fit is just a starting point.

Your physical condition is important, but your mental attitude is crucial when it comes to adjusting to the changes that will inevitably take place. Your genes and all the cultural baggage that you carry are factors, but you do have some choice about whether sex gets better for you as you age or it is something that flickers and fades.

At New Horizons, a Seattle-area swing club that strives for inclusivity, it was inspiring to see a very elderly woman, probably well into her eighties and in adult diapers, who continued to express her sexuality. We did not interview her, but we strongly suspect that her ability to embrace the erotic at such a late stage in life, and with so little inhibition about her age, was not just a choice but also the product of many choices she had made over the years. While some may find this anecdote somewhat discomfiting, we were moved.

We're getting a little bit ahead of ourselves. The important point is that barring significant health issues, you can continue to be a sexual being long after the ability or desire to reproduce has disappeared. Hormones and biology drive youthful sex, in men and women, regardless of orientation. While we may still be driven by these factors to some degree as we get older, all human beings experience a shift from something that is in large part biologically driven to something that is chosen.

Of all the changes, menopause is perhaps the most obvious and dramatic. While men go through hormonal changes at midlife and there have been attempts to apply the terms "andropause" or "male menopause" to the experience, these changes are considerably more subtle and do not signal the end of fertility. Strictly speaking, menopause is an event, the end of menstruation, but it is also a process that takes place over a number of years. It neither begins nor ends with the last period. Because there are associated and sometimes dramatic physical indications (hot flashes, for example), and because orthodox medicine has a long history of pathologizing female sexuality, there has been a tendency to view menopause as something akin to an illness. It is also often seen as the point at which female sexuality comes to an end. Postmenopausal sex can't be procreative, and there's still a cultural tendency to view nonprocreative sex as suspect. There is also the belief that male sexuality is driven by the desire to reproduce and that once a woman is no longer fertile, she is no longer desirable. For these reasons, among others, women are conditioned to think of menopause as an event that marks not only the end of their attractiveness but also of their own desire and erotic identities.

This is a very heavy psychological burden. While it is true that some women experience a decline in sexual desire after menopause, this is by no means always the case. For some, the ability to be sexual without worrying about pregnancy is liberating. In others, hormonal changes lead to increased libido. If you notice that your desire and responsiveness are starting to decline as you are going through menopause, you can continue to exercise your PC muscles, pleasure yourself, and choose to be sexual. You may find that it takes more time to get turned on, and you will probably need to use more lube. If you are not sleeping well because of hot flashes, be sure to explore a medical solution, and don't beat yourself up if you're not feeling particularly sexy. The decline in libido may be due to fatigue, not an actual loss of desire or ability to become aroused.

At times when sex just isn't working well, whether it's for reasons of fatigue or due to other factors, it may be appropriate to forgo it for a while. Severe illness, for instance, or a traumatic event can create circumstances in which you are compelled to take a break. Even if you're taking a break from sex, it's a good idea to do what you can to be sensual with each other and to remain erotically connected. Don't let the break go on for longer than is absolutely necessary. "Use it or lose it" applies to sexual functioning, especially as we age. Later in life, the vaginal musculature can start to atrophy without regular penetration, and in our experience, relatively frequent sex helps maintain good erectile function in men.[121]

It's important to note that if you're in an open relationship, taking a break can mean taking a break from being sexual outside the primary partnership. We know couples who have opened their relationships in midlife, after the kids are gone, and others who have used the menopause/andropause years as a time to focus on each other.

---

121 For vaginal atrophy: Shawna L. Johnston and Scott A. Farrell, "The Detection and Management of Vaginal Atrophy," *Society of Obstetricians and Gynaecologists of Canada Clinical Practice Guidelines,* No. 145, May 2004, available at http://www.sogc.org/guidelines/public/145E-CPg-May2004.pdf.

CLOSING AND REOPENING A RELATIONSHIP

Nina and Jay, a longtime open couple we know, went through several years of monogamy after their kids went to college, only to reopen their relationship and form a long-term attachment with another couple. They had this to say about their experience:

Jay

I fell wildly in love with Nina in high school on our first date. It was the most powerful experience I ever had. We only opened our relationship when we were in our thirties after twenty years of happy monogamy. A specific moment comes to mind. We were in the yard at the end of summer and Nina was sitting on my lap. We were talking about how we had everything: two kids, two careers, a wonderful home, great friends, and a still-juicy sex life. We wondered what was next. Shortly thereafter, we met another couple who suggested we become lovers. It was the trippiest experience to fall in love as a couple with another couple. And although that relationship didn't last, we continued being polyamorous for many years. We loved the feeling of being connected with "tribe." We never found another couple, so we dated single poly-amorous people. I think that was ultimately why we had to eventually close our relationship for a while. We had put so much time and energy into trying to satisfy the needs of our other partners that we robbed our marriage of the attention it needed. We had grown apart and distant. So, once the kids were out and it was obvious we weren't on the same page, we pulled the plug on the other relationships and focused on our marriage. We spent a lot of time just being together—making love, jogging, reconnecting. It took some time to regroup. Once we were back in the groove, we were feeling adventurous again, so I suggested we try swinging instead of polyamory, thinking we could keep more of the focus on ourselves. Ironically, very early in the process we met a couple who have been with us for five years. We don't have sex with anyone other than these partners and are very content.

Nina

I agree with Jay. We had never considered becoming nonmonogamous. I never even imagined experimenting. It was only through falling in love as a couple with another couple that I opened to the notion of expanding our marriage. And when that ended, I was heartbroken. We discovered that we liked having other partners around, and at heart I am a hippie, so sharing our lives came pretty easily to me. We ended up with partners who weren't significantly partnered with other people and it was ultimately unsustainable. It made for tensions between us—resentments on my part as Jay got so much love and attention from his partner, while I had problems with mine. Jay's partner flatly refused to date other people. I finally got very fed up and put my foot down. I sorely missed the intimacy with him that I had always enjoyed, and felt deeply alone. It was painful for me. We closed our relationship and went to marriage counseling. We were able to address some of the hurts we had unintentionally inflicted on each other. It was amazing how by not focusing on the problems outside of our sessions, but simply enjoying each other's company, we quickly found our way back to each other. We made up for lost time and had a blast. One of our experiments was to try swinging instead of polyamory. I wasn't keen on sex without connection, but I was happy to do something adventurous with Jay. And as fate would have it, we were lousy swingers. Before we knew it, we met a couple and settled down with them. A very happy ending.

Most people remain sexually active after their reproductive years have ended. Even between the ages of seventy-five and eighty-five, 38.9 percent of men and 16.8 percent of women continue to be sexually active with a partner, according to a study published in the *British Medical Journal*. The discrepancy between men and women is a function of the generally shorter life expectancy for men, and when adjusted for whether people had partners, the difference was not statistically significant.[122] Notwithstanding this fact, the idea of older people as sexually active is a source of mockery in many segments of popular culture. Even in this era of an increasingly aging population, it's still a controversial and unsettling topic for many.[123]

The aging process itself can lead to greater sexual fluidity, and curiosity about same-sex interactions sometimes emerges in middle age or even later. Various forms of open relating may be more common among the elderly than most would suspect. One small study found that over 50 percent of long-term, happy couples practiced some form of consensual nonmonogamy; several of these couples had opened their relationships while in their fifties.[124] Although the sample size was small and all of the participants were able-bodied, the findings suggest that nonmonogamous arrangements also make a good deal of sense in the context of aging and physical decline: Other people can substitute when systems fail. For example, sighted people can help the blind, and those who

---

122 Stacy Tessler Lindau and Natalia Gavrilova, "Sex, Health, and Years of Sexually Active Life Gained Due to Good Health: Evidence From Two US Population Based Cross Sectional Surveys of Ageing," *British Medical Journal* 340 (2010), c810, full text available at http://www.bmj.com/content/340/bmj.c810. The study also highlights the importance of health and fitness, especially later in life.

123 The recent, generally positive critical response to the film *Hope Springs* with Tommy Lee Jones and Meryl Streep suggests that some of these attitudes may be changing, or perhaps that more movie reviewers can identify with characters who are sexual in late middle age.

124 P. J. Kleinplatz, A. D. Ménard, N. Paradis, M. Campbell, T. Dalgleish, A. Segovia, and K. Davis, "From Closet to Reality: Optimal Sexuality Among the Elderly," *Irish Psychiatrist* 10, No. 1 (2009), 15–18. This small study involved twenty-five couples, mostly from the United States. All were over sixty-five, and all had been married for more than twenty-five years.

retain erectile function can substitute for those who do not. This is yet another example of the ways in which flexibility and a collaborative attitude can enrich your relationship, even very late in life.

We ourselves are in the process of making the transition into later-life sex, and we see it as an opportunity, even as we recognize that the changes will be substantial. While neither one of us longs to recapture the kinds of sexual experiences we had in our youth, and sex continues to get better for us, we do sometimes think it would be interesting if we could go back in time and apply some of what we've learned over the years. What we're finding as we get older is that our youthful sex was so experiential and hormonally driven that it lacked texture. Younger people don't have to give a lot of thought to sex, to consider its underlying meaning. Except perhaps during the years when HIV was killing large numbers of young people, those under the age of forty have generally lacked the maturity, self-awareness, and sense of mortality to think deeply about the meaning of sex or the many different reasons for having it.

In his influential book *Ecstasy Through Tantra*, Dr. Jonn Mumford discusses a number of different purposes for having sex, including procreation, recreation, relaxation, and consciousness expansion. In Tantra, the primary purpose of sex is consciousness expansion. This contrasts with most conventional beliefs about why people have sex, and we would argue that it is a very valuable model, whether or not you embrace any form of spirituality. In sex, there is the potential to be more fully ourselves and also to lose ourselves more fully than there is in virtually any other human activity. This transcendent dimension becomes more accessible and more poignant as we age.

In addition, as people get older and procreative sex is no longer an option, they have the opportunity to discover additional purposes. Most of us are brought up believing that you should only have sex if you are in love with someone and that sex is an expression of that love. Even as same-sex marriage becomes more widely accepted, opponents continue to insist that nonprocreative sex is inferior and morally suspect. Of course, young people too have sex for recreation, relaxation, or as a way of making up after an argument.

There's no age limit on having Tantric sex, and even a twenty-year-old can have mystical experiences and achieve altered states of consciousness. Similarly, older people can express their love through making love, can have makeup sex, and can pursue the mystical ecstasy and altered states that extended arousal can produce. At the same time, when you are older, sex can be stripped of all of that baggage. If you are lucky, you can begin to have sex for its own sake, for the pure experience of the emotions and sensations associated with it. This means that getting older can make you freer sexually. Even though the physical mechanics of sex get more complicated with age, the liberating potential is greater because you are choosing it and exercising your will and autonomy. It is not demanding your attention. When you reach a certain age sex will no longer be driving you; instead, you will be driving sex.

AGING: ONE MAN'S PERSPECTIVE

Dr. Kenneth Haslam very generously shared his firsthand perspective on how aging changes the male experience.

We need a lot more visual and auditory and physical stimulation to turn on. Porn is nice, as is an assertive partner. Low testosterone has a negative impact on our interest in sex. Personally, I find my own sex life turning more and more toward oral and manual sex. An enthusiastic blow job or a skilled hand job (and shared masturbation) can be more satisfying than old-fashioned PIV sex. These work when a full erection cannot be maintained for PIV sex. The end point when you age is not orgasm but shared intimacy and vulnerability. Wet sex is not what it used to be, while intimacy and touch are ever so much more precious. Yes, hot juicy sex is good once in a while, but the intimacy and vulnerability are still the top priorities. Genital touching always feels good even without the erection or sexual turn-on, and sometimes just caressing genitals without a turn-on is enough. Separating sexual touch from sex can be delightful, but it is difficult for folks to understand the difference. Genital touch does not always mean you want to get laid.

As the chances of illness and infirmity become more present, sex can become a powerful affirmation of life. In her important book *Naked at Our Age,* Joan Price describes her experience with a partner with whom she had fallen in love later in life. He had been diagnosed with cancer and was undergoing chemotherapy. Although the treatments left him feeling ill and anything but sexy, he wanted to make love as soon as he was physically able. This was an act of celebrating his humanity and his embodiment, of defying mortality, however briefly.

The reality is that, like anything else in life, your capacity to have genital sex will eventually end, whether due to incapacity or death. If you come to a place in your aging together where sexual function is impaired to such an extent that you can't have genital sex, the foundation and connection you have built over the years will help you move through that transition, and perhaps remain sensually engaged even when intercourse is no longer possible. Touch, including its erotic component, remains important even if sexual functioning is impaired, and many, if not most, elderly people are touch deprived.

We dream of a world that celebrates consensual human sexuality in its multitude of expressions, including among the elderly. Ours is a utopian vision, and we invite you to explore your own sexualities and revel in them as fully as you can, regardless of your current stage in life. There are challenges to doing this as we grow older, and you may encounter some resistance. Because sex is so hidden in our society, it is very easy for children to find the thought of their parents having sex unsettling at best and repulsive at worst.

This discomfort means that adult children can have a very hard time dealing with the idea that parents are sexual, and in the context of assisted living this discomfort can be damaging. Children may assume the role that parents of teenagers often play and abet the policing of their parents' sexuality by caregivers. The process of aging and becoming physically debilitated is in and of itself a kind of indignity. Not allowing older people to have some measure of sexual autonomy is a violation of their basic human rights. Of course, when dementia is involved and consent or lack thereof becomes an issue, the need for monitoring is real. If you have aging parents, we encourage you to celebrate the possibility that they are still sexual beings. If you are aging yourself, remember that erotic energy is what brought you into the world, and if you can keep your own sexual fires burning, even faintly, that warmth is likely to suffuse your later years, keeping you healthier, happier, and more attuned to each other.

RESOURCE GUIDE

It is easy to feel overwhelmed by the abundance of information about sexuality that's available online and in print. We have limited our coverage to North America, with a few exceptions. This material should be helpful, even if it only leads you to other resources that address your specific interests or concerns.

Our selections are somewhat biased toward the mid-Atlantic region and the West Coast; however, many of the websites we've listed have links that should help you locate local groups and events. (There are far too many to include here.) There are numerous Yahoo groups for polyamorous people and BDSM practitioners, and these can be a valuable resource. In addition, you can search the Internet to find local munches and meet and greets.

We cannot personally vouch for every listing. We have not, for example, attended all the events or visited all the shops and retreat centers. The books we recommend may not resonate with you, so trust your own judgment, be discerning, and find ones that do. On a related note, we assume that most of our readers are heterosexual or bisexual, so our selections tend to be focused on those orientations, though many of the educators we've listed may not so identify.

BOOKS

Aging

Better Than I Ever Expected: Straight Talk about Sex After Sixty, Joan Price (Seal Press, 2005).

Naked at our Age: Talking Out Loud About Senior Sex, Joan Price (Seal Press, 2011).

Anatomy and Human Sexuality

The Erotic Mind: Unlocking the Inner Sources of Sexual Passion and Fulfillment, Jack Morin, PhD (HarperCollins, 1995).

The G Spot and Other Discoveries about Human Sexuality, Alice Kahn Ladas, Beverly Whipple, and John D. Perry (Holt Paperbacks, 2004).

Out in the Open: The Complete Male Pelvis, R. Luis Schultz (North Atlantic Books, rev. ed., 2012).

The Science of Orgasm, Barry R. Komisaruk, Carlos Beyer

Flores, and Beverly Whipple (Johns Hopkins University Press, 2006).

Sex at Dawn: How We Mate, Why We Stray, and What It Means for Modern Relationships, Christopher Ryan and Cacilda Jethá (Harper Perennial, 2011).

Women's Anatomy of Arousal: Secret Maps to Buried Pleasure, Sheri Winston (Mango Garden Press, 2009).

Distractions and Disruptions

Hot Mamas: The Ultimate Guide to Staying Sexy Throughout Your Pregnancy and in the Months Beyond, Lou Paget (Gotham Books, 2004).

Money, Sex, and Kids: Stop Fighting about the Three Things That Can Ruin Your Marriage, Tina B. Tessina (Adams Media, 2008).

Erotica

Cleis Press has published many anthologies edited by people we respect: Tristan Taormino, Rachel Kramer Bussel, Susie Bright, Sinclair Sexsmith, and Violet Blue. So browse the Cleis catalog—you're sure to find some hot stories. www.cleispress.com

Riverdale Avenue Books is another great source for erotica. www.riverdaleavebooks.com

Kink

Dark Eros: The Imagination of Sadism, Thomas Moore (Spring, rev. ed., 1998).

Playing Well with Others: Your Field Guide to Discovering,

Exploring and Navigating the Kink, Leather and BDSM Communities, Lee Harrington and Mollena Williams (Greenery Press, 2012).

The Ultimate Guide to Kink: BDSM, Role Play, and the Erotic Edge, Tristan Taormino, ed. (Cleis Press, 2012).

When Someone You Love is Kinky, Dossie Easton and Katherine A. Liszt (Greenery Press, 2000).

Wild Side Sex: The Book of Kink: Educational, Sensual, and Entertaining Essays, Midori (Daedelus Publishing, 2006).

Open Relating

The Ethical Slut: A Practical Guide to Polyamory, Open Relationships, and Other Adventures, Dossie Easton and Janet W. Hardy (Celestial Arts, 2nd ed., 2009).

Open: Love, Sex, and Life in an Open Marriage, Jenny Block (Seal Press, 2009).

Opening Up: A Guide to Creating and Sustaining Open Relationships, Tristan Taormino (Cleis Press, 2008).

Pagan Polyamory: Becoming a Tribe of Hearts, Raven Kaldera (Llewellyn, 2005).

Relationships—General

Mating in Captivity: Unlocking Erotic Intelligence, Esther Perel (Harper Perennial, 2007).

Passionate Marriage: Keeping Love and Intimacy Alive in Committed Relationships, David Schnarch (W.W. Norton, reprint, 2009).

The Relationship Handbook: A Simple Guide to More Satisfying Relationships, George S. Pransky (Pransky and Associates, 2001).

The Seven Principles for Making Marriage Work: A Practical Guide from the Nation's Foremost Relationship Expert, John Gottman and Nan Silver (Three Rivers Press, 2000).

Ten Lessons to Transform Your Marriage: America's Love Lab Experts Share Their Strategies for Strengthening Your Relationship, John Gottman, Julie Schwartz Gottman, and Joan Declaire (Three Rivers Press, reprint, 2007).

Sex and Disability

The Ultimate Guide to Sex and Disability: For All of Us Who Live with Disabilities, Chronic Pain, and Illness, Miriam Kaufman, Cory Silverberg, and Fran Odette (Cleis Press, 2007).

Sex—Tips, Techniques, Practices

Anal Pleasure and Health: A Guide for Men, Women and Couples, Jack Morin (Down There Press, 4th rev. ed., 2010).

Dr. Sprinkle's Spectacular Sex: Make Over Your Love Life with One of the World's Great Sex Experts, Annie Sprinkle (Tarcher, 2005).

The Good Vibrations Guide to Sex: The Most Complete Sex Manual Ever Written, Cathy Winks and Anne Semans (Cleis Press, 2002).

Guide to Getting It On! A Book About the Wonders of Sex, Paul Joannides (Goofyfoot Press, 2012).

Nice Girl's Guide to Talking Dirty: Ignite Your Sex Life with Naughty Whispers, Hot Fantasies, and Screams of

Passion, Dr. Ruth Neustifter (Amorata Press, 2011).

Nina Hartley's Guide to Total Sex, Nina Hartley (Avery Trade, 2006).

Sexual Pleasure: Reaching New Heights of Sexual Arousal and Intimacy, Barbara Keesling (Hunter House, 2004).

She Comes First: The Thinking Man's Guide to Pleasuring a Woman, Ian Kerner (HarperCollins, 2004).

The Ultimate Guide to Anal Sex for Women, Tristan Taormino (Cleis Press, 2nd ed., 2006)

The Ultimate Guide to Cunnilingus: How to Go Down on a Woman and Give Her Exquisite Pleasure, Violet Blue (Cleis Press, 2010).

Ultimate Guide to Fellatio: How to Go Down on a Man and Give Him Mind-Blowing Pleasure, Violet Blue (Cleis Press, 2nd ed., 2010).

The Ultimate Guide to Prostate Pleasure: Erotic Exploration for Men and Their Partners, Charlie Glickman and Aislinn Emirzian (Cleis Press, 2013).

Sexual Trauma

Healing Sex: A Mind-Body Approach to Sexual Trauma, Staci Haines (Cleis Press, 2007).

Tantra

Desire: The Tantric Path to Awakening, Daniel Odier (Inner Traditions, 2001).

Great Sex Made Simple: Tantric Tips to Deepen Intimacy and Heighten Pleasure, Mark Michaels and Patricia Johnson (Llewellyn Worldwide, 2012).

Ecstasy Through Tantra, Dr. Jonn Mumford (Llewellyn Worldwide, 2002).

The Essence of Tantric Sexuality, Mark Michaels and Patricia Johnson (Llewellyn Worldwide, 2006).

Tantra for Erotic Empowerment: The Key To Enriching Your Sexual Life, Mark Michaels and Patricia Johnson (Llewellyn Worldwide, 2008).

Tantric Quest: An Encounter with Absolute Love, Daniel Odier (Inner Traditions, 1997).

Urban Tantra: Sacred Sex for the Twenty-First Century, Barbara Carrellas (Celestial Arts, 2007).

DATING AND SOCIAL NETWORK WEBSITES

www.adultfriendfinder.com—An adult dating site for all orientations, primarily aimed at the swing community.

www.blendr.com—Social network site and app. Often used for hooking up.

www.craigslist.com—The "Casual Encounters" section of this site is popular for hook-ups.

www.FetLife.com—The kinky answer to Facebook.

www.fling.com—Free, sexually oriented dating site for singles and swingers.

www.lifestylelounge.com—One of the many popular swingers' dating sites.

www.okcupid.com—An open relationship–friendly dating site.

www.Swinglifestyle.com—Bills itself as "the largest swingers' site in the world," and has very extensive event listings.

EVENTS

This list includes film festivals, meet and greets, conferences, and weekend retreats. FetLife is probably your best resource for kink events.

www.brevent.org—Black Rose, Washington, DC, long-running kink event

www.brimstonenj.com—Brimstone, New Jersey, kink-oriented hotel takeover

www.catalystcon.com—Catalyst, East and West Coast conferences aimed at "sparking communication in sexuality, activism and acceptance"

www.cinekink.com—CineKink, New York/touring kink-oriented erotic film festival

www.darkodyssey.com—Dark Odyssey, pansexual events in Maryland, Washington, DC, and San Francisco

www.turtlehillevents.org—The Free Spirit Sacred Sexuality Beltane Gathering, Maryland, Pagan-oriented

www.fetfest.com—FetFest, Maryland, kink-oriented event

www.thefloatingworld.org—The Floating World, New Jersey, kink event

www.frenchconnectionevents.com—New Orleans, long-running swingers' convention

www.nasca.com—North American Swing Club Association, convention listings

www.openloveny.com—Open Love New York hosts Poly Cocktails, a monthly meet and greet

www.pleasuresalon.com—Pleasure Salon, New York and other cities, monthly social gathering open to all alternative sexual communities

pbf.polyaustin.org—Poly Big Fun, Bastrop, Texas, polyamory retreat sponsored by Poly Austin

www.polycamp.net—Poly Camp East, Seneca Rocks, West Virginia, annual campground retreat sponsored by several poly groups, family-friendly

www.polycamp.org—Poly Camp Northwest, WA, all ages polyamory event

www.shibaricon.com—Shibari Con, Chicago, rope bondage educational conference

www.swingstock.com—Swingstock, Minnesota, outdoor swinger event

www.takeabiteoftheapple.com—TABOTA, swinger events in Canada

www.vegasexchange.com—Vegas Exchange, Las Vegas, Nevada, a new event in 2013 intended to replace Lifestyles, which was probably the longest running and best-known swing convention in the United States

GENERAL OPEN RELATING AND KINK RESOURCES

www.alfredpress.com—Coordinated by Raven Kaldera and Christina "slavette" Parker, "a writers' cooperative that publishes books on alternative relationship structures and alternative sexual lifestyles including polyamory, Dominant/submissive and Master/slave power dynamic relationships, transgender relationships, and sacred sexuality"

www.kinseyinstitute.org/library/haslam.html—The Kinsey

Institute's Polyamory Collection, established by Kenneth R. Haslam, MD

www.lifestylemagazine.com—A magazine for swingers distributed to swing clubs

www.lovemore.com—Loving More, founded in 1985, is the oldest polyamory organization in the country

www.openingup.net—Tristan Taormino's site includes listings and resources for all forms of nonmonogamy

http://groups.yahoo.com/group/Polygeezers/—A Yahoo group for older people exploring open relationships

www.soj.org—The Society of Janus, a San Francisco–based pansexual BDSM organization, has links to groups in other parts of the country

www.tes.org—Founded in 1971, the New York–based Eulenspiegel Society is "the oldest and largest BDSM support and education group in the country"

ONLINE EROTICA AND EDUCATION

dick-n-jane.com—We're advice columnists on this site along with a number of other educators. Also includes a blog, product reviews, and erotic materials

www.eroticmassage.com—The New School of Erotic Touch, Joseph Kramer's site, thirty-three online video classes

www.feministporn.net—Founded by Madison Young, this collective of sex-positive websites features "authentic chemistry, real couples, empowered women and genuine fetish play"

www.hotmoviesforher.com—Streaming videos, blogs, reviews. Handpicked "porn for women"

www.janesguide.com—This is a great resource that covers an array of sexual subjects

www.lovingsex.com—The Alexander Institute, producer of our instructional films among many others

www.kinkacademy.com—On-demand kink and sex education, featuring many of the top educators in the field

www.qualitysm.com—A site "woman owned and run since 1989" that focuses on kink

www.reclaimsex.com—A program for renewing sexual function and enjoyment after childbirth

www.scarletletters.com—Since 1998, a website that seeks to "break boundaries and bridge gaps, crashing the genre and gender barricades in favor of a collection of constantly updated work from some of the most inventive authors and artists online"

www.sexsmartfilms.com—This site preserves, archives, and showcases films addressing sexual health issues

www.thesexcarnival.com—A "link blog about sex and sexuality." Whatever your interests may be, you're sure to find something here that gets you going

RETREAT CENTERS AND RESORTS

The resorts and websites listed here include spiritually oriented retreat centers that offer the occassional Tantra workshop (but that may not be particularly sex-positive), clothing-optional resorts and spas, nudist and naturist organizations, and "lifestyle"-oriented all-inclusive facilities.

www.aanr.com—American Association for Nude Recreation, membership organization with links to clubs and clothing-optional events, limited listings of nude beaches

www.breitenbush.com—Breitenbush Hot Springs, Oregon, retreat center that offers couples massage and workshops on relationships and Tantra

www.calienteresorts.com—Lifestyle-friendly, clothing-optional resorts in Tampa, Florida, and the Domincan Republic

www.desireresorts.com—Desire, couples only, lifestyle-oriented resort in Mexico

www.esalen.org—Esalen, Big Sur, California, retreat and workshop center, the birthplace of the New Age movement

www.harbin.org—Harbin Hot Springs, clothing-optional retreat and workshop center in Northern California

www.hedonism.com—Hedonism II, Jamaica, venerable lifestyle-friendly resort with a clothing-optional area, for singles as well as couples

www.naturist.com—The Naturist Society, membership organization offers resources, guides to nude beaches, and information on nude recreation

www.eomega.org—Omega Institute, New Age retreat center in Rhinebeck, New York, offers workshops on sexuality, relationships, and Tantra

SAFER SEX RESOURCES

www.ashastd.org—American Social Health Association

www.stdtestexpress.com—Commercial STI testing service

www.cdc.gov/nchstp/od/nchstp.html—Centers for Disease

Control and Prevention

www.gmhc.org—Gay Men's Health Crisis

www.plannedparenthood.org—Planned Parenthood

SEX AND DISABILITY INFORMATION

www.sexualhealth.com/disabilities-chronic-conditions/

SEX-POSITIVE ORGANIZATIONS/DIRECTORIES—PROFESSIONAL, POLITICAL, EDUCATIONAL

www.aasect.org—American Association of Sexuality Educators, Counselors, and Therapists

www.biresource.org—Bisexual Resource Center

www.bisexual.org—American Institute of Bisexuality

www.bizone.org/bap/—Bisexuality-Aware Professionals

www.sexandculture.org—Center for Sex and Culture

www.ncsfreedom.org/—National Coalition for Sexual Freedom (NCSF); see their resource page for kink-aware professionals

http://www.polychromatic.com/pfp/main.php—Poly-Friendly Professionals

www.sexuality.org—Society for Human Sexuality

http://www.sexscience.org/–The Society for the Scientific Study of Sexuality (SSSS).

www.sstarnet.org—Society for Sex Therapy and Research

www.woodhullalliance.org—Woodhull Sexual Freedom Alliance

SEX SHOPS/ONLINE VENDORS/TOY MANU-FACTURERS/FETISHWEAR/BDSM SUPPLIES

Many of the sex shops listed here offer a wide variety of classes and have excellent educational information online. Most of these stores take orders over the Internet, but if there's one in your vicinity, there's no substitute for a visit. We've also included some web-based sources for high-quality toys.

www.a-womans-touch.com—A Woman's Touch, Madison, Wisconsin

www.aslanleather.com—Aslan Leather

www.aneros.com—Aneros, toy manufacturer

www.babeland.com—Babeland, stores in Seattle and New York

www.blowfish.com—Blowfish

www.comeasyouare.com—Come As You Are, Toronto

www.early2bed.com—Early to Bed, Chicago

www.evesgarden.com—Eve's Garden

www.forbiddenfruit.com—Forbidden Fruit, Austin, Texas

www.goodforher.com—Good for Her, Toronto

www.goodvibes.com—Good Vibrations, stores in San Francisco, Berkeley, Oakland, California, and Brookline, Massachusetts

www.grandopening.com—Grand Opening!

www.hustlerstore.com—Hustler, stores nationwide

www.liberator.com—Liberator Shapes, pillows, cushions, sex furniture

www.libida.com—Libida

www.loveashland.com—The Love Revolution, Ashland, Oregon

www.lovecraftsexshop.com—Lovecraft, Mississauga, Ontario

www.luminouslovetoys.com—Luminous Love Toys, rose quartz wand

www.madame-s.com—Madame S, kink-focused, San Francisco

www.njoytoys.com—njoy, beautifully crafted metal toys

www.nobessence.com/home.htm—NobEssence, sculpted hardwood toys

www.passionalboutique.com—Passional Boutique, Philadelphia

www.thepleasurechest.com—Pleasure Chest, New York, Chicago, Los Angeles, and West Hollywood

www.progressivepleasureclub.com—Home of the Progressive Pleasure Club, a network of independent brick-and-mortar sex shops, including some that are listed here

www.purplepassion.com—Purple Passion, New York

www.pyrexions.com—PyreXions Glass, artisan-crafted Pyrex toys

www.therubberrose.com—The Rubber Rose, San Diego

www.selfservetoys.com—Albuquerque, New Mexico

www.shebeoptheshop.com—She Bop the Shop, Portland, Oregon

www.smittenkittenonline.com—Smitten Kitten, Minneapolis, now offering "Ethical Porn on Demand"

www.stormyleather.com—Stormy Leather, kink and fetish wear

www.sugartheshop.com—Sugar, Baltimore, Maryland

www.venusenvy.ca—Venus Envy, Ottawa, Ontario, Halifax, Nova Scotia

www.womynsware.com—Womyn's Ware, Vancouver, British Columbia

SEXUALITY EDUCATORS, ADVOCATES, AND ALLIES

We're personally acquainted with and have learned from a majority of the people listed below. Some are good friends. We respect the minority we don't know based on reading their work, corresponding with them, or by reputation. Visit their websites to learn more.

www.dianaadamslaw.net—Diana Adams

www.ohmegan.com—Megan Andelloux

www.marciabaczynski.com—Marcia Baczynski

www.tinynibbles.com—Violet Blue

www.thehappyendingscompany.com—Sonia Borg, PhD

www.katebornstein.com—Kate Bornstein

www.gloriabrame.com—Gloria Brame, PhD

www.susiebright.com—Susie Bright

www.drpattibritton.com—Patti Britton, PhD

www.dodsonandross.com—Betty Dodson, PhD

www.charlieglickman.com—Charlie Glickman, PhD

www.amyjogoddard.com—Amy Jo Goddard

www.lovemakingdances.com—Zahava Griss

www.nina.com—Nina Hartley

www.vanguardleather.com—Lady Hilary

www.missjaiya.com—Jaiya

www.passionandsoul.com—Lee Harrington

www.pauljoannides.com—Paul Joannides, PsyD

www.ravenkaldera.org—Raven Kaldera

www.shannakatz.com—Shanna Katz

www.goodinbed.com—Ian Kerner, PhD

www.martyklein.com—Marty Klein, PhD

www.beingshameless.com—Pamela Madsen

www.missmaggiemayhem.com—Maggie Mayhem

www.FHP-inc.com—Midori

www.reidaboutsex.com—Reid Mihalko

www.polyweekly.com—Cunning Minx

www.sabrinamorgan.com—Sabrina Morgan

www.drtammynelson.com—Tammy Nelson, PhD, LPC

www.exploringintimacy.com—Ruth Neustifter, PhD

www.expandingsextherapy.com—Gina Ogden, PhD, LMFT

www.estherperel.com—Esther Perel, MA, LMFT

www.joanprice.com—Joan Price

www.audaciaray.com—Audacia Ray

www.thesexsurrogate.com—Tamar Reilly

www.mrsexsmith.com—Sinclair Sexsmith

www.brutalaffection.com—Felice Shays

www.corysilverberg.com—Cory Silverberg

www.sarahsloane.net—Sarah Sloane

www.anniesprinkle.org—Annie Sprinkle, PhD

www.puckerup.com—Tristan Taormino

www.missvera.com—Veronica Vera

www.practicalpolyamory.com—Anita Wagner Illig

www.jamyewaxman.com–Jamye Waxman

www.winstonwilde.com—Winston Wilde

www.mollena.com—Mollena Williams

www.intimateartscenter.com—Sheri Winston

www.leatheryenta.com—Lolita Wolf

TANTRA AND SACRED SEXUALITY RESOURCES

If you are interested in learning more about Tantra, the links below should be useful for getting started. In the past decade, the number of teachers and "Tantric healers" has grown dramatically, as various schools and individuals began offering teacher trainings and certifications. The field is entirely unregulated, and there's no guarantee that a "certified" teacher is a knowledgeable or competent one. We've included some of the teachers we respect in this section, some who focus on the sexual aspects and others who do not. The fact that we respect a teacher doesn't mean he or she will be right for you. If at all possible, try to attend an introductory workshop before signing on to something more ambitious. This may not always be an option, especially if you're thinking about taking an extended, residential training in a faraway location. Always check the teacher's credentials and experience; caginess about training or background may be a warning sign.

http://www.sacredjourneyhealing.com—Kyle Applegate
www.kalirisingthebook.com—Dr. Rudy Ballentine
www.thebodyelectricschool.com—The Body Electric School
www.barbaracarrellas.com—Barbara Carrellas
www.sacredintimateonline.com—Arabella Champaq
www.intimacyretreats.com—Richard and Diana Daffner
www.shivashakti.com—Hindu Tantrik home page, a good
    source of classical texts
www.annamarti.com—Anna Marti
www.jonnmumfordconsult.com—Dr. Jonn Mumford (Swami

Anandakapila Saraswati)

www.danielodier.com—Daniel Odier

www.sacredtantra-club.com/—Sacred Tantra Club, Portland, Oregon

www.sexyspirits.com—Sexy Spirits, New York

www.tantra.com—Comprehensive site with teacher listings, streaming video, and other resources

SELECTED BIBLIOGRAPHY

For the sake of brevity and simplicity, this bibliography includes all book-length works referenced or consulted. Specific references to journal articles, websites, music, and personal communications are included in the footnotes, and suggestions for further reading, audiovisual materials, and Internet resources can be found in the Resource Guide.

American Psychiatric Association. *Diagnostic and Statistical Manual of Psychiatric Disorders: DSM IV-TR.* 4th ed. Arlington, VA: American Psychiatric Association, 1994.

———. *Diagnostic and Statistical Manual of Psychiatric Disorders: DSM-5.* 5th ed. Arlington, VA: American Psychiatric Association, 2013.

Barrs, Patchen. *The Erotic Engine: How Pornography has Powered Mass Communication, from Gutenberg to Google.* Toronto: Anchor Canada, 2010.

Bergstrand, Curtis R., and Jennifer Blevins Sinski. *Swinging in America: Love, Sex, and Marriage in the 21st Century.* Westport, CT: Praeger, 2009.

Blanton, Brad. *Radical Honesty: How to Transform Your Life by Telling the Truth.* Rev. ed. Stanley, VA: Sparrowhawk Publications, 2005.

Block, Jenny. *Open: Love, Sex, and Life in an Open Marriage.* Berkeley, CA: Seal Press, 2008.

Block, Joel. *The Art of the Quickie: Fast Sex, Fast Orgasm, Anytime, Anywhere.* Gloucester, MA: Quiver, 2006.

Bodansky, Vera, and Steve Bodansky. *To Bed or Not to Bed:*

What Men Want, What Women Want, How Great Sex Happens. Alameda, CA: Hunter House, 2006.

Britton, Patti. *The Art of Sex Coaching: Expanding Your Practice*. New York: W.W. Norton, 2005.

Byrne, Rhonda. *The Secret*. New York: Atria Books, 2006.

Carrellas, Barbara. *Ecstasy Is Necessary: A Practical Guide*. Carlsbad, CA: Hay House, 2012.

———. *Urban Tantra: Sacred Sex for the Twenty-First Century*. Berkeley, CA: Celestial Arts, 2007.

Chopra, Deepak. *Soulmate: A Novel of Eternal Love*. New York: Putnam Adult, 2001.

Clayton, Anita, and Robin Cantor-Cook. *Satisfaction: Women, Sex, and the Quest for Intimacy*. New York: Ballantine Books, 2007.

Cohen, Bruce J. *Theory and Practice of Psychiatry*. New York: Oxford University Press, 2003.

Constantine, Larry L., and Joan M. Constantine. *Group Marriage: Marriages of Three or More People, How and When They Work*. New York: MacMillan and Company, 1973.

Coontz, Stephanie. *Marriage, a History: How Love Conquered Marriage*. New York: Penguin Books, 2005.

Daedone, Nicole. *Slow Sex: The Art and Craft of Female Orgasm*. New York: Grand Central Publishing, 2011.

Dodson, Betty. *Liberating Masturbation: A Meditation on Self-Love*. New York: Body Sex Designs, 1974.

———. *Self-Love and Orgasm*. New York: Privately Printed, 1983.

———. *Sex for One: The Joy of Self-Loving*. New York:

Harmony Books, 1987.

Easton, Dossie and Janet W. Hardy. *The Ethical Slut: A Guide to Infinite Sexual Possibilities*. San Francisco: Greenery Press, 1997.

———. *When Someone You Love Is Kinky*. Eugene, OR: Greenery Press, 2000.

Edwards, Logan. *Secrets of the A Game: How to Meet and Attract Women Anywhere, Anyplace, Anytime*. Venice, CA: Sweetleaf Publishing, 2008.

Federation of Feminist Women's Health Centers. *A New View of a Woman's Body: A Fully Illustrated Guide*. New York: Simon and Schuster, 1981.

Einstein, Albert, and George Bernard Shaw. *Cosmic Religion: With Other Opinions and Aphorisms*. New York: Dover Publications, 2009.

Fein, Ellen, and Sherrie Schneider. *The Rules: Time-Tested Secrets for Capturing the Heart of Mr. Right*. New York: Warner Books, 1997.

Fisher, Helen. *The Anatomy of Love: A Natural History of Mating, Marriage, and Why We Stray*. New York, Ballantine, 1994.

Ford, Arielle. *The Soulmate Secret: Manifest the Love of Your Life with the Law of Attraction*. New York: HarperOne, 2008.

Gay, Peter, ed. *The Freud Reader*. New York: W.W. Norton, 1989.

Giles, Lionel, trans. *The Sayings of Lao-Tzu*. London: The Orient Press, 1904.

Gilligan, Carol. *In a Different Voice: Psychological Theory and Women's Development*. Cambridge, MA: Harvard University Press, 1993.

Gottman, John. *What Predicts Divorce: The Relationship Between Marital Processes and Marital Outcomes*. Hillsdale, NJ: Lawrence Earlbaum Associates, 1994.

Gottman, John, Julie Schwartz Gottman, and Joan DeClaire. *10 Lessons to Transform Your Marriage: America's Love Lab Experts Share Their Strategies for Strengthening Your Relationship*. New York: Crown Publishers, 2006.

Gottman, John, and Nan Silver. *The Seven Principles for Making Marriage Work: A Practical Guide from the Country's Foremost Relationship Expert*. New York: Three Rivers Press, 1999.

Gray, John. *Men Are from Mars, Women Are from Venus: A Practical Guide for Improving Communication and Getting What You Want in Your Relationship*. New York: HarperCollins, 1993.

Griffiths, T. H. *The Ramayan of Valmiki*. London: Trubner and Co., 1870.

Hartley, Nina, with I. S. Levine. *Nina Hartley's Guide to Total Sex*. New York: Penguin, 2006.

Heinlein, Robert A. *Stranger in a Strange Land*. New York: Ace Trade, 1991.

Hicks, Jerry, and Esther Hicks. *The Law of Attraction*. Carlsbad, CA: Hay House, 2007.

Holy Bible: The New King James Version.

James, E. L. *Fifty Shades of Grey: Book One of the Fifty Shades Trilogy*. New York: Vintage, 2012.

Joannides, Paul. *Guide to Getting It On! A Book About the*

Wonders of Sex. 7th ed. Oregon: Goofyfoot Press, 2012.

Jones, Ernest. *Sigmund Freud: Life and Work.* New York: Basic Books, 1981.

Kaldera, Raven. *Dark Moon Rising: Pagan BDSM and the Ordeal Path.* Hubbardston, MA: Asphodel Press, 2006.

———. *Pagan Polyamory: Becoming a Tribe of Hearts.* Woodbury, MN: Llewellyn Worldwide, 2005.

Keesling, Barbara. *Sexual Pleasure: Reaching New Heights of Sexual Arousal and Intimacy.* Alameda, CA: Hunter House, 1993.

Kerner, Ian. *She Comes First: The Thinking Man's Guide to Pleasuring a Woman.* New York: William Morrow, 2010.

Kennedy, Adele P., and Susan Dean. *Touching for Pleasure: A 12-Step Program for Sexual Enhancement.* Chatsworth, CA: Chatsworth Press, 1988.

Khaneman, Daniel. *Thinking Fast and Slow.* New York: Farrar, Straus and Giroux, 2011.

Kirshenbaum, Mira. *I Love You But I Don't Trust You: The Complete Guide to Restoring Trust in Your Relationship.* New York: Berkeley Publishing Group, 2012.

Klein, Marty. *Sexual Intelligence: What We Really Want from Sex—and How to Get It.* New York: HarperOne. 2012.

Komisaruk, Barry R., Carlos Beyer-Flores, and Beverly Whipple. *The Science of Orgasm.* Baltimore: The Johns Hopkins University Press, 2006.

Ladas, Alice Kahn, Beverly Whipple, and John D. Perry. *The G Spot and Other Discoveries About Human Sexuality.* New York: Dell Publishing, 1982.

Langley, Liz. *Crazy Little Thing: Why Love and Sex Drive*

Us Mad: How Your Hormones and Neurotransmitters Make You Do Really Stupid Things. Berkeley, CA: Cleis Press/Viva Editions, 2011.

Laqueur, Thomas. *Making Sex: Body and Gender from the Greeks to Freud.* Cambridge, MA: Harvard University Press, 1990.

Lewis, Thomas, Fari Amini, and Richard Lannon. *A General Theory of Love.* New York: Random House, 2000.

Love, Patricia, and Steven Stosny. *How to Improve Your Marriage Without Talking About It.* New York: Broadway Books, 2007.

Lu, Henry C. *Traditional Chinese Medicine: How to Maintain Your Health and Treat Illness.* Laguna Beach, CA: Basic Health Publications, 2005.

Maines, Rachel P. *The Technology of Orgasm: "Hysteria," the Vibrator, and Women's Sexual Satisfaction.* Baltimore: Johns Hopkins University Press, 2001.

Masters, William H., and Virginia E. Johnson. *Human Sexual Response.* Boston: Little, Brown and Co., 1966.

Masters, William H., Virginia E. Johnson, and Robert C. Kolodny. *Masters and Johnson on Sex and Human Loving.* Boston: Little, Brown and Company, 1988.

McGinnis, Thomas, and Dana Finnegan. *Open Family and Marriage: A Guide to Personal Growth.* St. Louis: C.V. Mosby, 1976.

Michaels, Mark A., and Patricia Johnson. *The Essence of Tantric Sexuality.* Woodbury, MN: Llewellyn Worldwide, 2006.

———. *Tantra for Erotic Empowerment.* Woodbury, MN:

Llewellyn Worldwide, 2008.

———. *Great Sex Made Simple: Tantric Tips to Deepen Intimacy and Heighten Pleasure.* Woodbury, MN: Llewellyn Worldwide, 2012.

Moore, Thomas. *Dark Eros: The Imagination of Sadism.* Dallas: Spring Publications, 1990.

———. *The Soul of Sex: Cultivating Life as an Act of Love.* New York: HarperCollins, 1998.

Morin, Jack. *Anal Pleasure and Health: A Guide for Men, Women, and Couples.* 7th ed. San Francisco: Down There Press, 2010.

———. *The Erotic Mind: Unlocking the Inner Sources of Sexual Passion and Fulfillment.* New York: HarperCollins, 1995.

Mumford, Jonn (Swami Anandakapila Saraswati). *Ecstasy Through Tantra.* 3rd rev. ed. St. Paul, MN: Llewellyn Worldwide, 1988.

Nelson, Tammy. *Getting the Sex You Want: Shed Your Inhibitions and Reach New Heights of Passion Together.* Beverly, MA: Quiver, 2008.

———. *The New Monogamy: Redefining Your Relationship after Infidelity.* Oakland, CA: New Harbinger Publications, 2013.

Neustifter, Ruth. *The Nice Girl's Guide to Talking Dirty: Ignite Your Sex Life with Naughty Whispers, Hot Fantasies and Screams of Passion.* Berkeley, CA: Amorata Press, 2011.

Newman, Felice. *The Whole Lesbian Sex Book: A Passionate Guide for All of Us.* 2nd rev. ed. Berkeley, CA: Cleis Press, 2004.

Nietzsche, Friedrich Wilhelm. *The Gay Science.* New York: Vintage Books, 1974.

Odier, Daniel. *Desire: The Tantric Path to Awakening.* Rochester, VT: Inner Traditions, 2001.

———. *Tantric Quest: An Encounter with Absolute Love.* Rochester, VT: Inner Traditions, 1997.

O'Neill, Nena, and George O'Neill. *Open Marriage: A New Life Style for Couples.* New York: Avon Books, 1972.

Ogden, Gina. *Women Who Love Sex: An Inquiry into the Expanding Spirit of Women's Erotic Experience.* Rev. ed. Cambridge, MA: Womanspirit Press, 1999.

———. *The Heart and Soul of Sex.* Boston: Trumpeter Books, 2006.

———. *The Return of Desire: A Guide to Rediscovering Your Sexual Passion.* Boston: Trumpeter Books, 2008.

———. *Expanding the Practice of Sex Therapy: An Integrative Model for Exploring Desire and Intimacy.* New York: Routledge, 2013.

Paget, Lou. *Hot Mamas—The Ultimate Guide to Staying Sexy Throughout Your Pregnancy and the Months Beyond.* New York: Gotham Books, 2005.

Perel, Esther. *Mating in Captivity: Reconciling the Domestic and the Erotic.* New York: HarperCollins, 2006.

Plato. *The Symposium.* New York: Penguin Classics, 2002.

Porst, H., and J. Buvat, eds. *ISSM (International Society of Sexual Medicine) Standard Committee Book, Standard Practice in Sexual Medicine.* Oxford, UK: Blackwell, 2006

Price, Joan. *Better Than I Ever Expected: Straight Talk About Sex After Sixty.* Berkeley, CA: Seal Press, 2006.

———. *Naked at Our Age: Talking Out Loud About Senior Sex*. Berkeley, CA: Seal Press, 2011.

Random House Unabridged Dictionary. 2nd ed. New York: Random House, 1993.

Restak, Richard. *The Secret Life of the Brain*. Washington, DC: Joseph Henry Press, 2001.

Richardson, Diane. *Slow Sex: The Path to Fulfilling and Sustainable Sexuality*. Rochester, VT: Destiny Books, 2011.

Reich, Wilhelm. *The Function of the Orgasm: Sex-Economic Problems of Biological Energy*. New York: Touchstone, 1974.

Riley, Kerry and Diane Riley. *Sexual Secrets for Men: What Every Woman Will Want a Man to Know*. Sydney: Random House Australia, 1995.

Rimmer, Robert. *The Harrad Experiment*. Amherst, NY: Prometheus Books, 1990.

Rinella, Jack. *Partners in Power: Living in Kinky Relationships*. Eugene, OR: Greenery Press, 2003.

Ryan, Christopher, and Cacilda Jethá. *Sex at Dawn: How We Mate, Why We Stray, and What It Means for Modern Relationships*. New York: HarperCollins, 2010.

Schnarch, David. *Passionate Marriage: Love, Sex, and Intimacy in Emotionally Committed Relationships*. New York: W.W. Norton, 1997.

Santayana, George. *The Life of Reason; or the Phases of Human Progress*. Vol. 1. New York: Scribner's, 1905.

Schultz, R. Lewis. *Out in the Open: The Complete Male Pelvis*. Berkeley, CA: North Atlantic Books, 2012.

Shakespeare, William. *The Complete Works of William Shakespeare.* Vol. 3: Tragedies. Roslyn, NY: Walter J. Black, 1937.

Singh, Jaideva, trans. *The Yoga of Delight, Wonder, and Astonishment: A Translation of the Vijnana-bhairava.* Albany, NY: State University of New York Press, 1991.

Stockham, Alice Bunker. *Karezza: The Ethics of Marriage.* Chicago: Stockham Publishing Co., 1896.

Stolorow, Robert D., Bernard Brandchaft, and George Atwood. *Psychoanalytic Treatment: An Intersubjective Approach.* Hillsdale, NJ: The Analytic Press, 1987.

Strauss, Neil. *The Game: Penetrating the Secret Society of Pickup Artists.* New York: It Books, 2005.

Sundahl, Deborah. *Female Ejaculation and the G-Spot: Not Your Mother's Orgasm Book.* Alameda, CA: Hunter House, 2003.

Tannen, Deborah. *You Just Don't Understand: Women and Men in Conversation.* New York: William Morrow and Co., 1990.

Taormino, Tristan. *The Anal Sex Position Guide: The Best Positions for Easy, Exciting, Mind-Blowing Pleasure.* Minneapolis: Quiver, 2009.

———. *Opening Up: A Guide to Creating and Sustaining Open Relationships.* Berkeley, CA: Cleis Press, 2009.

———. *The Ultimate Guide to Anal Sex for Women.* 2nd ed. Berkeley, CA: Cleis Press, 2006.

———. *The Ultimate Guide to Kink.* Berkeley, CA: Cleis Press, 2012.

Tessina, Tina. *Money, Sex, and Kids: Stop Fighting about the*

Three Things That Can Ruin Your Marriage. Avon, MA: Adams Media, 2007.

Thomas, Patti. *Recreational Sex: An Insider's Guide to the Swinging Lifestyle*. Cleveland, OH: Peppermint Publishing Company, 1997.

Tyler, Alison. *Never Have the Same Sex Twice*. Berkeley, CA: Cleis Press, 2008.

Von Sacher-Masoch, Albert. *Venus in Furs*. Charleston, SC: Biblioczar, 2006.

White, David Gordon. *Kiss of the Yogini: "Tantric Sex" in its South Asian Contexts*. Chicago: University of Chicago Press, 2006.

Winks, Cathy, and Anne Semans. *The Good Vibrations Guide to Sex*. 3rd ed. Berkeley, CA: Cleis Press, 2002.

Winston, Sheri. *Women's Anatomy of Arousal: Secret Maps to Buried Pleasure*. Kingston, NY: Mango Garden Press. 2010.

Wolf, Naomi. *Vagina: A New Biography*. New York: HarperCollins, 2012.

Yogananda, Paramahansa. *Autobiography of a Yogi*. 13th rev. ed. Los Angeles: Self-Realization Fellowship, 2000.

ACKNOWLEDGMENTS

We're deeply grateful to Tristan Taormino for introducing us to Cleis Press. Tristan has been an inspiration and a source of support since we first met her in 2005. Dr. Jonn Mumford has guided us, influenced our thinking, and supported our work for over a decade. He continues not only to inspire us but also to provide us with new insights and information. Barbara Carrellas is a great friend, colleague, and sometime collaborator. She was there to lift our spirits whenever we hit a rough spot in the writing process, and her specific comments on the BDSM/kink were particularly helpful. Dr. Tammy Nelson's enthusiasm and input are much appreciated, as is her foreword.

Thanks to Malaga Baldi, our agent, and Kim Dower (Kim from LA), our publicist, for all their efforts on our behalf, and to Kyle Applegate, Jochen Buck, Simon Hay, Anita Wagner Illig, Raven Kaldera, Maggie Mayhem, Midori, Reid Mihalko, Dr. Ruthie Neustifter, Raymond and Tamar Reilly, Murray Schechter, Shibari_Warrior, Lolita Wolf, Luc Wylder, and Alexandra Silk for their professional insights, suggestions, and contributions to this book. Thanks also to our parents.

Our knowledge of anatomy, physiology, and neuroscience is limited, so we are profoundly grateful to Dr. Barry Komisaruk, Nan Wise, MSW, and Talli Rosenbaum, M. Sc. They provided helpful explanations, gave us feedback on some of the scientific material, and recommended several references.

Kenneth R. Haslam, MD, generously shared his thoughts about open relationships and his perspective on aging. We're grateful for his input and his wisdom. Peggy Kleinplatz, PhD, was kind enough to share some insights on her study that revealed a surprisingly high rate of open relationships among the elderly.

While some of our interviewees would have been comfortable with seeing their real names in print, others expressed a desire to protect their privacy, so we opted to use pseudonyms in most instances. Aviator, Carole and Michael, Diane and Jack, Don and Eve, Francesca and Caroline, Isadora and Armand, Jed, Jennifer and David, Karen and Oliver, Kathleen and Jason, Kendra and Robert, Karl and Christopher, Nina and Jay, and Ted generously shared their personal stories and perspectives. Their thought-provoking contributions are much appreciated. Thanks to Eileen Zidi for helping us find the perfect couple we needed for one last sidebar.

Our students have always been a source of inspiration.

We've learned a great deal from this give-and-take, whether online, in private, or in workshops. Although we've tended to discuss our students' negative patterns of interacting more than their positive ones, this is not an accurate representation of what we encounter. We're not therapists, so we've had the good fortune to work with many people who are satisfied with their relationships and are looking for ways to make them even better. Even if we haven't specifically emphasized these positive ways of relating, we have been affected and influenced by them.

Thanks also to our Facebook friends and Twitter followers for their observations about NRE and their definitions of sex.

Adrian Buckmaster, Arabella Champaq, Damon Ginandes, Lolita Wolf, Amie Ziner, and Marnie Miller-Keas provided very helpful feedback on the manuscript, and their perspectives were invaluable. Dvora and Paul Konstant have been great supporters of our teaching, and we can't thank Dvora enough for her meticulous reading of the penultimate draft and her thoughtful feedback.

Hurricane Sandy hit three days before the deadline for submitting our manuscript, leaving us without power or Internet for ten days. We're indebted to Jonathan Pratt and Peter Pratt's Inn for sheltering us after the storm. The generator at Pratt's enabled us to complete the draft and submit it on time.

Finally, thanks to Felice Newman, Cleis Press, and especially to Brenda Knight for her support and enthusiasm about our concept. While this book had been percolating in our minds for many years, it wasn't until we pitched Brenda at Book Expo America in 2011 that our ideas began to take shape.

ABOUT THE AUTHORS

MARK A. MICHAELS and **PATRICIA JOHNSON** have won numerous awards for their work. They are a devoted married couple and have been collaborators since 1999. In addition to *Partners in Passion,* they are the authors of *Great Sex Made Simple: Tantric Tips to Deepen Intimacy and Heighten Pleasure* (Llewellyn, 2012, Winner: *Independent Publisher*/IPPY Award; Winner: International Book Award; Silver Medalist: *ForeWord Reviews* Book of the Year Award; Silver Medalist: Living Now Awards; Honorable Mention: Eric Hoffer Award), *Tantra for Erotic Empowerment: The Key to Enriching Your Sexual Life* (Llewellyn, 2008, Winner: *USA Book News* National Best Books Award; Finalist: *ForeWord Reviews* Book of the Year Award; Finalist: Indie

Excellence Awards), and *The Essence of Tantric Sexuality* (Llewellyn, 2006, Winner: *USA Book News* National Best Books Award). The couple's meditation CD set *Ananda Nidra: Blissful Sleep* (Projekt Records, 2011) was a COVR Visionary Awards finalist.

They are senior students of Tantric pioneer Dr. Jonn Mumford (Swami Anandakapila Saraswati), who has named them his lineage holders for the Americas and Europe. In addition, the two are cofounders of the Pleasure Salon, a monthly gathering in New York City that brings together sex-positive people and pleasure activists from a variety of communities.

Michaels and Johnson have taught throughout the United States, as well as in Canada, Europe, and Australia. They have been featured on television and radio and in numerous publications, including *The Village Voice, Metro, Latina, Ebony, Cosmopolitan, Jane, Rockstar, Breathe, Redbook, The Complete Idiot's Guide to Tantric Sex*, and *The Complete Idiot's Guide to Enhancing Sexual Desire*. They have written and appeared in two instructional films, *Tantric Sexual Massage for Lovers* and *Advanced Tantric Sex Secrets* (Alexander Institute, 2008).

Michaels is a graduate of New York University School of Law and holds master's degrees in American Studies from NYU and Yale. A playwright and translator, he translated and adapted Goldoni's *The Mistress of the Inn* for New York's Roundabout Theatre company and cowrote *The Thrill of Victory, The Agony of Debate*, which premiered at New York's Primary Stages.

Johnson is a retired professional operatic soprano who toured extensively throughout the United States, Europe, and South America and performed with the New York City Opera, the Houston Grand Opera, and the Komische Oper Berlin, among other companies.

INDEX

THE ULTIMATE GUIDES

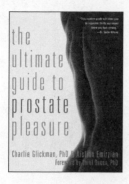

The Ultimate Guide to Prostate Pleasure
Erotic Exploration for Men and Their Partners

Charlie Glickman, PhD and Aislinn Emirzian

$17.95, 6" x 9", 368 Pages,
Health/Sexuality,
ISBN: 978-1-57344-904-5,
Trade Paper, 32/case,
Rights: World

The Ultimate Guide to Kink
BDSM, Role Play and the Erotic Edge

Tristan Taormino

$19.95, 6" x 9", 464 Pages,
Sexuality,
ISBN: 978-1-57344-779-9,
Trade Paper, 28/case,
Rights: World

The Ultimate Guide to Orgasm for Women
How to Become Orgasmic for a Lifetime

Mikaya Heart

$17.95, 6" x 9", 272 Pages,
Health/Sexuality,
ISBN: 978-1-57344-711-9,
Trade Paper, 40/case,
Rights: World

The Ultimate Guide to Cunnilingus
How to Go Down on a Woman and Give Her Exquisite Pleasure

Violet Blue

$16.95, 6" x 9", 200 Pages,
Sexuality,
ISBN: 978-1-57344-387-6,
Trade Paper, 52/case,
Rights: World

The Ultimate Guide to Fellatio
How to Go Down on a Man and Give Him Mind-Blowing Pleasure

Violet Blue

$16.95, 6" x 9", 272 Pages,
Sexuality,
ISBN: 978-1-57344-398-2,
Trade Paper, 36/case,
Rights: World

THE ULTIMATE GUIDES

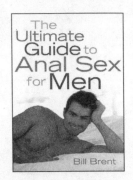

The Ultimate Guide to Anal Sex for Women
Tristan Taormino

$16.95, 6" x 9", 240 Pages,
Sexuality,
ISBN: 978-1-57344-221-3,
Trade Paper, 40/case,
Rights: World

The Ultimate Guide to Pregnancy for Lesbians
How to Stay Sane and Care for Yourself from Pre-conception Through Birth
Rachel Pepper

$17.95, 6" x 9", 288 Pages,
Health/Pregnancy & Childbirth,
ISBN: 978-1-57344-216-9,
Trade Paper, 36/case,
Rights: World

The Ultimate Guide to Anal Sex for Men
Bill Brent

$16.95, 6" x 9", 272 Pages,
Sexuality,
ISBN: 978-1-57344-121-6,
Trade Paper, 36/case,
Rights: World

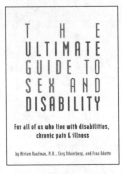

The Ultimate Guide to Sexual Fantasy
How to Turn Your Fantasies into Reality
Violet Blue

$15.95, 6" x 9", 272 Pages,
Sexuality,
ISBN: 978-1-57344-190-2,
Trade Paper, 32/case,
Rights: World

The Ultimate Guide to Sex and Disability
For All of Us Who Live with Disabilities, Chronic Pain and Illness
Miriam Kaufman, M.D., Cory Silverberg and Fran Odette

$18.95, 6" x 9", 360 Pages,
Health/Sexuality,
ISBN: 978-1-57344-304-3,
Trade Paper, 24/case,
Rights: World

"A welcome resource.... This book will be a worthwhile read for anyone who lives with a disability, loves someone with a disability, or simply wants to be better informed sexually."
—Curve

Classic Sex Guides

Buy 4 books,
Get 1 *FREE**

The Smart Girl's Guide to the G-Spot
Violet Blue

It's not a myth, it's a miracle, the G-spot, that powerhouse of female orgasm. With wit and panache, sex educator and bestselling writer Violet Blue helps readers master the sexual alphabet through G.
ISBN 978-1-57344-780-5 $14.95

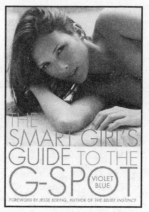

The Smart Girl's Guide to Porn
Violet Blue

As seen on the Oprah Winfrey show!
Looking for authentic sex scenes? Thinking of sharing porn with a lover? Wonder which browser is safest for Internet porn surfing? *The Smart Girl's Guide to Porn* has the answers.
ISBN 978-1-57344-247-3 $14.95

The Adventurous Couple's Guide to Sex Toys
Violet Blue

Feeling adventurous? In this witty and well-informed consumer guide, bestselling author and sex educator Violet Blue shows couples how to choose and use sex toys to play and explore together—and have mind-blowing sex.
ISBN 978-1-57344-972-4 $14.95

The Adventurous Couple's Guide to Strap-On Sex
Violet Blue

"If you're seriously considering making it a part of your sexual repertoire, *The Adventurous Couple's Guide to Strap-On Sex* will give you all the advice you need to enjoy it in a safe and satisfying fashion." —*Forum UK*
ISBN 978-1-57344-278-7 $14.95

Seal It With a Kiss
Violet Blue

A great kiss can stop traffic, start a five-alarm fire, and feel like Times Square on New Year's Eve. Get your smooch on with all the different tricks and tips found in *Seal It with a Kiss*.
ISBN 978-1-57344-385-2 $12.95

Bestselling Erotica for Couples

Sweet Life
Erotic Fantasies for Couples
Edited by Violet Blue

Your ticket to a front row seat for first-time spankings,
breathtaking role-playing scenes, sex parties, women who
strap it on and men who love to take it, not to mention
threesomes of every combination.
ISBN 978-1-57344-133-9 $14.95

Sweet Life 2
Erotic Fantasies for Couples
Edited by Violet Blue

"This is a we-did-it-you-can-too anthol-
ogy of real couples playing out their fantasies." —Lou Paget, author of *365 Days of
Sensational Sex*
ISBN 978-1-57344-167-4 $15.95

Sweet Love
Erotic Fantasies for Couples
Edited by Violet Blue

"If you ever get a chance to try out your
number-one fantasies in real life—and I assure you, there will be more than one—say
yes. It's well worth it. May this book, its
adventurous authors, and the daring and
satisfied characters be your guiding inspiration."—Violet Blue
ISBN 978-1-57344-381-4 $14.95

Afternoon Delight
Erotica for Couples
Edited by Alison Tyler

"Alison Tyler evokes a world of heady sensuality where fantasies are fearlessly explored and dreams gloriously realized."
—Barbara Pizio, Executive Editor, *Pent-
house Variations*
ISBN 978-1-57344-341-8 $14.95

Three-Way
Erotic Stories
Edited by Alison Tyler

"Three means more of everything. Maybe
I'm greedy, but when it comes to sex, I like
more. More fingers. More tongues. More
limbs. More tangling and wrestling on the
mattress."
ISBN 978-1-57344-193-3 $15.95

Best Erotica Series

"Gets racier every year."—*San Francisco Bay Guardian*

Buy 4 books,
Get 1 *FREE**

Best Women's Erotica 2013
Edited by Violet Blue
ISBN 978-1-57344-898-7 $15.95

Best Women's Erotica 2012
Edited by Violet Blue
ISBN 978-1-57344-755-3 $15.95

Best Women's Erotica 2011
Edited by Violet Blue
ISBN 978-1-57344-423-1 $15.95

Best Bondage Erotica 2013
Edited by Rachel Kramer Bussel
ISBN 978-1-57344-897-0 $15.95

Best Bondage Erotica 2012
Edited by Rachel Kramer Bussel
ISBN 978-1-57344-754-6 $15.95

Best Bondage Erotica 2011
Edited by Rachel Kramer Bussel
ISBN 978-1-57344-426-2 $15.95

Best Lesbian Erotica 2013
Edited by Kathleen Warnock.
Selected and introduced by
Jewelle Gomez.
ISBN 978-1-57344-896-3 $15.95

Best Lesbian Erotica 2012
Edited by Kathleen Warnock.
Selected and introduced by
Sinclair Sexsmith.
ISBN 978-1-57344-752-2 $15.95

Best Lesbian Erotica 2011
Edited by Kathleen Warnock.
Selected and introduced by Lea DeLaria.
ISBN 978-1-57344-425-5 $15.95

Best Gay Erotica 2013
Edited by Richard Labonté.
Selected and introduced by Paul Russell.
ISBN 978-1-57344-895-6 $15.95

Best Gay Erotica 2012
Edited by Richard Labonté.
Selected and introduced by
Larry Duplechan.
ISBN 978-1-57344-753-9 $15.95

Best Gay Erotica 2011
Edited by Richard Labonté.
Selected and introduced by
Kevin Killian.
ISBN 978-1-57344-424-8 $15.95

Best Fetish Erotica
Edited by Cara Bruce
ISBN 978-1-57344-355-5 $15.95

Best Bisexual Women's Erotica
Edited by Cara Bruce
ISBN 978-1-57344-320-3 $15.95

Best Lesbian Bondage Erotica
Edited by Tristan Taormino
ISBN 978-1-57344-287-9 $16.95

* Free book of equal or lesser value. Shipping and applicable sales tax extra.
Cleis Press • (800) 780-2279 • orders@cleispress.com
www.cleispress.com

Ordering is easy! Call us toll free or fax us to place your MC/VISA order.
You can also mail the order form below with payment to:
Cleis Press, 2246 Sixth St., Berkeley, CA 94710.

ORDER FORM

QTY	TITLE	PRICE
_____	_____	_____
_____	_____	_____
_____	_____	_____
_____	_____	_____
_____	_____	_____
_____	_____	_____
_____	_____	_____
_____	_____	_____

SUBTOTAL _____

SHIPPING _____

SALES TAX _____

TOTAL _____

Add $3.95 postage/handling for the first book ordered and $1.00 for each additional
book. Outside North America, please contact us for shipping rates. California residents
add 9% sales tax. Payment in U.S. dollars only.

* Free book of equal or lesser value. Shipping and applicable sales tax extra.

Cleis Press • Phone: (800) 780-2279 • Fax: (510) 845-8001
orders@cleispress.com • www.cleispress.com
You'll find more great books on our website

Follow us on Twitter @cleispress • Friend/fan us on Facebook